Performance testing, cognition and assessment:Selected papers from the 15th Language Testing Research Colloquium (LTRC), Cambridge and Arnhem

ISS

STUDIES IN LANGUAGE TESTING...3
Series editor: Michael Milanovic

Also in this series:

Performance testing, cognition and assessment:Selected papers from the 15th Language Testing Research Colloquium (LTRC), Cambridge and Arnhem

CAMBRIDGE
UNIVERSITY PRESS

Desktop published by Dave Smith

Published by the Press Syndicate of the University of Cambridge
The Pitt Building, Trumpington Street, Cambridge CB2 1RP
40 West 20th Street, New York, NY 10011–4211. USA
10 Stamford Road, Oakleigh, Melbourne 3166, Australia

First published 1996

Printed in Great Britain at the University Press, Cambridge

British Library cataloguing in publication data

University of Cambridge, Local Examinations Syndicate
Performance testing, cognition and assessment:Selected papers from the 15th Language
Testing Research Colloquium (LTRC), Cambridge and Arnhem

1. Education. Assessment 2. Education. Tests. Setting

ISBN   0 521 48169 4 hard cover
       0 521 48465 0 paperback

Contents

Introduction

Michael Milanovic and Nick Saville
University of Cambridge Local Examinations Syndicate

The background to the first LTRC in Europe

The papers presented in this volume are a selection from the 15th Language Testing Research Colloquium (LTRC), the first to be held outside North America. It was jointly hosted in August 1993 by The University of Cambridge Local Examinations Syndicate (UCLES) in Cambridge and CITO in Arnhem, the Netherlands.

The very first LTRC was held in 1979 during the TESOL convention in Boston, papers were presented and discussions held to plan future activities. Since then an annual colloquium has been organised and from the handful of original organisers the group has grown steadily with participants now coming from many parts of the world.

With the growing international participation, the idea of holding the colloquium outside of North America was discussed, and at the colloquium hosted by ETS in Princeton 1991, it was suggested that LTRC could be held in Europe in August 1993 prior to the AILA Conference in Amsterdam. Offers to host the event came from The University of Cambridge Local Examinations Syndicate (UCLES) and CITO. In Vancouver the following year it was agreed that the colloquium should be jointly hosted by these two organisations.

This precedent having been set, there are now plans for LTRC to take place outside North America once every three years at the time of the AILA Conference. At the time of writing, plans are well underway for the colloquium to return to Europe in 1996 in Finland, and offers to host the event in Japan 1999 have already been forthcoming.

1993 – Anniversaries in Cambridge and Arnhem

The two institutions, UCLES and CITO, both had particular reasons to mark 1993 as a special year and the hosting of a major language testing conference seemed an appropriate way to do so.

For UCLES, 1993 was the 80th anniversary of the administration of its first English as a Foreign Language examination, the Certificate of Proficiency in

English (CPE). UCLES was established as a department of the University of Cambridge in 1858 in order to conduct examinations for schools in England. It first began examinations in EFL in 1913 with the introduction of the CPE. (For an historical overview see Spolsky in Bachman *et al.* 1995:1–13.) After eighty years, UCLES now offers a range of English as a foreign language examinations which were taken by over 400,000 candidates in 1993.

For CITO, 1993 marked the 25th anniversary of its establishment as the National Institute for Educational Measurement in the Netherlands. It was founded in 1968 as a non-profit-making educational institution by the Dutch Ministry of Education and Science. As well as designing and developing achievement and proficiency tests, CITO is also in charge of the implementation of programme evaluation at local and national levels.

Both UCLES and CITO are members of the Association of Language Testers in Europe (ALTE) which has as its principal objective the establishment of a framework of examination levels for European languages (see ALTE Document 1).

Themes of the Colloquium

As the colloquium was to be held at two venues, it was decided that the focus of the two events should be different, with an opportunity to present more papers than normal. The colloquium in Cambridge had 'Performance testing' as a broad theme, although proposals for papers on other topics were also invited. This theme of performance testing reflected the interest in recent years in the assessment of spoken and written language and is also relevant to the debates on, for example, the development of rating scales, on backwash and 'systemic validity'.

Furthermore, the direct testing of oral and writing skills has historically been an integral part of the approach adopted by UCLES in assessing English as a Foreign Language. For example, John Roach, an UCLES officer from 1925 to 1945, was one of the first language testers to document an approach to standardising oral assessment using recorded examples of speech to train examiners. In 1944 he experimented with using gramophone records to standardise the assessment of Polish officers taking the Lower Certificate in English (the predecessor to the First Certificate in English – FCE).

The colloquium in Arnhem had 'Communication, cognition and assessment' as the theme; it was thought this might allow for the possibility of speakers in related disciplines, perhaps already in the Netherlands for AILA, to contribute. In particular, the cognitive dimension was thought to be relevant, as were a number of wider issues of assessment related to language testing (e.g. L1 skills testing, bilingualism and translation).

Format of the Colloquium

The Cambridge sessions of the colloquium were held on Tuesday 3 and Wednesday 4 August thus leaving Thursday 5 August free so that participants could transfer to CITO in Arnhem, where two further days of the colloquium were held. As planned, many participants then went on to AILA which was being held in Amsterdam.

Over the four days of the colloquium a total of 51 papers, posters and workshops were held and approximately 200 people attended (with a core of over 100 attending the event at both venues).

All the titles of the papers, posters, etc. and the authors are listed in the Appendix.

Format of the book

At the colloquium, presenters were asked to submit their papers for inclusion in a volume of selected papers from the colloquium as a whole. The selection of 16 papers which appear in this volume has been made from those which were submitted by their authors. Some authors chose to submit elsewhere and some papers which were presented have already appeared in print, notably in the journal *Language Testing*.

The final selection was not made in order to provide a comprehensive set of proceedings as this was not possible. Apart from the fact that not all papers were available, a limitation of space would not allow for more than a selection. However, the final decision to include the papers which appear was made with a desire to maintain a flavour of the key issues which were discussed at the 1993 LTRC and to reflect the proceedings in a representative way.

Performance testing – An historical note

The concept of language as performance has been discussed at length by linguists over the past 30 years. In Chomsky's seminal work (Chomsky 1965), performance, in terms of the language actually produced by people, is contrasted with competence, which is the underlying knowledge of a language. When taken up by applied linguists, the concept of performance was elaborated within the notion of communicative competence (Hymes 1967, 1972), and this in turn led to the development of communicative approaches to teaching language in the 1970s. As is often the way, language testing followed in the wake of language teaching, and by the late 1970s there was considerable interest in testing communicative competence and in performance tests.

A performance test is based on a testing procedure which requires the candidate to produce a sample of language, either in writing or speech (e.g. essays and oral interviews). While traditional approaches to assessment have relied on this method, the influence of the communicative movement introduced concepts of authenticity and contextual considerations surrounding the performance. This gave rise to an interest in procedures designed to replicate language performance in non-test contexts, sometimes referred to as the 'real life' approach (Bachman 1990: 304–5).

Within an historical perspective, it is interesting to look back at the first LTRC held in Boston in February 1979. The proceedings were edited by Palmer, Groot and Trosper (1981) and appeared as a volume entitled *The Construct Validation of Tests of Communicative Competence*. This volume is in two sections with 12 papers including an introduction. The titles of the papers are as follows:

Classification of oral tests

A theoretical framework of communicative competence

Beyond faith and face validity: the multitrait-multimethod matrix and convergent and discriminant validity of oral proficiency tests

Convergent and discriminant validation of integrated and unitary language skills: the need for a research model

Structure of the oral interview and content validity

A study of the reliability and validity of the Ilyin Oral Interview

Inter-rater and intra-rater reliability of the oral interview and concurrent validity with cloze procedure

Assessing the oral proficiency of prospective foreign teaching assistants: instrument development

Measurements of reliability and validity of two picture-description tests of oral communication

An experiment in a picture-stimuli procedure for testing oral communication

A multitrait-multimethod investigation into construct validity of six tests of speaking and reading

The focus was predominantly on oral assessment procedures, and while there were important contributions looking at construct validity (as the title of the volume suggests), there was also emphasis on testing method and a traditional concern for reliability. In looking at the titles which appear in the present volume and by reviewing the LTRC archives since 1979, it can be seen that there have clearly been changes in emphasis over 15 years – from LTRC 1 to LTRC 15.

During LTRC 1 in 1979 in their paper entitled 'A theoretical framework of communicative competence' Canale and Swain presented their model of communicative language ability which later appeared in the first edition of the journal *Applied Linguistics* in 1980 (Vol 1, No 1). Drawing on the work of many scholars (Allen, Stern, Halliday, Hymes, Morrow, Johnson, Wilkins, Widdowson and others), this initial framework became highly influential in the 1980s, in both teaching and testing. Further versions of the model were proposed by Canale himself in 1983 and by Bachman in 1990. In particular, the discussion surrounding these models of communicative language ability has helped to bring performance to the centre of attention in language testing.

From the titles in the present volume, it can be seen that the facets of performance testing apply to the assessment of both speech and writing and that the potential interactions between these facets are in fact very complex. Within a contemporary approach to language testing, it is now taken for granted that performance testing has an important role to play. This approach needs to incorporate current views of validity as a unitary concept (Messick 1989) and the need to separate method from construct.

It has become axiomatic in language testing that the definition of language ability to be tested (the constructs) should be kept distinct from the test method used. In the case of performance testing, such as oral assessment, it is essential to be able to specify the construct (e.g. in terms of a model of language ability) and to be able to account for test method factors, such as the tasks and raters, which might confound the interpretation of the scores.

Bachman (1990, Ch. 5), sets out his framework of test method facets (or characteristics) and discusses an application of this framework to language testing. When applied to performance testing, not only are the tasks and participants aspects of the method, but there are many variables which combine to create a testing event.

Facets of performance testing

In order to provide an overview of the variables which interact in performance testing, the following model can be used as a conceptual framework and a characterisation of the different avenues of research which are possible. (A version of this model was presented by Milanovic and Saville during the conference in 1993.)

The diagram in Figure 1 is applicable to both spoken and written assessment and can be interpreted in the following way.

The examination developer specifies a procedure to test spoken or written performance for use with candidates under particular assessment conditions. The procedure must result in some form of a score or description of performance which can be interpreted by the intended test user. In order to produce a suitable sample of language, appropriate assessment conditions and test tasks have to be developed to meet the assessment context.

In oral and written assessment, unlike most tests of reading or listening, the candidates produce samples of language under specified performance conditions and these samples have to be rated by an examiner. The rating needs to be carried out by trained examiners using specially designed 'assessor-oriented' rating scales (Alderson 1991). Traditionally, testing research has concentrated on the assessment criteria (e.g. the rating scales and descriptors) and the problem

Figure 1

Diagram showing interaction of facets

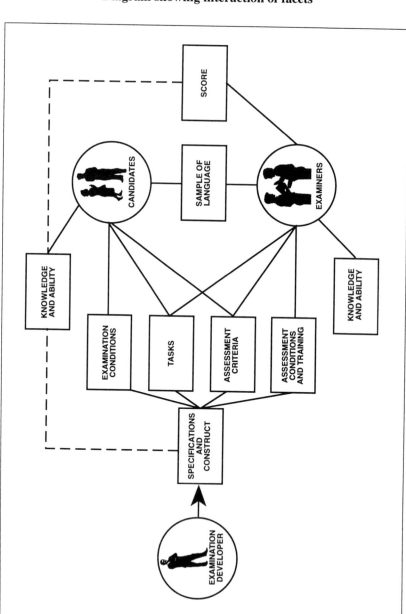

of getting examiners to agree on their interpretation. The problem was largely conceived of as one of reliability.

When emphasis switches to the process of the assessment itself, it is clear that there are complex interactions between the variables which need to be anticipated by the test designer. In many cases, however, the effect of these interactions on the process of assessment and the resulting score are not well understood. Because of the complexity of the issues, different areas of the process presented in Figure 1 require extensive research before clear answers emerge. The extent to which these issues are important will also be determined by the language skill that is being assessed – speaking or writing. The face-to-face conditions of an oral proficiency interview raise questions concerning a real–time, live event where the examination conditions are created and enacted by the participants. This differs from the conditions of assessment for compositions or tape-mediated semi-direct oral tests where the sample of language constitutes a permanent record of the performance which is marked at a distance (in space and time) from the actual performance by the candidate. Both sets of circumstances pose different problems and different kinds of interaction between the variables.

An expanded list of the facets of performance tests is presented in Table 1 on page 8.

In relation to Tasks, the specific points noted in Table 1 apply mainly to oral assessment contexts. When tasks are presented in the written form as prompts for Writing Tests, the full range of test method characteristics, which apply to input on other paper-and-pencil tests, also apply to this case.

A number of issues relating to a research agenda suggested by the framework in Figure 1 were presented at the conference and are reflected in the papers collected in this volume.

The relationship between test-tasks (as used within the performance conditions created by the assessment environment) and the use of language for communication in situations outside of the examination room, raises important questions regarding authenticity and interpretation of test scores. A number of the papers address these issues.

In order to investigate these interaction between facets, a variety of research methods are required which can be both quantitative and qualitative in nature. New statistical procedures can be usefully applied to the data obtained from performance assessments (e.g. Generalizability Theory, Brennan 1983; Many-faceted Rasch measurement, Linacre 1989) and research methods can be borrowed from related disciplines, such as sociology, ethnography and psychology, and used to investigate the interactions between linguistic, cognitive and contextual factors (e.g. techniques for conversation analysis, protocol analysis, observation schedule, focus-group interviews, etc.).

Table 1

Expanded list of facets

General specification of the assessment procedure
 format
 length
 type of tasks
 number of tasks

Features of the assessment environment
 where the assessment procedure test takes place (venue, rooms, etc.)
 when the assessment takes place (day/time)

Candidates
 background, e.g., age, sex, nationality, L1, etc.
 general behaviour and attitude, e.g., shy, confident, etc.
 personality
 the sample of language elicited

Examiners
 background, e.g., age, sex, education, etc.
 training and specific experience
 general behaviour/attitude
 personality
 their familiarity with candidates:
  – general candidate-type, e.g., from a familiar nationality/L1 group
  – specific candidates, e.g., from the same school
 their ratings of candidates – interlocutor decision-making behaviour
 their role or relationship with other examiners

For oral assessment only:
 the language model (L1, dialect/accent, degree of fluency, etc.) presented to candidates
  through the interlocutor's own speech
 the language used for:
  – instructions to candidates – interlocutor frame (rubric)
  – verbal prompts – interlocutor frame (integral to a phase/task)
  – spontaneous talk – interlocutor support/unplanned talk

Tasks
 spoken (verbal) prompts
  – fixed format
  – free format
 visual prompts
  – written
  – pictorial
 time allowed – 'real time' constraints on candidates
 preparation time

Ratings
 where the ratings are made
 when the ratings are made
 nature of scales
 number of scales
 length of scales
 number of ratings/raters

Cognition and assessment

A number of the papers included in this volume deal specifically with cognitive aspects of assessment in relation to performance testing.

One of the changes which came about in relation to the model of communicative language ability during the 1980s was a change of emphasis from socio-linguistic aspects to the area of cognitive processing. This is illustrated by the expanded model proposed by Bachman (1990), in which he develops the notion of strategic competence. For Canale and Swain (1980), strategic competence was conceptualised as a linguistic ability. It concerned the extent to which a language user is able to compensate for deficiencies in other areas of competence by employing strategies to maintain or 'repair' the communication. For Bachman (1990: 102–106), strategic competence is not part of linguistic competence but is concerned with a cognitive capacity which enables the speaker to make most efficient use of language abilities under performance conditions. In his model, he seeks to account for the ways in which the speaker's psycho-physiological mechanisms interact with the context of language use to produce appropriate language.

Given that one of the fundamental variables in performance testing is the rater, it is important to focus not only on the unobservable mental processes of language users being assessed, but also on the judgements and decision-making behaviour of raters.

Overview of the papers

In relation to direct performance testing, in terms of testing of the productive skills of speaking and writing, four of the papers deal with spoken language performance, and four deal with writing. These papers cover a range of the issues suggested by the framework in Figure 1, and touch on cognitive as well as linguistic and measurement issues.

In relation to less direct tests, two papers deal with the assessment of reading comprehension within broad educational contexts and several papers are concerned with the design of tests for more limited or specific testing contexts, where notions of authenticity and content validity are particularly important.

In relation to the topic of cognition and mental processes, one paper deals with early bilingualism and metacognitive development, and the final paper in the volume addresses the issue of translation from L1 to L2 and an appropriate rating instrument to assess this ability.

Speaking

Lazaraton's paper makes use of qualitative data obtained from recordings and transcriptions of a standardised oral assessment procedure – the Cambridge Assessment of Spoken English – CASE. She uses conversation analysis to focus on the language of examiners. Results indicated that there was significant variation in the wording of prompts, in the degree to which particular prompts were used and avoided and in the ways that candidates responded to modifications. Based on the findings, a 'template' was developed to provide feedback to examiners on how they might improve their examining technique and monitor their performance.

Berwick and Ross focus on the language of candidates in a speaking test and the question of cross-cultural pragmatics. Their study showed that strategies used by examiners in conducting interviews may be linked to underlying cultural and pragmatic phenomena. As with Lazaraton an implication is that rater training should focus on the language of the examiner in order to determine the extent to which accommodation is appropriate.

Both Pollitt and Murray and Chalhoub focus on the raters – Pollitt and Murray in relation to their decision-making behaviour in the use of rating scales and Chalhoub in relation to candidates performing different tasks.

In their study, Pollitt and Murray make use of Thurstone's paired comparison technique for accurate measurement of psychological dimensions and also Kelly's Personal Construct Theory, which they suggest provide useful tools to investigate the behaviour of raters.

Chalhoub focused on learners of Arabic and aimed to derive holistic oral scores using three elicitation tasks across three rater groups. She employed multi-dimensional scaling techniques and was able to show that the three rating groups used dimensions differentially to assess the learners' speech. A conclusion of her work is that scales need to be empirically derived according to the tasks and the audience.

Writing

Milanovic, Saville and Shen focus on raters in the context of assessing compositions produced by candidates taking Cambridge FCE and CPE examinations. Like Pollitt and Murray, their study was carried out to explore the decision-making behaviour of raters in relation to a number of variables. They propose a model of the rating process, and, in particular, they investigate the different approaches to marking which the raters in their study employed. They also look at other variables such as the linguistic elements which the raters focused on when marking the compositions, as well as the raters' background, their marking speed, and the proficiency level of the scripts to be marked. In order to collect data they employed a range of techniques, including retrospective written reports, think-aloud verbal protocols and group interviews.

Taylor, Lukmani and Hamp-Lyons look at the assessment of writing ability in academic contexts.

Taylor reports on a project to develop academic writing tasks for assessment used in a specific EAP domain. Stage one of the project is described in the paper, including the work carried out to identify the kinds of writing tasks that are actually required of college and university students in the USA. Her concern is with content validity, and the research is characterised by the involvement of test users in the test development process.

Lukmani looks at the role of English and the ability to write effectively in relation to academic success in a university context where English is the medium of instruction. Her concern is with the writing of freshman-level students at the University of Bombay and, in particular, her paper focuses on the relative roles of accuracy and coherence in the assessment of student performance in content subjects.

Hamp-Lyons in her paper looks at the use of portfolios as an approach to ESL performance assessment, particularly as applied to academic contexts in the United States. Specifically, she is concerned with ways in which ethical assessment of ESL writing can be achieved using portfolio-based methods.

Reading

Davies and Irvine describe a project to develop and validate a set of achievement tests of extensive reading. In particular, their concern is with content validity, test difficulty and the dependability of judgements made by the tests (i.e. assignment of readers to levels of reading ability).

Van Krieken considers the issue of equating tests of reading comprehension within the context of national examinations in the Netherlands. He describes two projects which led to important decisions being made as to how standards should be maintained over time by making use of equating procedures.

Test purpose and context of use

Wesche, Paribakht and Ready present a comparative study of four placement *tests* asking the question, which is the best possible test? (rather than which is the best test possible).

Teasdale describes an approach to defining what is to be tested in a very specific testing context – a test of the English language requirements of Air Traffic Controllers (ATCs) in Europe. He is concerned with the issue of authenticity and of achieving high content validity. The aim of the project is to develop a measurement framework to allow for valid decisions to be made about the competence of the newly qualifying ATC officers on the basis of test scores.

Test validation using statistical procedures

Brown and Ross investigate the reliability of TOEFL in a number of ways using large data-sets from the May 1991 administration. In particular, they investigate the relative contributions to score dependability of various numbers of items and sub-tests and also the decision dependability at different cut-points. In addition to classical statistics, they use generalisability theory and decision dependability [phi(lambda)] estimates to estimate various cut points.

Lee describes the use of the Many-faceted Rasch model and the FACETS program (Linacre 1991) in the validation of an ESL placement test. A number of facets were investigated including the two sub-tests in the battery which were designed to measure grammatical accuracy and discourse sensitivity.

Bilingualism

Verhoeven describes a project to assess early bilingual proficiency of groups of Antillean, Moroccan and Turkish children in the Netherlands. A bilingual proficiency test was used to monitor metacognitive and language development and a range of techniques, including IRT and analysis of variance, were used to analyse the results. The results support the view that there is interdependency in bilingual development and that high proficiency in either language is related to a high level of metalinguistic awareness.

Translation

Cascallar, Cascallar, Lowe and Child describe an inter-agency project in the USA to develop rating scales and descriptors for the assessment of translation ability. These developments are based on a new theoretical model that conceptualises the translation process in cognitive terms. The scales cover both the assessment of proficiency in reading the 'donor' language and of proficiency in writing in the 'receptor' language. In addition, there is a new congruity scale designed to deal with the product of the translation.

Appendix

Alphabetical list of all papers, posters, and workshops

presented at the

15th Language Testing Research Colloquium

Cambridge and Arnhem

August 2–7, 1993

Lyle F. Bachman, Brian Lynch and Maureen Mason
Investigating Variability in Tasks and Rater Judgements in a Performance Test of Foreign Language Ability

Jared Bernstein
Performance Testing with Speech Recognition: Methods and Validation

Richard Berwick and Steven Ross
Cross-cultural Pragmatics in Oral Proficiency Interview Strategies

Jean-Guy Blais and Michel Laurier
The Dimensionality of a Placement Test Components

Sarah L. Briggs
Using 'Real Life' Academic Challenges for Evaluating Communicative Skills in English

Annie Brown
The Effect of Rater Variables in the Development of an Occupation-Specific Language Performance Test

James Dean Brown and Jaqueline A. Ross
Decision Dependability of Item Types, Sections, Tests, and the Overall TOEFL Test Battery

Eduardo C. Cascallar
A New Cognitive Approach for the Assessment of Language Aptitude

Eduardo C. Cascallar and Marijke I. Cascallar
New Technologies for the Assessment of Oral Proficiency in Second Language Learners

Eduardo C. Cascallar, Marijke I. Cascallar, Pardee Lowe and James Child
Development of New Proficiency and Performance-Based Skill Level Descriptors for Translation: Theory and Practice

Micheline Chalhoub-Deville
Performance Assessment and the Components of the Oral Construct Across Different Tasks and Rater Groups

Marcia J. Reeves
The Impact of Rater Quality Control and Training/Retraining Procedures on Rater Reliability in Scoring Test of Spoken English Response Tapes

Elana Shohamy, Smadar Donitsa-Schmidt and Ronit Waizer
The Effect of the Elicitation Modes on the Oral Language Obtained on Language Tests

Bernard Spolsky
Testing the English of Foreign Students in 1930

Marie-Christine Sprengers
The Feasibility of the Guided Summary as a Test of Reading Comprehension

Charles W. Stansfield and Dorry Mann Kenyon
Evaluating the Efficacy of Rater Self-Training

Carol Taylor
A Study of Writing Tasks Assigned in Academic Degree Programs

Alex Teasdale
Content Validity in Tests for Well-Defined LSP Domains: An Approach to Defining What is to be Tested

Ludo Verhoeven
Early Bilingualism, Cognition and Assessment

Marjorie Wesche, T. Sima Paribakht and Doreen Ready
A Comparative Study of Four Placement Instruments

Gillian Wigglesworth and Kieran O'Loughlin
An Investigation into the Comparability of Direct and Semi Direct Versions of an Oral Interaction Test

Elaine Wylie
An Aspect of the Reliability of the Speaking Test of the International English Testing System (IELTS)

Susan A. Zammit
Motivation, Test Results, Gender Differences and Foreign Languages: How do they Connect?

References

Alderson, J. C. 1991. Bands and Scores. In J. C. Alderson and B. North (eds.), *Language Testing in the 1990s.* London: Macmillan.

ALTE Document 1. 1994. *European language examinations.* University of Cambridge Local Examinations Syndicate.

Bachman, L. F. 1990. *Fundamental Considerations in Language Testing.* Oxford: Oxford University Press.

Bachman, L. F., F. Davidson, K. Ryan and I. Choi. 1995. *An Investigation into the Comparability of Two Tests of English as a Foreign Language: The Cambridge-TOEFL Comparability Study.* Cambridge : UCLES.

Brennan, R. L. 1983. *Elements of generalizability theory.* Iowa City, IA: The American College Testing Program.

Canale, M. 1983. From communicative competence to communicative language pedagogy. In J. C. Richards and R. W. Schmidt (eds.), *Language and Communication.* London: Longman.

Canale, M. and M. Swain. 1980. Theoretical bases of communicative approaches to second language teaching and testing. *Applied Linguistics* 1 (1): 1–47.

Chomsky, N. 1965. *Aspects of the Theory of Syntax.* Cambridge, MA: MIT Press.

Hymes, D. H. 1967. Models of the interaction of language and social setting. *Journal of Social Issues.* 23 (2): 8–38.

Hymes, D. H. 1972. On communicative competence. In J. B. Pride and J. Holmes (eds.), *Sociolinguistics: Selected Readings.* Harmondsworth, Middlesex: Penguin.

Messick, S. 1989. Validity. In R. L. Linn (ed.), *Educational Measurement.* Third Edition. New York: Macmillan.

Linacre, J. M. 1989. *Many-faceted Rasch measurement.* Chicago, IL: MESA Press.

Linacre, J. M. 1991. *Facets for PC-Compatibles (Computer Program).* Chicago, IL: MESA Press.

Palmer, A. S., P. J. M. Groot and G. A. Trosper. 1981. *The construct validation of tests of communicative competence.* Washington, DC: TESOL.

Roach, J.O. 1945. *Some problems of oral examinations in modern languages: an experimental approach based on the Cambridge Examinations in English for foreign students, being a report circulated to oral examiners and local examiners for those examinations.* Cambridge: Local Examinations Syndicate.

Spolsky, B. 1995. A not-too-special relationship. In L. F. Bachman, F. Davidson, K. Ryan and I. Choi, *An Investigation into the Comparability of Two Tests of English as a Foreign Language: The Cambridge-TOEFL Comparability Study.* Cambridge: UCLES.

1

A qualitative approach to monitoring examiner conduct in the Cambridge assessment of spoken English (CASE)

Anne Lazaraton
The Pennsylvania State University

Introduction

In our attempts to understand communicative competence and to promote its development in second language learners, one area of second language acquisition research has attempted to describe and to analyze both the language used by L2 speakers in communicative interaction, and the ways that they are accommodated by their more proficient native speaker interlocutors (see, for example, Day 1986; Chaudron 1988; Larsen-Freeman and Long 1991). Until recently though, little attention has been paid to one very important form of native-speaker non-native-speaker interaction, that which occurs in oral proficiency assessment contexts. Certainly, a considerable amount of interest has been shown in the measurement of this spoken language proficiency, especially by the ACTFL/ETS Oral Proficiency Interview (OPI) (ACTFL 1986) and its variants. An extensive body of research exists on oral interview validity (e.g., Bachman and Palmer 1981; Henning 1992), reliability (e.g., Magnan 1987; Reeves 1993; Wylie 1993), and rating procedures (e.g., Adams 1980; Brown 1993; Shohamy 1983), on its comparisons with other oral testing methods (e.g., Clark 1988; Stansfield and Kenyon 1992); and on some perceived objections to the OPI itself (e.g., Bachman 1988; Lantolf and Frawley 1985; Raffaldini 1988; Shohamy 1988).

Nevertheless, it is only recently that any empirical attempts have been made to look beyond the oral proficiency interview product – outcome ratings – to the actual interviewing process in order to understand how the participants behave in this context, and how this behavior might or might not impact on eventual assessment outcomes. Young and Milanovic's (1992) analysis of the interview section of the Cambridge FCE indicated that the resulting interviewer-candidate discourse was highly asymmetrical in terms of features of dominance, contingency, and goal orientation. In Ross and Berwick's (1992) study, OPI interviewers were shown to use features of control (e.g., topic nomination) and accommodation (e.g., speech modifications) for different purposes, such as supporting the interview process and gauging language proficiency. In another study, Ross (1992) analyzed OPI interviewer accommodation in terms of 'antecedent triggers' in the candidates' talk. Ross suggests that the degree of interviewer accommodation should be considered in the assignment of final ratings to candidates.

Although quantitative approaches to test development and validation are usually employed in language testing research, there has been a call in recent years to include qualitative analyses in research and development (Bachman 1989; van Lier 1989). This suggests another promising avenue of inquiry into the issue of interview discourse and interaction, one that has been used successfully by Lazaraton (1991), who employed conversation analysis techniques to understand various aspects of the interaction in a corpus of language assessment interviews, including interviewer question formulation and modification, assessments of language ability, and the overall structural organization of the interviews. Other qualitative approaches to understanding the oral interviewing process have been used by Berwick and Ross (1993) in examining pragmatic aspects of the OPI; by He (1994) in describing elaborated answers in the FCE oral interview; and by Ross (1994) in demonstrating formulaic speech in the OPI.

An important finding to emerge from the research on interview discourse and interaction is that by looking only at the 'product' of these assessments – the assigned ratings – we are left with an incomplete understanding of the assessment process itself, and how it impacts on rating outcomes. In fact, the achievement of consistent ratings is highly dependent on the achievement of consistent examiner conduct during the procedure, since we cannot ensure that all candidates are given the same number and kinds of opportunities to display their abilities unless oral examiners conduct themselves in similar, prescribed ways. More importantly, it may be that final ratings and the descriptions of candidate ability which are derived from them are, in reality, a collaborative, interactional accomplishment between the tester and the testee (see Marlaire 1990, and Marlaire and Maynard 1990 on this point).

As a first step in the process of coming to a fuller understanding of examiner conduct in the oral interview, a descriptive analysis of 58 Cambridge Assessment of Spoken English (CASE) audiotape transcripts (see a description of the CASE procedure in Appendix 1) was undertaken in order to examine CASE assessor behavior for consistency across candidates and across assessors in terms of adherence to the prespecified CASE Interlocutor Frame, a written agenda that prescribes both the wording of and the order in which question prompts ought to occur during the assessment. Although the CASE procedure consists of three phrases, only the Stage 1 Interview, in which one candidate is interviewed by one examiner, was analyzed, since it is the only section in which the assessor participates in the interaction (s/he merely facilitates the interaction between pairs of candidates in subsequent phases).

The results of this study are useful for monitoring the behavior of and providing feedback on the conduct of the five assessors who took part in this test administration. The study also has broader implications, in that it may suggest possible modifications to the existing CASE Interlocutor Frame, if certain prompts are not functioning well or are being overlooked by the assessors. In addition, it provides a method whereby future examiners can be monitored for consistent behavior during training, certification, and live encounters. Finally, it is hoped that this type of monitoring procedure can be adapted for other face-to-face oral examinations. This information on examiner conduct in the examination process, in conjunction with more traditional 'product' ratings, can give a more accurate estimate of reliability in oral assessment contexts.

Method

The data analyzed for this study were collected during one CASE administration in Tokyo, Japan in September 1992. All 58 assessments were audio-taped with a table-top recorder, and video-recorded with a fixed, wide-angle video camera on a tripod.

Candidates

Fifty-eight part-time language school students at the Suntory Cambridge English School took part in the assessments. They ranged in age from 18–55, with an average age of 29; 24 were male and 34 were female.

Examiners

A total of ten examiners took part in the administration, but only the five who administered Stage 1 (the Interview) of the procedure are considered in this paper. All of the examiners had some experience in administering and rating CASE assessments. They are identified below and subsequently by initial:

A	(female)	16 interviews
B	(female)	6 interviews
C	(female)	18 interviews
H	(male)	12 interviews
W	(male)	6 interviews

Transcripts

The 58 audiotapes were transcribed, using conversation analysis conventions (Atkinson and Heritage 1984), by two graduate students at The Pennsylvania State University under the supervision of the researcher. Transcripts were carefully checked, and corrected where necessary. Approximately six of the 58 audiotapes were incomplete due to recording difficulties; this fact accounts for some of the results being based on less than the total 58 assessments.

Results

An analysis of stage 1 interlocutor frame adherence

The occurrence of and variations in each of the 26 prompts suggested by the Interlocutor Frame for Stage 1 (labelled as 1c–6b from this point on) was tallied for each examiner and across examiners, and a percentage of occurrence figure was computed for each prompt. It should be noted that there are actually 31 prompts in Stage 1, but the first three and the last two, which do not require candidate responses, were not analyzed.

The first part of the interview deals with introductions. The four prompts that required a verbal student response in the first part of the interview were used 94% to 100% of the time by the five examiners who acted as interlocutors for this part of the assessment. The problems that arose were not with examiners avoiding the prompts, but with students understanding them, especially prompt 1e.

1e What would you prefer me to call you?

Although this prompt occurred in 56 of the 57 interviews (98%) it caused more misunderstanding than any other prompt in the interview. 22 of the 44 candidates who responded to this particular wording misunderstood this question, the meaning of which often required several turns to negotiate. I believe the misunderstanding is due in part to unfamiliarity with the lexical item 'prefer' and its non-salient perceptual position in the question. Again, time spent negotiating this prompt would be better spent on some of the prompts at the end of the interview which are ignored due to lack of time. Therefore, it might be beneficial to reword it to something like 'Can I call you ____' or 'May I call you ____', wordings that were used successfully seven times by Interviewer H. This formulation would allow for a simple 'yes' or 'no' response.

The rest of the interview deals with giving information about self. These prompts comprise the following topic areas: job, travel, language learning, career prospects and personal interests. In relation to prompts dealing with current job there was a fair amount of variation in the rate of occurrence of these prompts, ranging from 100% adherence for 2a *What's your job?* to 45% for 2f *What makes you say that?* as a follow-up to yes/no question.

The prompts in the section on travel occurred between 72% and 95% of the time, and all three showed great variability in their wording e.g.

3b If you could choose, where would you go?

Where have you been/where will you go?

This prompt occurred in 42 of the 58 encounters (72%), 11 of which were worded exactly. However, although this prompt showed a significant amount of variation in wording, there were a few misunderstandings. It functions as a follow-up to question 3a but also requires elaboration through its wh-form. Therefore, it is important to ask, although its frequency of occurrence in this dataset indicates that examiner adherence is sufficient.

The prompts in the section on language learning showed a great deal of variability in their frequency of occurrence, from 89% for 4a to 39% for 4e. Wording modifications, however, were not frequent.

4a Is English the only foreign language you speak?

This prompt was used 51 times in the interviews (89%), 40 with its exact wording. Of these 40, seven were misunderstood; other minor modifications were not problematic in terms of misunderstanding. This prompt seemed to function well, but it could be modified to 'Do you speak any other foreign languages', wording used successfully by Interviewer C 6 times. This would put 'foreign languages' in the perceptually salient final position in the question, rather than embedded as it is in the original prompt.

4e Who do you generally speak English with?

This prompt occurred only 22 times in the 57 interviews (39%) and only seven times with this exact wording. It was probably skipped due to lack of time, but because it requires little work to answer, it could be dropped in order to allow time for other, later questions to be asked.

The section of the interview dealing with career prospects received the least coverage in the encounters. While question 5a occurred in 47 of the 57 interviews (82%), prompt 5b wasn't used at all, and the remaining three were used less than 35% of the time. Undoubtedly, this occurred because time was running out, which is unfortunate since these more speculative and hypothetical questions can discriminate students at higher proficiency levels.

5a How do you see your career developing?
What do you see yourself doing in the future?

This prompt occurred in 47 of the 57 interviews (82%) but proved to be difficult for the candidates. With its exact wording it was misunderstood in over half of the encounters in which it was used. 'Career developing' and 'see yourself doing' are both probably unfamiliar, idiomatic expressions for these candidates. Interestingly, three candidates, hearing 'career developing', interpreted 'career' as 'Korea' and went on to talk about Korea's development in the future! Other minor wording variations were used with some success. Based on its frequency of occurrence, it is probably not necessary to check that it is used, but it might be advisable to reword it to avoid unnecessary misunderstanding, unless it is seen as a good prompt for discriminating proficiency levels.

I believe it is beneficial to end the encounter on a positive note. The questions about personal interests were used often and were rarely misunderstood, giving most candidates the impression that the encounter ended well.

Summary

To summarize the findings in this section, the following observations and recommendations were made for the 26 prompts in this stage of the assessment:

1c: aim for consistency in wording

1d: aim for consistency in wording

1e: difficult to understand; consider rewording to 'May/Can I call you ...'

1f: fine as is

2a: fine as is; check for use

2b: fine as is; check for use

2c: check for use; consider rewording to 'Why did you decide on/choose ...'

2d: consider rewording to wh-question 'How long have you ...'

2e: fine as is

2f: check for use; consider rewording to 'Why do you say that'

2g: fine as is

3a: fine as is

3b: fine as is

3c: aim for consistency in wording

4a: consider rewording to 'Do you speak any other foreign languages'

4b: fine as is

4c: fine as is

4d: check for use

4e: fine as is

5a: difficult to understand; may want to reword; see 5c

5b: was not used; drop from Frame?

5c: check for use; may be able to replace 5a and 5c with 'What are your plans for the future'

5d: rarely used

5e: rarely used

6a: fine as is

6b: fine as is

An analysis of individual examiner performance in stage 1

The results of the tally of the 26 Stage 1 prompts for each of the five examiners appear in Table 1.

Table 1

Interlocutor Frame for Stage 1 Interview

Interviewer	Assessments	Mean	s.d.	Minimum	Maximum
A	15	18.6	2.13	15	22
B	6	20.0	1.67	18	22
C	17	19.8	2.33	14	24
H	12	15.8	2.21	11	19
W	6	17.0	2.37	14	20

As can be seen from the table, the interviewers as a group averaged between 16 and 20 of the 26 prescribed prompts, with Examiners B and C using the most and Interviewer H using the least. To better understand their individual performance during Stage 1, comments on their style and a table showing their adherence to the Interlocutor Frame for each candidate (C#) they interviewed are given below.

Interviewer A

C#	1c d e f	2a b c d e f g	3a b c	4a b c d e	5a b c d e	6a b	Total
25	+ + + +	+ + + + +	+ +	+ + + +	+	+	17
26	+ + + +	+ + + + + +	+ + +	+ + + +	+	+	20
27	+ + + +	+ + + + +	+ + +	+ + +	+	+ +	18
28	+ + + +	+ + + + + +	+ + +	+ + + +	+ +	+ +	21
29	+ + + +	+ + + +	+ + +	+ +	+	+	15
30	+ + + +	+ + + + + +	+ + +	+ +	+	+	18
43	+ + + +	+ + + + +	+ + +	+ + + +	+	+ +	19
45	x x x x	+ + + + +	+ + +	+ + +	+	+	--
46	+ + + +	+	+ + +	+ + + +	+ +	+	15
48	+ + + +	+ + + + + +	+ + +	+ + + +	+	+ +	20
55	+ + + +	+ + + + + +	+ + +	+ + +	+ + +	+ +	21
56	+ + +	+ + + + + + +	+ +	+ +	+	+ +	17
57	+ + + +	+ + + + + +	+ + +	+ + + +	+ +	+	20
58	+ + + +	+ + + + + + +	+ + +	+ + +		+ +	19
59	+ + + +	+ + + + + +	+ +	+ +	+	+ +	17
60	+ + + +	+ + + + + +	+ + +	+ + + +	+ +	+ +	21

The letters 1c to 6b represent the 26 prompts recommended by the Interlocutor Frame.

Sixteen interviews were conducted by Interviewer A. She had no problem covering the questions in the first two sections, but achieved a rate of less than 50% for the last two prompts in language learning (4d, 4e), and for all the prompts in future career prospects. Probably the most notable feature of A's speech behavior was her tendency to slow her rate down considerably when asking questions.

Suggestions: A could use her time more efficiently, and try to maintain a normal rate of speaking, if possible, even when candidates seem to misunderstand questions.

Interviewer B

C#	1c d e f	2a b c d e f g	3a b c	4a b c d e	5a b c d e	6a b	Total
49	x x + +	+ + + + +	+ + +	+ +	+ +	+ +	18
50	x + + +	+ + + + + + +	+ + +	+ + + +	+	+ +	21
51	+ + + +	+ + + +	+ + +	+ + + +	+ +	+ +	20
52	+ + +	+ + +	+ + +	+ + + +	+ +	+ +	18
53	+ + + +	+ + + + + + +	+ + +	+ + + +	+	+ +	21
54	+ + + +	+ + + +	+ + +	+ + + +	+	+ +	19

Interviewer B conducted six interviews. The prompts that were used 50% or less of the time were 2b and 2f in current job, 4e in language learning, and all the prompts in future career prospects except 5a. Her frequent laughter with the candidates or in response to their answers indicates either that she was nervous, or that she needs to strive for a more detached, objective tone.

Suggestions: B could also use her time more efficiently and refrain from laughing so often.

Interviewer C

C#	1c d e f	2a b c d e f g	3a b c	4a b c d e	5a b c d e	6a b	Total
1	x + + +	+ + + + +	+ +	+ + + +	+ +		17
3	+ + + +	+ + + + + + +	+ +	+ + +	+ +		18
2	+ + + +	+ + + + +	+ +	+ + + + +	+ + + + +	+ +	23
4	+ + + +	+ +	+ + +	+ + + +	+	+ +	17
5	+ + + +	+ + + + + + +	+ + +	+ + + + +	+ +	+ +	23
6	+ + + +	+ + + + + + +	+ + +	x x x x x	x x x x x	x x	--
13	+ + + +	+ + + + +	+ + +	+ + + +	+ +	+ +	21
14	+ + + +	+ + + +	+ + +	+ + + + +	+ +	+ +	21
15	+ + + +	+ + + +	+ + +	+ + + +	+ +	+ +	20
16	+ + + +	+ + + + + +	+ + +	+ + + +	+ + +	+ +	22
17	+ + + +	+ + + + +	+ + +	+ + + +	+ + +	+ +	21
18	+ + + +	+ + + + +	+ + +	+ + + +	+ +	+ +	20
19	+ + + +	+ + + + + + +	+ +	+ + +	+ +	+ +	20
20	+ + +	+ +	+ + +	+ +	+	+ +	14
21	+ + + +	+ + + + + + +	+ +	+ + + +	+ +	+ +	21
22	+ + + +	+ + + +	+ +	+ + + + +	+ +	+ +	19
23	+ + + +	+ + + + +	+ +	+ + +	+ +	+	17
24	+ + + +	+ + + + + + +	+ +	+ + + +	+	+ +	20

Interviewer C conducted 18 interviews, the most of any of the five examiners. Her adherence to the Interlocutor Frame was admirable; only 4d in language learning and three prompts in the future career prospects section were covered less than 50% of the time (5b, 5c, 5e). She laughed occasionally during the assessments.

Suggestions: No suggestions for Interviewer C.

Interviewer H

C#	1c d e f	2a b c d e f g	3a b c	4a b c d e	5a b c d e	6a b	Total
7	+ + + +	+ + + +	+ +	+ + +	+	+ +	16
8	+ + + +	+ + + + +	+ + +	+ + +	+ +	+ +	19
9	+ + + +	+ + +	+ +	+ + +	+ + +	+ +	17
10	+ + + +	+ + + +	+ +	+ + +		+ +	15
11	+ + + +	+ + + +	+	+ + +	+	+ +	15
12	+ + + +	+ + + +	+ +	+ + + +		+ +	16
37	+ + + +	+ + + + +	+ + +	+ + + + +	+	+	19
38	+ + + +	+ + +	+ + +	+ +	+ +	+ +	16
39	+ + + +	+ + +	+ +	+ + +	+ +	+ +	16
40	+ + + +	+ + +	+	+ + +	+	+ +	14
41	+ + + +	+ +	+ + +	+ +	+	+ +	14
42	+ + + +	+ + + +	+	+ + +	+ +	+ +	16

Interviewer H served as the interlocutor in 12 interviews, and he had trouble using prompts in all of the sub-areas of the interview, but especially in current job and future career prospects (2b, 2c, 2f, 2g, 3b, 4d, 5a, 5b, 5c, 5d). In fact, H's style can best be characterized as chatty and conversational; whether this served the candidates well is not clear.

Suggestions: H could be more serious about adhering to the Interlocutor Frame, not just in using the prompts, but in wording them without random modifications. In general, his interviewer stance, as objective and detached, could be improved.

Interviewer W

C#	1c d e f	2a b c d e f g	3a b c	4a b c d e	5a b c d e	6a b	Total
31	+ + + +	+ + +	+ + +	+ + +	+	+ +	16
32	+ + + +	+ + + +	+ + +	+ + + + +	+ +	+ +	20
33	+ + + +	+ + + +	+ +	+ +	+	+ +	15
34	+ + + +	+ + + + +	+ + +	+ + + +	+ +	+	19
35	+ + + +	+ + + + + +	+ +	+ + + +	+ +	+	18
36	+ + +	+ + + +	+ +	+ + +		+ +	14

Interviewer W conducted 6 interviews, and had problems covering prompts in current job (2c, 2f, 2g), language learning (4d), and future career prospects (all but 5a). A notable feature of W's speech was his consistent repetition of words or entire candidate responses in each of his six interviews.

Suggestions: W could use his time more efficiently and avoid repeating candidate responses, perhaps by withholding verbal reactions as much as possible.

Summary

This brief description of the behavior of the five CASE examiners during Stage 1 is neither as comprehensive nor as detailed as it might be, but it does exemplify the sort of feedback that might be given to assessors after a test administration. It is also a useful starting point for noting the sorts of behaviors that might be included in a template to monitor assessor performance in the future.

Discussion

The analysis of adherence to the Stage 1 Interlocutor Frame indicated that certain prompts were not used consistently, or were worded in ways that substantially deviated from the prescribed wording of the Frame. It was proposed, based on prompt usage and wording in these data, that examiners should be checked to see whether they are using those prompts, and with the prescribed wording. It seemed that particular prompts, such as those about future career prospects, were skipped across the board, because time ran short. The fact that other prompts were avoided may be more a matter of individual style, and cannot be remedied by changing the structure of the interview or its time allotment.

In fact, what is needed is more emphasis in CASE assessor training on the role of the interlocutor in the assessment, and the behaviors that are part of and appropriate in that role. A great deal of time is devoted to training assessors to rate candidate language samples, and for some, that is all they will ever do; they will never act as an examiner in a CASE assessment. But for those who will, more time needs to be spent on the issue of sticking to the Interlocutor Frame, in terms of both using the required prompts and wording them as given. A good start in this direction would be to revise the Training Manual to include a section on assessor behavior, using material that is based on empirical findings as well as common sense notions of what constitutes acceptable behavior in this context.

In addition, more thought should go into monitoring the behavior of examiners after training; this is where an evaluation template would be useful. A form which evaluates the performance of CASE examiners in three broad areas – *Interlocutor Frame Adherence*, *Speech Behavior*, and *Rater Reliability* – seems advisable. These happen to coincide with the three-part ACTFL tester evaluation scheme (Buck 1989) which assigns points in the three areas of Interview Structure, Elicitation Technique, and Rater Reliability in order for ACTFL OPI testers to become certified. In terms of the specifics of the evaluation form, the first section, *Interlocutor Frame Adherence*, could contain all 26 Stage 1 prompts, or just those that were shown to be problematic in this study. I believe it is important to capture the rewordings that examiners use; therefore, there should be a column to make notes on this aspect of the assessment. Of course, the prompts would actually be listed, perhaps as they are in the CASE Assessment Booklet; that format could be modified for this purpose. Since adherence to the Frame was only analyzed for the Stage 1 Interview, further research is needed to determine whether and how examiners intervene during the last two parts of the assessment.

The second section, *Speech Behavior*, would be evaluated using a checklist where the evaluator assesses the frequency with which certain speech behaviors occur during the assessment. These behaviors are ones that were shown to occur with some regularity in another report on these data (Lazaraton 1993) and include rephrased and slowed down rate of asking questions, as well as repetitions, completions, corrections, and evaluations of candidate answers; others may suggest themselves in subsequent research. Finally, *Rating Reliability* would be evaluated for the chosen assessments, according to criteria developed by the CASE administrators and trainers. Since this facet of CASE assessment was not dealt with in this study, no suggestions are made regarding how this might be evaluated.

The proposed evaluation form might be used as follows. After a CASE administration, tapes of the assessments would be selected for evaluation. Perhaps one third of the assessments by experienced examiners, and one half of those by new examiners would be analyzed. Although analysis via transcripts of the assessments would be most efficient, the evaluation could be done with just the tapes. The CASE trainer would evaluate each of the chosen assessments using the evaluation form; the results would constitute feedback to the examiner, as well as evidence that raters are capable of conducting the assessments in an appropriate manner. Ideally, during CASE training, trainees would take part in some mock assessments, after which the form could be used to provide suggestions for improving their interviewing techniques.

Whether or not it is actually feasible to enact this sort of evaluation procedure would have to be determined by UCLES. Nevertheless, I believe that this effort to make examiners accountable for their ratings as well as their behavior in the assessments would help to make CASE a more reliable and valid oral assessment procedure. Of course, it is hoped that this same procedure could be carried out with other oral proficiency examinations, resulting in templates appropriate for those contexts. Although the specifics may vary from context to context, it is likely that the same types of examiner behaviors exist, and should be monitored, in most face-to-face oral tests.

Proposed CASE examiner evaluation template

Examiner Name:
Assessment #:

I. Interlocutor frame adherence

Stage 1 Prompts	Used as is	Reworded as	Skipped
1c Would you tell me your name please			
.			
.			
6b Are there any new activities you would like to take up			
Comments on adherence:			

II. Speech behaviors

Stage 1 Behaviors	Rare	Occasional	Frequent	Excessive
laughing				
correcting responses				
repeating answers				
slowing rate/increasing pitch				
completing utterances				
stating prompts				
rephrasing questions				
evaluating answers				
other:				

Comments on speech behavior in Stage 1:

Stage 2 Behaviors	Rare	Occasional	Frequent	Excessive
intervening to encourage talk				
explaining vocabulary				
explaining procedures				
prompting a focus on task				
asking questions				
suggesting questions				
other:				

Comments on speech behavior in Stage 2:

III. Rater reliability

Appropriate information to be recorded here from monitoring of the assessments made by the examiner.

Conclusion

This study is but a small step towards understanding the role the native speaker examiner plays in the interaction in the oral assessment context. Although descriptive in nature, it has shed light on several of issues that arise in face-to-face testing, using techniques that are not normally adopted in language testing research, but ones that are uniquely suited to looking 'inside' the assessment process. Whether revising some of the prompts in the Interlocutor Frame would actually lead to less misunderstanding by the candidates, whether actual feedback to examiners, based on the evaluation form, would lead to improved performance in the assessments, and whether consistent performance has any effect on candidate ratings, are questions which await further study. In any case, it is critical that more studies on interview interaction be undertaken on other widely used oral proficiency examinations. As a result, the outcomes of these examinations will be better understood, not just in terms of how 'reliable' and 'valid' the ratings are, but in terms of whether, and if so, the degree to which such measures of proficiency in a second or foreign language are collaborative accomplishments between examiner and candidate.

Appendix 1   CASE Description

Adapted from pp. 3.16–3.17 of CASE Manual (UCLES, 1992))

The Cambridge Assessment of Spoken English (CASE) is a test of oral proficiency designed to assess both the linguistic and communicative skills necessary for oral communication between non-native and other speakers of English in a wide variety of contexts. CASE sponsors may be managers and employers, as well as educational institutions where English is an important or the main medium of communication. CASE provides an overall measure of spoken English language proficiency, as well as individual profile reports which describe the candidates' spoken language proficiency in terms of specific areas of ability, including grammar, vocabulary, pronunciation, organization, communication strategies and interaction, and task achievement.

CASE is a two-stage oral assessment, carried out by two trained examiners with groups of six candidates; the entire procedure takes less than two hours. In Stage 1 candidates are assessed individually by an interlocutor and by a second assessor who observes, but does not take part in, the interaction. In this five-minute interview the emphasis is on drawing out the candidate to demonstrate his/her ability to speak English, so an initial impression check can be made. In Stage 2 the candidates take part in a 13–15 minute task-based interaction where they are assessed on the basis of their interaction with a fellow candidate. The pairs, and the particular tasks in which they engage, are based on a variety of factors, including overall ability, gender, etc. In the first part of Stage 2 the candidates take turns making presentations to their partners; upon completion the listener asks questions of the presenter. In the second part, the candidates work together on a task which requires discussion and negotiation; the assessors listen but do not take part.

Assessors are trained to meet the needs of local testing centers. Assessor training is in three stages. The first is participation in two half-day intensive group training sessions. These training sessions are followed by standardization exercises, and then a certification tape and score grid. On rating the certification tape successfully, assessors are certified for a set period of one year.

References

Adams, M.L. 1980. 'Measuring foreign language speaking proficiency: A study of agreement among raters' in J.L.D. Clark (ed.), *Direct Tests of Speaking Proficiency: Theory and Application* (pp. 129–49). Princeton, NJ: Educational Testing Service.

American Council on the Teaching of Foreign Languages. 1986. ACTFL/ETS *Oral Proficiency Guidelines*. Hasting-on-Hudson, NY: ACTFL.

Atkinson, J.M. and J. Heritage (eds.) 1984. *Structures of Social Action*. Cambridge: Cambridge University Press.

Bachman, L.F. 1988. Problems in examining the validity of the ACTFL oral proficiency interview. *Studies in Second Language Acquisition* 10, 149–64.

Bachman, L.F. 1989. Language testing – SLA research interfaces. *Annual Review of Applied Linguistics* 9: 193–209.

Bachman, L.F. and A.S. Palmer. 1981. The construct validation of the FSI oral interview. *Language Learning* 31: 167–86.

Berwick, R. and S. Ross. 1993. *Cross-cultural pragmatics in oral proficiency interview strategies*. Paper presented at the 15th LTRC, Cambridge, UK: August.

Brown, A. 1993. *The effect of rater variables in the development of an occupation-specific language performance test*. Paper presented at the 15th LTRC, Cambridge, UK: August.

Buck, C. (ed.) 1989. *The ACTFL OPI: Tester Training Manual*. Yonkers, NY: ACTFL.

Chaudron, C. 1988. *Second Language Classrooms*. New York, NY: Cambridge University Press.

Clark, J.L.D. 1988. Validation of a tape-mediated ACTFL/ILR scale based test of Chinese speaking proficiency. *Language Testing* 5: 187–205.

Day, R.R. (ed.) 1986. *Talking to Learn: Conversation in Second Language Acquisition*. Rowley, MA: Newbury House.

He, A. 1994. *Elicited vs. volunteered elaboration: talk and task in language proficiency interviews*. Paper presented at AAAL, Baltimore, MD: March.

Henning, G. 1992. The ACTFL oral proficiency interview: Validity evidence. *SYSTEM* 20: 365–72.

Lantolf, J.P. and W. Frawley, 1985. Oral-proficiency testing: A critical analysis. *Modern Language Journal* 69: 337–45.

Larsen-Freeman, D. and M.H. Long 1991. *An Introduction to Second Language Acquisition Research*. London: Longman.

Lazaraton, A. 1991. *A conversation analysis of structure and interaction in the language interview*. Unpublished Ph.D. dissertation, University of California at Los Angeles.

Lazaraton, A. 1993. *The development of a quality control template based on the analysis of CASE transcripts.* Report prepared for the EFL Division, University of Cambridge Local Examinations Syndicate, Cambridge, UK.

van Lier, L. 1989. Reeling, writhing, drawling, stretching, and fainting in coils: Oral proficiency interviews as conversation. *TESOL Quarterly* 23: 489–508.

Magnan, S.S. 1987. Rater reliability of the ACTFL oral proficiency interview. *Canadian Modern Language Review* 43: 525–37.

Marlaire, C.L. 1990. On questions, communication, and bias: Educational testing as "invisible" collaboration. *Perspectives on Social Problems* 2: 231–58.

Marlaire, C.L. and P.W. Maynard. 1990. Standardized testing as an interactional phenomenon. *Sociology of Education* 63: 83–101.

Raffaldini, T. 1988. The use of situation tests as measures of communicative ability. *Studies in Second Language Acquisition* 10: 197–216.

Reeves, M.J. 1993. *The impact of rater quality control and training/retraining procedures on rater reliability in scoring Test of Spoken English response tapes.* Paper presented at the 15th LTRC, Cambridge, UK: August.

Ross, S. 1992. Accommodative questions in oral proficiency interviews. *Language Testing* 9: 173–86.

Ross, S. 1994. *Formulaic speech in language proficiency interviews.* Paper presented at AAAL, Baltimore, MD: March.

Ross, S. and R. Berwick, 1992. The discourse of accommodation in oral proficiency interviews. *Studies in Second Language Acquisition* 14 (2): 159–76.

Shohamy, E. 1983. The stability of oral proficiency assessment in the oral interview testing procedures. *Language Learning* 33 (4): 527–40.

Shohamy, E. 1988. A proposed framework for testing the oral language of second/foreign language learners. *Studies in Second Language Acquisition* 10: 165–79.

Stansfield, C.W. and D.M. Kenyon. 1992. Research on the comparability of the oral proficiency interview and the simulated oral proficiency interview. *SYSTEM* 20: 347–64.

University of Cambridge Local Examinations Syndicate. 1992. *Cambridge Assessment of Spoken English: CASE.* Cambridge: UCLES.

Wylie, E. 1993. *An aspect of the reliability of the speaking test of the International English Language Testing System (IELTS).* Paper presented at the 15th LTRC, Cambridge, UK: August.

Young, R. and M. Milanovic, 1992. Discourse variation in oral proficiency interviews. *Studies in Second Language Acquisition* 14: 403–24.

2 Cross-cultural pragmatics in oral proficiency interview strategies

Richard Berwick
University of British Columbia
Steven Ross
University of Hawaii at Manoa

Introduction

Tests of second language proficiency can be enormously consequential to second language learners. Because such tests are routinely used to open, restrict or deny educational or employment opportunities, test developers are obliged to construct their instruments within established norms of validity and reliability in order to limit the effects of *arbitrary assessment*. No one sets out to create an arbitrary instrument or assessment procedure, although it is clear that as our understanding of the construct of proficiency changes over time and we acquire fresh perceptions about the ecology of proficiency testing, it becomes increasingly important, perhaps even ethically compelling, to consider approaches to aligning the instrument or procedure with the new knowledge.

This is precisely the position oral proficiency assessment in general now assumes with respect to the body of research developed during the past two decades into face-to-face cross-cultural exchanges in gatekeeping contexts (Ericson 1976, 1979; Fiksdal 1988, 1990; Marlaire and Maynard 1990; Scollon and Scollon 1981), especially those intended to support oral proficiency ratings (Ross and Berwick 1992; van Lier 1989) entailing an interviewer's use of accommodation and control strategies (i.e., broadly, *foreigner talk*; Ferguson 1971, 1975; Freed 1978). The orientation to examination of oral proficiency as a rule-governed cross-cultural encounter has received little attention within the traditional psychometric framework of the oral proficiency movement (see Bachman 1988; Valdman 1988), nor has the status of oral proficiency interviews as instances of extended, asymmetric discourse (van Lier, 1989; Young and Milanovic 1992) been expanded to scrutinize cross-cultural effects on the texts interviewers and interviewees construct in test settings.

This paper builds upon a relatively small body of work that has examined potential threats to the validity of the Oral Proficiency Interview[1] based on the use of arbitrarily constructed rating scales (Lantolf and Frawley 1985, 1988; also Bachman 1988; Bachman and Savignon 1986; Clark and Clifford 1988; *cf.* Dandonoli and Henning 1990) and, more recently, upon the frequently naive (from the interviewer's point of view) use of accommodation and control during the interview procedure (Ross and Berwick 1992), particularly in interviewer strategies for framing interview questions (Ross 1992).

Although the OPI gains much of its reliability (Lowe 1987) from the fact that it is organized around an interview protocol, and claims both face and content validity from its appearance as a series of conversational exchanges around a variety of interviewer-induced probes (Educational Testing Service 1982), it is ironically the conversational qualities of the procedure that we have found comprise the most serious challenge to the ecological validity of interviewers' ratings and perhaps also to the validity of the construct underlying the procedure. Our initial study examined the relationship between various features of accommodation interviewers employed during the OPI – including requests for clarification, propositional reformulation and grammatical simplification that normally form the core of contingent, non-test conversational management between native speakers and non-native speakers – and the award of ratings associated with global oral proficiency descriptions on the 11-point (0 to 5, including plus points) ACTFL/ETS scale. Findings suggested the tendency of interviewers to over-accommodate at the lower to intermediate levels and to effectively tutor production of the 20-minute speech sample. Under these circumstances, truly conversational performance which normally leaves participants unaware of their accommodative behavior would seem to be a dysfunctional element of a procedure expressly intended at the outset of the interview to guide interviewees into displaying the limits of their knowledge of the language of the interview.

We also speculated about the effects of interviewers' interest in controlling topical development specifically and exercising control over the interview structure generally through such features of control as topic nomination, topic abandonment, propositional reformulation and expansion of an interviewee's utterances. Here we noted the possibility that the ambivalence created when *both* conversational and interview values are instantiated into the speech setting might affect the ways in which the interviewee interprets and responds to the interviewer. To the extent that one's culture provides patterns for interpretation and responsiveness during face-to-face encounters of the sort encompassed by the OPI, it is also possible to speculate that ratings of exchanges between interviewers and interviewees from various cultures will profoundly and perhaps unwittingly reflect the orientations to talk participants bring to the interview context (Labov 1972; Gumperz 1978; 1982a, 1982b). To put the point more explicitly into the framework of oral assessment, interviewer-raters may be unaware of the constraints their own cultural background imposes on the sample of speech produced by interviewees who function within a different framework for what constitutes responsive speech in interview or test settings – or for appropriate verbal behavior in tasks imposed during the period of assessment. Given the largely universal, effectively culture-neutral stance of the interview procedure and rating guidelines, that is, the implied logic that a particular rating awarded to different interviewees from different cultural backgrounds on different occasions describes the same level of proficiency in the language of the interview, evidence of cultural variability would pose questions about the validity of the procedure across cultures. How are we to treat ratings based on very different perceptions of what interviewees must produce in order to provide evidence of their oral proficiency?

Ratings accomplished within a standard protocol and with reference to established guidelines appear to afford protection from arbitrary assessment at the relatively formal procedural level. At the discourse level, however, research has shown significant variability of native-non-native talk in both non-test and test settings in response to a variety of features of the speech setting, including task (Berwick 1988; Douglas and Selinker 1985; Long, 1980; Porter 1983; Tarone 1985, 1988; Young and Milanovic 1992) and gender (Young and Milanovic 1992; see also Gass and Varonis 1986 re: non-native/non-native exchanges). Although the responsiveness of OPI discourse to cultural background and its unintended effects on ratings have been more suggested than examined systematically, studies of interethnic communicative systems and cross-cultural pragmatics within the context of native-non-native dyadic exchanges in a variety of non-test settings strongly implicate a role for culture in determining how interviewers and interviewees build their talk, exchange and clarify information and accomplish their goals.

Along these lines, Brown and Levinson (1978) and Scollon and Scollon (1981), for example, have examined the potential of interethnic communication to produce miscommunication in terms of misfit between *politeness systems* which are deployed in order to assert or maintain face. Interactants' perceptions of the power and distance relationships within the setting trigger use of a natural (i.e., 'appropriate') system from the user's perspective. Reciprocity between systems is possible at the outset of interaction (the systems are 'symmetric'): system elements may be shared and individuals may have more than one system at their disposal for different settings or for the demands of interaction within a setting. Failure to achieve reciprocity (the systems are 'asymmetric'), however, is not so much a failure to negotiate a common interpretation of meanings within the discourse as it is the inability to satisfy a partner's expectations about the treatment of face or even to perceive that these expectations have not been met. From this point of view, then, the communicative systems in play during a gatekeeping interview extend, as Scollon and Scollon (1981) note, well beyond the set of objective procedures normally developed to eliminate overt discrimination (p. 4) or to ensure reliability of assessment. They provide the literally unremarkable structures through which interviewers and interviewees engage in purposeful talk and draw unarticulated inferences about each other's capacity to conduct social life.

These 'unarticulated inferences' are central to the position developed thus far with respect to the influence of communicative systems and discourse frames (such as tasks) on talk produced during the OPI. Some of the effects of cross-cultural variation that may bear upon the OPI have also been pointed out in studies of cross-cultural pragmatics, specifically those dealing with what Blum-Kulka, House, and Kasper (1989; also Brown and Levinson 1978) describe as face-threatening speech acts such as requests and apologies conducted within interactants' cultural frameworks for the exercise of power and perception of social distance. The relevance of dominance, in particular, to the conduct of oral proficiency interviews also forms a key element of Young and Milanovic's (1992) analysis of native-non-native interview discourse which they cast in terms of the *contingent,* specifically, *reactive,* utterances made in response to the content or perhaps form of a prior utterance. Their empirical study found significant interviewee reactivity to interviewer control over topics and goal orientation, that is, evidence for 'assymmetical contingency' (also, Jones and Gerard 1967).

What emerges from examining the various approaches to study of the cross-cultural dimensions of communicative style, whether at the level of communicative system, contingent discourse or speech act, is a focus on power and distance relations, and the ways in which participants attempt to maintain and develop an image of themselves through discourse.

Extending this convergence of viewpoint, we turn now to a comparative case study of accommodation and control exercised cross-culturally and attempt to outline several fundamental differences in the way OPI ratings at a nominally equivalent level are worked out by two interviewers from different cultures. We first compare the interviewers' management of the assessment procedure through several non-parametric tests of the null hypothesis that there are no differences in the ways the interviewers accommodate to their interviewees and control the interview. We then move to a microanalysis of discourse which depicts the use of these strategies in context.

The use of statistical analysis to compare the two cases and then to suggest points in the discourse that distinguish them is not intended to advance general claims about the ways interviewers from different cultures achieve ratings. On the contrary, we are interested in initiating, first, an approach to the study of cross-cultural pragmatic behavior during oral proficiency interviews and, second, developing a set of empirically-based speculations about face-to-face interviews conducted by Japanese- and English-speaking interviewers that may prove useful to others in generating research hypotheses.

Approach

Raters and ratings

The possible influence of cross-cultural phenomena on the oral proficiency interviewer is most validly examined directly in the context of the interview itself. To this end, six English as a second language (ESL) and six Japanese as a second language (JSL) OPIs were matched for the purpose of comparing two interviewers' approaches to accommodating towards their interviewees and controlling the development of the interview. Each of the six interviews for each target language was administered by the same interviewer.

The ESL interviews were conducted by an American male initially trained and certified by Educational Training Service staff and retrained by an ETS-certified rater at a large Japanese company which conducts numerous English language courses for its employees. The OPI is routinely used at the company as an adjunct to placement and end-of-course examinations. Rated audio cassette tapes of English language OPIs were archived at the company and form the pool from which the Japanese tapes used in this study were drawn.

Interviewees were all company employees taking the OPI as an end-of-course examination.

The JSL interviews were conducted by a Japanese male trained with others by an ETS-certified rater as part of a study of Japanese language proficiency gain during a three-month period of residence in Japan for grade 11 and 12 students of Japanese at secondary schools in British Columbia. Rated audio cassette tapes for the present study were selected from the archived Japanese OPI tapes produced during the gain study.

The proficiency level samples used for the matching included five 1+ (high intermediate) and one 2 (advanced) interviews recorded on cassette tape. Each interview was transcribed and analyzed by two researchers independently following the features of interview accommodation and control outlined in Ross and Berwick, 1992 (also Appendix A). The average number of tallied features per interview was used as the basis for comparing the two sets of interviews in the analysis[2].

Given the small number of matched interviews considered for analysis, the difference between the JSL and ESL interviews was tested with non-parametric procedures. We employed the Mann-Whitney U Test to examine the hypothesis that the observed differences in the frequencies of the features of accommodation and control were a matter of random chance. The criterion for significance was set at .01 in order to protect against Type I error.

Findings

Categorical comparisons

Accommodation

Table 1 lists the features of accommodation that differentiate the JSL and ESL interview phenomena. Although the JSL interviewer used all ten of the accommodative moves more frequently than did the ESL interviewer, three met our criterion probability of .01: display questions, over-articulation and lexical simplification. A strong trend towards grammatical simplification also distinguished the Japanese from the English language interviews. Overall, the Japanese interviewer employed accommodation more frequently both pre-emptively (within turns) and responsively (across turns) during the course of the six interviews.

Table 1

Features[3] of Accommodation: JSL and ESL

	JSL	ESL	p
Display Question	19	2.5	.008
Clarification Requests	20.5	16	.464
Or-Questions	29.5	18	.376
Fronting	19.5	11	.180
Grammatical Simp.	12.5	4.5	.075
Slow-Down	31.5	10	.128
Over-Articulation	28	9	.010
Other-Expansion	27.5	20.5	.194
Lexical Sima.	29	8	.008

Control

In previous research on the role of interviewer efforts to control the focus and content of the oral interview we found that the major control strategies do not appear to be related to subsequent rating outcomes (Ross and Berwick 1992). The potential for systematic cross-cultural and cross-linguistic differences between interviewers in the use and extent of control is nevertheless a possibility worth exploring. The forms of control examined here include interviewer moves to nominate new topics in the discourse, to abandon previously nominated topics when they generate insufficient interviewee talk, to extend and alter the interviewer's immediately preceding utterance in order to shape the interviewee's next turn and to reformulate the propositional content of topics to which there has been an apparent under-elaboration provided by the interviewee. All of these moves converge on the interviewers' compelling need to obtain a ratable sample of speech and form the core of strategies intended to advance the interview (Ross and Berwick 1992). Table 2 provides the results for analysis of the control strategies.

None of these features of control reaches our criterion of .01. There is still a trend consistent with the inter-rater differences observed in use of the accommodation strategies. The JSL interviewer offered a larger number of topics as focal points for the interview and was readier to pursue topics for which interviewee responses were not deemed elaborate enough for adequate evaluation of oral proficiency. These trends, when matched with the results for accommodation, suggest that the interviewers followed different paths to accomplishing their ratings. They also suggest that the interviewers may have developed disparate forms of evidence for allocating their interviewees' behavior to nominally equivalent levels of second language ability within the rating scale descriptions.

Table 2

Features of Control: JSL and ESL

	JSL	ESL	*p*
Self-Repetition	26	16	.295
Topic Nomination	49	54	.625
Topic Abandonment	35	25	.038
Self-Expansion	46	53	.687
Propositional Reformulation	42	18	.023

Discussion: The discourse of accommodation and control

Our analysis thus far has revealed several significant and reliable categorical differences in the use of accommodation, in addition to trends which suggest different approaches to the exercise of control during the interview. Beyond the interviewers' common interest in preserving a kind of generic question-and-answer format to guide elicitation of interviewee speech, the specific differences encountered in the Japanese and English interviews profile a distinct contrast between the interviewers' strategies in assisting their interviewees to understand problematic material, find a way through a problem when it arises and follow an agenda that is intended to move the interviewee across major boundaries of the assessment procedure – from small-talk to level check, into and out of probes and into a wind-down. How are these differences elaborated pragmatically within the interview context? How do they function as contrasting communicative styles with reference points in two cultures?

To a large extent the two languages of the interviewers provide templates of opportunity for accommodation and control which permit, and may require, quite different treatment of problems arising during exchanges across turns. For example, an English-speaking interviewee may demonstrate difficulty with the frequent lack of explicit initial and secondary subject reference in Japanese; this may provide the Japanese interviewer an occasion to supply it in what would normally be inappropriate contexts of use. Similarly, Japanese post-position verbal inflections may signal solidarity or deference, or may indeed be altered to enforce the submissive position of an interviewee in ways which are simply unavailable to English-speaking interviewers. Cross-cultural pragmatic differences may also be evinced beyond the semantic properties of language structures and be conveyed through the ways the discourse is organized to achieve both the goals of the interview and the contingencies of topical development. The following excerpts illustrate some of what we think are reliable differences in the interviewers' approaches to accommodating the interviewees and directing their talk.

Excerpt 1 depicts the preference of the Japanese interviewer (T) for an intense, closely managed, lexically and phrasally responsive accommodation to the interviewee. It contrasts rather prominently with the American interviewer's (P's) attempt in Excerpt 2 to provide the interviewee sufficient conversational resources to find a path out of lexical difficulty.

Excerpt 1

01)	T	:Gakko de donna benkyo shitaka oshiete kudasai.:
		Would you please tell me what sort of things you studied at school?
02)	A >	:Dona? [donna] (2) Taitei Nihongo...:
		Wha- Kind? (2) Basically Japanese
03)	T	:Nihongo, sore kara...:
		Japanese and...
04)	A >	:Mmm, ryoko? Uh, ry-ryo-ri?:
		Mmm, travel? Uh, co- cook-ing?
05)	T	:Ryori:
		Cooking
06)	A >	:to shodo, to bigitsu [bijutsu]:
		and tea ceremony and art
07)	T	:Bijutsu:
		art
08)	A	/:bijutsu, to taiku:
		/art and P.E.
09)	T	:Bijitsu wa donna koto oshiemashita?:
		What sort of art were you taught?

Excerpt 2

01)	P	And, uh, do you do aerobics or anything, or
02)		anything else?
03)	T >	/I'm sorry
04)	P	Do you do, you do any other kind of sports?
05)		like aerobics or ...
06)	T	aerobics. Ah, yes. I have tried aerobics before

In both cases, the interviewees' indications of lexical uncertainty (>) were noticed and handled within a turn-relinquishing (question-and-response) framework. The American interviewer, however, attempts to clarify by suggesting an 'index' of categories that might offer assistance indirectly, including supply of or-questions and self-expansion; the more directive style of the Japanese interviewer relies heavily on other-correction and other-repetition in a kind of try-it-and-I'll-let-you-know-if-it's-right style of exchange. Although we did not code for other-correction, inspection of the transcripts indicates that the general preference for self-correction in conversation (Schegloff, Jefferson, and Sacks 1977) was overturned relatively frequently in the Japanese interviewer's rejoinders to his interviewee's responses, but that the American interviewer avoided other-correction in order to accommodate through negotiated exchange.

Interviewers' treatment of the interview as an instructional venue and use of accommodation in the form of an instructional tactic when presented with evidence of misunderstanding is a problem we noted in our earlier study (Ross and Berwick 1992; see also Berwick 1988). In the present case, both interviewers also served as teachers of their own language, so it came as no surprise to observe them both attempting to instruct when the opportunity presented itself. The Japanese language interviews, however, show a frequent and preferred use of accommodation to instruct, especially when the problem involved evidence of lexical uncertainty, and included reliance on other-correction and definitions, as well as use of over-articulation and display questions. Excerpts 3 and 4 illustrate the use of other-correction, Excerpt 5, over-articulation and Excerpt 6, display questions.

Excerpt 3

01)	B >	:...taikitsu?:
		[?]
02)	T	:taiku, hai, taiku:
		physical education, OK, physical education
03)	B >	:...to biji-, biju-:
		and ar- ar-
04)	T	:Bijutsu, hai:
		Art, right

Excerpt 4

01)   B >   :Tokoro wa takusan sakana:
                       The place with lots of fish

02)   T   :Sakana, ah, 'aquarium', ne, suizokukan, desu ne:
                       Fish, oh, aquarium, right, you mean 'aquarium'

Excerpt 5

01)   B >   :kaimono [slurred] ni ikimashita:
                       I went shopping

02)   T: :Donna KAImono...: Shopping for what?

Excerpt 6

01)   T >   :Ja desu, ne, computaa wa doko ni arimasu ka?:
                       All right, >where is the computer?

02)   S   :Tsukue o, tsukue no ue ni arimasu:
                       The desk, it's on top of the desk

03)   T >   :Soo desu ne. Kore wa nan desu ka?: [taps desk twice with pen or pencil]
                       That's right. What's this?

04)   S >   :Wakarimasen:
                       I don't know

05)   T >   :Kore wa (1) purintaa desu ne. Computaa
06)   >   no purintaa. Computaa no purintaa wa doko ni
07)   arimasu ka?:
                       This is a printer, isn't it. A computer printer. Where is the computer printer?

The didactic quality of these excerpts has been described elsewhere as a relatively efficient approach to conveying instructional goals (Berwick 1988, 1993) in the sense that they avoid the apparently more roundabout negotiation of meaning evident in tasks which proceed via reciprocal information exchange. What makes the Japanese interviews unique as didactic transactions is the contingent nature of the instruction. That is, the instructionally focused sequences develop from within the discourse; they are not tied to any objectives which have been determined prior to the engagement of interviewer and interviewee. To this extent, the Japanese interviewer has effectively transformed accommodation to the interviewee into a means of exercising control from moment-to-moment without relying on the more marked tactics of control, including topic-initiation, topic-abandonment or reformulation of propositions produced by either the interviewee or the interviewer.

    The oral interview can now be viewed as a complex process in which nominally conversational forms of accommodation have the potential to serve some of the major goals of oral assessment by a rapid, rather nimble leading of the interviewee through troubled waters. Conversational values can be re-worked, in effect, to cast them into the unaccustomed role of providing the level of asymmetry necessary to produce quick convergence on a topical focus and controlled elicitation. This kind of *tutored* accommodation – a potential source of unreliability in the OPI context – is not, as we have noted, ordinarily tolerated in conversational exchange, a compelling function of which is the *cooperative* weaving of common indexical threads across turns. The Japanese interviews demonstrate competent attention to both senses of accommodation, the English interviews largely to the latter.

Construction and reformulation of propositional nodes also distinguishes the two sets of interviews. In the OPI frame of reference, an interviewer's intro-duction and reformulation of periodic probes are crucial elements in determining the limits of an interviewee's oral proficiency. A good interviewer is supposed to be able to establish a rough idea of a candidate's level with reference to the descriptive rating scales and then attempt to push through this level to the point at which the candidate's speech begins to break down. Reaching this point is demonstrably traumatic for some people. It is still very much an open question, however, whether the effects of this conspicuous exercise of control over the interview vary systematically by culture, although we have speculated (Ross and Berwick 1992) about the possibility that members of cultures which observe a norm of harmonious, uncontentious dialogue in face-to-face interaction (*cf.* Scollon and Scollon 1981 re: 'deference politeness', p. 175f) may be unprepared to either enforce or respond 'appropriately' to the demands of the probe.

Our observations in the present case indicate that the Japanese interviewer exercised considerable control over the direction of the interviews and quality of responses by negotiating a series of information resources about the interview-ee's recent experience and then committing the interviewee to dealing with an aspect or implication of the established resource. Functionally, this is equivalent to setting up a propositional node across several turns for further topical development. At no point did the Japanese interviewer launch a probe that appeared intended to destabilize an interviewee's performance at the current level. The American interviewer, on the other hand, attempted to organize probes which contained most of their rhetorical force in large monologue-like construc-tions and to reformulate these constructions during their delivery. It will not be especially useful here to examine the extent to which propositions formulated in this way succeeded in challenging the limits of the interviewees' current oral performance, except to note, as we have previously (Ross and Berwick 1992), that the potential for confusion, for ambiguous interpretation, or threats to face may increase with the growing complexity of the proposition.

The following excerpts exemplify this contrast in communicative style.

Excerpt 7

01)	T	:Eeeto, sore dewa desu ne. Ima Steveston de,
02)		ee to, Nihongo no benkyo shiteimasu ne.:
		Uh, all right then. You study Japanese at Steveston, right?
03)	S	[:?:]
04)	T	:Hai. Maishu, nankai Nihongo no benkyoshimasu
05)		ka? (2) Maishu, nankai kurasu ga arimasuka?:
		Yes. How many times a week do you study Japanese?
		(2) How many classes do you have per week?
06)	S	: (2) mm (2) uh (3) Getsuyobi kara (1) kinyobi
07)		made (1) Nihongo (1) benkyo shimasu.:
		(2) mm (2) uh (3) From Monday (1) to Friday (1) I study [1]
		Japanese.
08)	T	:Hai. Ja, isshukan, ikkai, nikai, sankai,
09)		yonkai, gokai, nankai benkyo shimasu ka?:
		All right, then. Once, twice, three times, four times, five times—
		how many times do you study in a week?
10)	S	:Uh, mainichi:
		Uh, every day
11)	T	:Mainichi benkyo shimasu, ah soo desu ka.
12)	>	Ee to, uh, S-san wa naze (1) Nihongo no benkyo
13)		shimasu ka?:
		Every day, I see. OK, uh, why (1) do you study Japanese?
14)	S	:(3) Moo ichi doo?:
		Once more?
15)	T >	:Hai. S-san wa *naze* ima Naze ima Nihohgo no benikyoshite imasu ka?
16)		imasu ka?:
		OK. S-san, *why* are you studying Japanese now?
17)	S	:(5) Wakarimasen:
		(5) I don't understand.
18)	T	:Hai. *Naze* to iyu no wa 'why' to iyu koto desu ne.:
		OK. 'NAZE' means *why*, right?
19)	S	:Uh, Nihongo ga suki desu.:
		Uh, I like Japanese.
20)	T >	:Naze suki desu ka?:
		Why do you like it?
21)	S	:(10) Manga ga suki desu.:
		(10) I like [Japanese] comics.
22)	T	:*man*ga. Donna manga ga suki desu ka?:
		Comics! What kind of comics do you like?

23) S   :(3) Takusan:
          Lots of them.
24) T   :Takusan. Ah so desu ka.:
          Lots. Oh, I see.

The probe which is formally initiated at line 15 ('*why* are you studying Japanese?') is apparently intended to be comprehensible from the outset. Beyond the careful, turn-based resolution of ancillary information leading to the question itself, the interviewee's trouble over the key word 'why' occasions a direct translation from Japanese to English and a temporary ratcheting up of the level of formal politeness. There are rough equivalents of this available to native English interviewers, including occasional code-switching, although in practice it would be difficult to avoid the rather heavy-handed, prosecutorial style that is conveyed when intense, turn-based propositional development in English becomes the norm for the interview. What works in Japanese with English-speaking interviewees apparently fails in English with Japanese-speaking interviewees.

The final excerpt points to an alternative approach to probing, to within-turn reformulation, preference for winding up to 'pitch a strike' to the interviewee and tolerance for awaiting the conclusion of an interviewee's turn that has the potential to develop into an extended monologue. The American interviewer expends no effort in responding contingently to the errors or mis-statements or other evidence of trouble, but focuses wholly on propositional content. It is an open question here whether the increasing weight of the proposition clarifies or obscures it for the interviewee.

Excerpt 8

01) P   And um (2) could you (2) maybe within the
02)   last, uh (1)last year or so, uh (5) excuse
03)   me, within the last year or so, uh, the land
04)   prices in, uh, Japan have been a subject in
05)   the news, and, uh, the land prices, the price
06)   of land
07) N   /um
08) P   Uh could you tell me where, where in Japan
09)   is the most expensive to buy land?
10) N   Uh, Tokyo
11) P   Tokyo
12) N   Uh (2) I, I hear Tokyo, uh, in Tokyo, uh, one,
13)   one Tsubo, uh, one (3) one, uh, one Tsubo is
14)   uu, three point three, uh, square meter
15) P   mm hm
16) N   uh, more than, uh, uh (2) several thousandu (3)
17)   several thousand million yen . .

[75 seconds]

18)	P		In general, my question that I want to ask you
19)		>	in general is, uh, do you think it's fair that
20)			thee, uh, normal person cannot buy land, that
21)			the normal, average worker, uh, cannot buy
22)			enough land to build a house, or to, or
23)			actually buy a house?
24)	N		Uh
25)	P		/Because land pri-, because the price of land
26)			is so expensive, uh, >do you think it's fair, uh,
27)	N		/mm
28)	P		or what do you think, uh, about the fact that
29)			thee average worker, the average person, uh,
30)	N		/mm
31)	P		has a very difficult time, uh, affording land?
32)		>	Do you think that's bad?

Conclusion

We conclude that communicative styles represented in the discourse of these interviews extend authority over the interviewee in very different ways, the Japanese style emphasizing authority through attention to form and a kind of 'instructional care-taking', the American style focusing on control through attention to content and reliance on the interviewee's willingness to observe a conversational style that 'engages the issues'. We suggest that if these interviewer differences are reliably distributed by culture, as we think they may be, ratings which result from the interview process are likely to be based on disparate kinds of evidence for oral proficiency. More extensive sampling of contrastive interviews, matched according to proficiency ratings, should provide the kind of evidence necessary to test this hypothesis.

The analyses of the JSL and ESL interviews suggest also that the role of cultural background of the interviewer and the apparent differences in pragmatic strategies for dealing with interlocutor attempts to manage the interview may lead to dramatic differences in the interviewer's understanding of what sort of proficiency is being demonstrated. In addition to the observed pattern that JSL interviewees can be much less fluent and demonstrate less control over the morphosyntax of their second language than their ESL counterparts in achieving comparable ratings of proficiency, it appears that there may be an underlying assumption that the form of the response is critical in the JSL interviews – more so perhaps than the content of the response is in the ESL interviews. This pattern, if shown to be consistent with further sampling of cross-linguistic interviews, may suggest a degree of cultural/pragmatic relativity in the oral interview procedure that has not been explored to the extent necessary to match the broad attribution of face validity the OPI has thus far received.

The implication of systematic cultural variation in interviewers' approaches to conducting the OPI suggests, beyond further focused, empirical study of actual interviews, a practical reformulation of training procedures for raters. Explicit attention to cross-cultural factors may be a useful general emphasis during interviewer training, as might the possibility of developing particular strategies for the contingent conduct of the interview based on our knowledge of politeness systems deployed during gatekeeping interviews. For example, if a universal prototype for conducting an oral interview – such as deference politeness – is tenable and does produce reliable interviewer behavior across cultures, it may be desirable to instruct candidate interviewers on how to apply it during their interviews.

At a more fundamental level, however, it may be more appropriate to consider whether attempting to obviate cultural differences through recourse to a universal protocol is what we really want to undertake. One of the practical implications for assessment of research in cross-cultural pragmatics and communicative systems is that norms for intracultural verbal exchange in natural, non-test settings are frequently extended to participants engaged in intercultural verbal exchange. If learners' developing pragmatic competence in a second language is part of the object of assessment in test settings, then it would seem odd to enforce an approach to assessment that fails to engage that competence.

Does this mean then that we are headed towards a kind of chaotic approach to oral proficiency testing in which local norms for the organization and enforcement of oral behavior overturn the relative certainty a single protocol provides? If rating scales are unsatisfactory now because of their arbitrary and open-ended characteristics, are we going to have to construct novel rating descriptions for all possible combinations of intercultural encounter between interviewers and interviewees? These problems may appear intractable given the often conflicting demands of validity, reliability and practicality which lead us to exact compromises in all of our approaches to assessment. The issue of validity in cross-cultural oral proficiency assessment therefore raises two additional questions for further examination, one empirical and the other axiological: how influential are cultural differences among interviewers and what do we think we should do about them?

Notes

1   Although the OPI is one among several leading, systematic approaches to oral proficiency assessment used worldwide, we have noted (Ross and Berwick 1992) that 'perhaps the most carefully crafted and widely employed approach to oral proficiency assessment in what Valdman (1988), Bachman (1988) and others have termed the oral proficiency movement is the group of rating levels, descriptive rating guidelines and specific procedures developed over the years by the joint efforts of the U. S. Foreign Service Institute (FSI), American Council on Teaching Foreign Languages (ACTFL) and the Educational Testing Service (ETS). It will be convenient, although somewhat inexact, to refer to the class of oral proficiency interview conducted within the protocols and with reference to the guidelines as the Oral Proficiency Interview, or, simply, OPI.' (American Council on the Teaching of Foreign Languages 1987; Educational Testing Service 1982.)

2   Interrater reliabilities were calculated using an analysis of variance procedure (Woods, Fletcher and Hughes 1986). For the features of accommodation meeting the criterion alpha = .01, the repeated measures reliabilities were .838 (display question), .746 (over-articulation) and .859 (lexical simplification).

3   The figures in Table 1 are not whole numbers because the features used for the analysis were averages of the two independent tallies derived from the discourse analyses of the interviews.

Appendix A

Features of accommodation and control used in the study

Accommodation

Feature	Definition
Display question	The interviewer asks for information which is already known to the interviewer or which the interviewer believes the interviewee ought to know.
Comprehension check	The interviewer checks on the interviewee's current understanding of the topic or of the interviewer's immediately preceding utterance.
Clarification request	The interviewer asks for a restatement of an immediately preceding utterance produced by the interviewee.
Or-question	The interviewer asks a question and immediately provides one or more options from which the interviewee may choose an answer.
Fronting	The interviewer provides one or more utterances to foreground a topic and set the stage for the interviewee's response.
Grammatical simplification	The interviewer modifies the syntactic or semantic structure of an utterance so as to facilitate comprehension.
Slowdown	The interviewer reduces the speed of an utterance.
Over-articulation	The interviewer exaggerates the pronunciation of words and phrases.

Other-expansion	The interviewer draws on the perceived meaning of the interviewee's utterance and elaborates on words or phrases within the utterance.
Lexical simplification	The interviewer chooses what is assumed to be a simpler form of a word or phrase which the interviewer believes the interviewee is unable to comprehend.

Control

Feature	**Definition**
Topic nomination	The interviewer proposes a new topic by foregrounding information not previously introduced in the discourse. This typically leads to a question which may be introduced by informative statements and which requires no link to previous topic development.
Topic abandonment	The interviewer unilaterally ends a current topic even though the interviewee may still show evidence of interest in further development.
Self-expansion	The interviewer extends and alters the content of the interviewer's immediately preceding utterance so as to accomplish interview objectives.
Propositional reformulation	The interviewer refocuses the interviewee's attention on a previously nominated topic or issue which has not produced enough language to confirm a rating for the interviewee.

References

American Council on the Teaching of Foreign Languages. 1987. ACTFL Lincolnwood IL: proficiency guidelines. In H. Byrnes and M. Canale (eds.), *Defining and Developing Proficiency: Guidelines, Implementations and Concepts*. Lincolnwood IL: National Textbook Company.

Bachman, L. 1988. Problems in examining the validity of the ACTFL oral proficiency interview. *Studies in Second Language Acquisition* 10: 149–64.

Bachman, L. and S. Savignon. 1986. The evaluation of communicative language proficiency: A critique of the ACTFL oral interview. *Modern Language Journal* 70: 380–90.

Berwick, R. F. 1988. *The effect of task variation in teacher-led groups on repair of English as a foreign language*. Unpublished doctoral dissertation, The University of British Columbia, Vancouver, British Columbia.

Berwick, R. F. 1993. Towards an educational framework for teacher-led tasks. In G. Crookes and S. Gass (eds.), *Tasks in a Pedagogical Context*, Clevedon, Avon: Multilingual Matters.

Bilmes, J. 1988. The concept of preference in conversation analysis, *Language in Society* 17.

Blum-Kulka, S., J. House and G. Kasper. 1989. Investigating cross-cultural pragmatics: An introductory chapter. In S. J. Blum-Kulka, House and G. Kasper (eds.), *Cross Cultural Pragmatics: Requests and Apologies*, Norwood, NJ: Ablex.

Brown, P. and S. Levinson. 1978. Universals in language usage: Politeness phenomena. In E. Goody (ed.), *Questions and Politeness: Strategies in Social Interaction*. Cambridge: Cambridge University Press.

Clark, J. L. D. and R. T. Clifford. 1988. The FSI/ILR/ACTFL proficiency scales and testing techniques: Development, current status and needed research. *Studies in Second Language Acquisition* 10.

Dandonoli, P. and G. Henning 1990. An investigation into the construct validity of the ACTFL guidelines and oral interview procedure. *Foreign Language Annals* 23.

Douglas, D. and L. Selinker. 1985. Principles for language tests within the 'discourse domains' theory of interlanguage: Research, test construction and interpretation. *Language Testing* 2: 205–26.

Educational Testing Service (ETS). 1982. *ETS Oral Proficiency Testing Manual*. Princeton, NJ: ETS.

Erickson, F. 1976. Gatekeeping encounters: A social selection process. In P. R. Sanday, (ed.), *Anthropology and the public interest: Fieldwork and theory*. New York: Academic Press.

Erickson, F. 1979. Talking down: Some cultural sources of miscommunication of interracial interviews. In A. Wolfgang (ed.), *Nonverbal Behavior:*

Applications and Cultural Implications. New York: Academic Press.

Ferguson, C. A. 1971. Absence of copula and the notion of simplicity. In D. Hymes (ed.), *Pidginization and the Creolization of Language.* Cambridge: Cambridge University Press.

Ferguson, C. A. 1975. Towards a characterization of English foreigner talk. *Anthropological Linguistics* 17.

Fiksdal, S. 1988. Verbal and nonverbal strategies of rapport in cross-cultural interviews, *Linguistics and Education* 1.

Fiksdal, S. 1990. *The Right Time and Pace: A Microanalysis of Cross-cultural Gatekeeping Interviews.* Norwood, NJ: Ablex.

Freed, B. 1978. *Foreigner talk: A study of speech adjustments made by native speakers of English in conversation with non-native speakers.* Unpublished doctoral dissertation, The University of Pennsylvania, Philadelphia.

Gass, S. and E. M. Varonis. 1986. Sex differences in NSS/NSS interactions. In R. Day (ed.), *Talking to Learn: Conversation in Second Language Acquisition.* Rowley, MA: Newbury House.

Gumperz, J. J. 1978. The conversational analysis of interethnic communication. In L. E. Ross (ed.). *Interethnic Communication.* Athens, GA: University of Georgia Press.

Gumperz, J. J. 1982a. *Discourse Strategies.* Cambridge: Cambridge University Press.

Gumperz, J. J. 1982b. *Language and Social Identity.* Cambridge: Cambridge University Press.

Jones, E. E. and H. B. Gerard. 1967. *Foundations of Social Psychology.* New York: Wiley.

Labov, W. 1972. *Sociolinguistic Patterns.* Philadelphia, PA: University of Pennsylvania Press.

Lantolf, J. P. and W. Frawley. 1985. Oral-proficiency testing: A critical analysis. *Modern Language Journal* 69 (4): 337–45.

Lantolf, J. P. and W. Frawley. 1988. Proficiency: Understanding the construct, *Studies in Second Language Acquisition* 10.

Levinson, S. 1983. *Pragmatics.* Cambridge: Cambridge University Press.

van Lier, L. 1989. Reeling, writhing, drawling, stretching and fainting in coils: Oral proficiency interviews as conversation. *TESOL Quarterly* 23 (3): 489–508.

Long, M. H. 1980. *Input, interaction, and second language acquisition.* Unpublished doctoral dissertation, The University of California, Los Angeles.

Lowe, Pardee. 1987. Interagency language roundtable oral proficiency interview [Review of the LPI]. In J. C. Alderson, K. J. Kranke and C.W. Stansfield (eds.), *Reviews of English Language Proficiency Tests,* Washington, DC: TESOL.

Marlaire, C. and D. Maynard. 1990. Standardized testing as an interactional phenomenon. *Sociology of Education* 63: 83–108.

Porter, P. A. 1983. *Variations in the conversations of adult learners of English as a function of the proficiency level of the participants.* Unpublished doctoral dissertation, Stanford University, Palo Alto, CA.

Ross, S. 1992. Accommodative questions in oral proficiency interviews, *Language Testing* 9: 173–86.

Ross, S. and R. F. Berwick. 1992. The discourse of accommodation in oral proficiency interviews. *Studies in Second Language Acquisition* 14 (2): 159–76.

Schegloff, E. A. 1988. From interview to confrontation: Observations on the Bush/Rather encounter. *Research on Language and Social Interaction* 22.

Schegloff, E. A., G. Jefferson and H. Sacks. 1977. The preference for self-correction in the organization of repair and conversation. *Language* 53.

Scollon, R. and S. B. K. Scollon. 1981. *Narrative, Literacy and Face in Interethnic Communication.* Norwood, NJ: Ablex.

Tarone, E. 1985. Variability in interlanguage use: A study of style-shifting in morphology and syntax. *Language Learning* 35.

Tarone, E. 1988. Task-related variation in interlanguage: The case of articles. *Language Learning* 38.

Valdman, A. 1988. Introduction. *Studies in Second Language Acquisition* 10.

Woods, A., P. Fletcher and A. Hughes. 1986. *Statistics in Language Studies.* Cambridge: Cambridge University Press.

Young, R. and M. Milanovic. 1992. Discourse variation in oral proficiency interviews. *Studies in Second Language Acquisition* 14 (4): 403–4.

3 Performance assessment and the components of the oral construct across different tests and rater groups

Micheline Chalhoub-Deville
University of Minnesota

Theoretical background

Second language (L2) oral testing increasingly calls for more performance-based tests. Performance-based tests require students to produce complex responses integrating various skills and knowledge and to apply their target language skills to life-like situations. In addition, these tests often employ more than one test method and call for human raters' judgement. Consequently, these two factors, the test method and the rater, have become integral components of performance-based tests, influencing test scores. As in all forms of assessment, the issue of the validity of scores obtained from these tests is paramount. What do total scores obtained from L2 oral tests mean? Validity researchers concur that the primary 'purpose of construct validity is to justify a particular interpretation of a test score by examining the behaviour that the test score summarizes' (Moss 1992: 233). The fundamental requirement for establishing the validity of L2 oral performance test scores, therefore, is defining the L2 oral construct.

According to Messick (1993), the purpose in construct validation studies is 'for construct-relevant variance to cumulate capitalizing on the positive features of each response format [method], while biases attendant upon the smaller construct-irrelevant variance would not cumulate as much' (p. 62). In construct validation, therefore, researchers need to specify the attributes of the construct and minimize factors that confound test score interpretation. In L2 oral language testing research, two important factors influence and potentially confound the scores reflecting the learners' oral construct: the test method and the rater.

A potential source of confounding and irrelevant variance in language test scores is the task or test method. It is well known that different elicitation tasks and test methods influence results differentially, limiting interpretation of constructs (see Chapter 5 in Bachman 1990). Second language acquisition (SLA) researchers document that diverse elicitation tasks produce variations in speech products (Ellis 1985, 1987; Larsen-Freeman and Long 1991; Tarone

1983, 1989). Tarone (1989) writes that '[t]here can be no doubt now that the linguistic forms produced by second language learners vary markedly as those learners move from one situation to another and one task to another' (p. 13).

Furthermore, L2 testing researchers concur that a test score is influenced to a large degree by the method used to measure the trait (Bachman 1990; Bachman and Palmer 1981; Clifford 1981; Henning 1983; Shohamy 1984; Shohamy, Reves and Bejerano 1986). Clifford (1981), reviewing multitrait-multimethod studies, argues that researchers fail to provide evidence of construct validity for the traits the test purports to measure because they fail to account for the effects of test methods on test scores. In summary, both SLA and L2 testing researchers document the effect of tasks and test methods on learners' test scores. In investigating the L2 oral construct, therefore, information from diverse test methods is needed in order to arrive at a richer and more dynamic picture of the construct.

Although much thought should be given to the selection of tests used to elicit L2 oral samples, scoring procedures are also critical. Test scoring is another potential source of irrelevant variance that affects score use and interpretation. L2 oral tests are usually human-scored, meaning that raters assign scores. The influence of the rater on scores obtained, therefore, is a potential source of error that may influence learners' scores of L2 oral ability.

Trained teachers are usually asked to assess learners' L2 ability. Teacher training, however, may influence teachers' assessment and render their judgement different from non-teaching native raters (Engber 1987; Shohamy, Gordon and Kraemer 1992) with whom many L2 learners wish to communicate. Diverse rater groups may differ in judging learners' L2 ability depending on their background and the set of criteria with which they operate.

In L2 oral testing, research shows that trained teachers and non-teaching native speakers differ in their assessment of learners' L2 oral ability (Barnwell 1989; Galloway 1980; Hadden 1991). In addition, Galloway (1980) has documented a difference between non-teaching native speakers residing in the learners' community and those living in the target language community. It is plausible that native speakers residing in the learners' community may have become accustomed to dealing with non-native speakers both linguistically and culturally, which may influence their ability to evaluate learners' L2 oral ability.

Consequently, assessment of learners' L2 oral ability obtained from different native speaking groups may provide varied perspectives of the L2 oral construct. In summary, both test methods and raters warrant attention as to their potential influence on the use and interpretation of L2 oral test scores.

Purpose

The purpose of this study is to derive the dimensions salient to diverse rater groups when assessing learners' L2 oral performance across various test methods. The present study addresses the following research questions:

1 What are the dimensions that underlie L2 oral ratings across three test techniques – oral interview, narration, and read-aloud?

2 What are the relative weights of the derived dimensions for each of the following groups of native speakers of Arabic – teachers of Arabic as a foreign language (AFL) in the US, non- teaching Arabs residing in the US for at least one year, and non-teaching Arabs living in Lebanon?

Methodology

Speech samples

Six subjects provided the speech data for this study. The six subjects were AFL students. They all had completed at least four quarters of college-level study of modern standard Arabic (MSA), and were enrolled at the time of the experiment in an intermediate level Arabic language class. Two of the subjects were males and four were females. Their ages ranged from 23 to 33.

The six subjects were audio-taped performing three tests: a modified oral proficiency interview, a narration of pictures depicting a story, and a read-aloud of a text. These tests were chosen to elicit a variety of speech products in order to tap a wide range of the subjects' L2 oral language abilities.

The subjects were interviewed by an ACTFL-certified oral proficiency tester of Arabic. The modified oral proficiency interview, which lasted approximately ten minutes, was employed to elicit the subjects' most spontaneous speech (Omaggio 1986). A two-minute segment, judged by the investigator and the ACTFL interviewer as representative of each subject's performance, was included on the tape used for rating. These segments were selected from the middle portions of the interviews. Thus, speech from the warm-up and wind-up stages, which are meant to make subjects feel comfortable and permit subjects to leave the interview situation with a sense of accomplishment, was not included.

The narration test was based on a sequence of six cartoon drawings depicting a story of an encounter between a female and a male bicycling in a park. This test was considered relatively more controlled than the interview, but still effective in providing subjects with the 'opportunity for personal expression and interpretation' (Underhill 1987: 67).

The third test involved reading aloud a short news-like printed passage. Although more constrained, this technique was considered appropriate for 'assessing the mechanical skills of language production' (Underhill 1987: 77).

A stimulus tape containing the 18 speech samples (six subjects each performing three tests) was put together. In order to curtail a carry over of one subject's rating on a certain test to a succeeding subject, an adaptation of the matched-guise technique (Lambert 1967) was used to randomize the samples. As such, similar tests or subjects were not placed in sequence on the stimulus tape.

Raters

The stimulus tape of the randomly ordered 18 speech samples was presented to 82 native speakers of Arabic for evaluation. The raters consisted of three groups:
i   15 native speakers teaching AFL in the US;
ii 31 non-teaching native speakers of Arabic who had been residing in the US for a period of at least one year. Raters within this group were all university students in central Ohio; and
iii 36 non-teaching native speakers of Arabic who were living in Lebanon. All raters within this group were also university students.

Ratings

After listening to each speech sample, raters were given time – usually one minute was sufficient – to provide their ratings. Anchored nine-point scales were used for the ratings, one indicating the lowest performance level and nine the educated native speaker. Each of the raters was requested to i) provide a holistic score reflecting his/her overall impression of the L2 oral ability level of each of the 18 speech samples; and ii) provide ratings for each speech sample on specific unidimensional scales typically used in L2 oral assessment (e.g., see ACTFL 1986; Albrechtsen, Henriksen, and Faerch 1980; Bachman 1990; Brown *et al.* 1984; Canale 1983; Canale and Swain 1980; Fayer and Krasinski 1987; Harlow and Caminero 1990; Shohamy 1983; Underhill 1987). These unidimensional scales included intelligibility, linguistic, and personality variables. As shown in Table 1, five of these unidimensional scales were common across all three tests, while the other unidimensional scales were test specific. The scales were presented to raters in Arabic.

Table 1

Scales included in the rating instrument

Scales common across the three tests
1 Fluency
2 Pronunciation
3 Grammatical accuracy
4 Comprehensibility of student's speech to the rater
5 Confidence

Test specific scales Interview
1 Length of student's responses
2 Linguistic maturity (simple versus complex)
3 Vocabulary
4 Appropriateness of the language used with the topic
5 Student's understanding of interviewer
6 Student's attempts to get the meaning across
7 Ability to converse on diverse topics
8 Giving detail unassisted

Narration
1 Vocabulary
2 Linguistic maturity (simple versus complex)
3 Student's attempts to get the meaning across
4 Adequacy of information in student's narration
5 Proper temporal shift
6 Ability to tell a story
7 Creativity

Read aloud
1 Student's ability to melodize the script to make reading meaningful

Research design

In order to delineate the dimensions that raters considered when rating subjects' overall L2 oral language ability, multidimensional scaling (MDS) was employed. More specifically, individual differences scaling (INDSCAL) that 'accounts for individual differences in the perceptual or cognitive processes that generate the responses [ratings]' (Young and Harris 1990: 428) was deemed as the most appropriate MDS technique to specify the salience of each of the derived dimensions for each of the three rater groups.

The averaged holistic scores provided by each of the three rater groups were used to construct three proximity matrices, the rows and columns of which represented the 18 speech samples. The three matrices were submitted for analysis using the INDSCAL model within the ALSCAL MDS program of SPSS-X (1990) in order to derive the dimensions salient to the raters and to specify the extent to which each of the three rater groups relied on each of the derived dimensions. It is important to note, therefore, that the multidimensional solution was generated using dissimilarity matrices, which were based on holistic scores and not unidimensional scale ratings (see Table 2).

In order to facilitate the interpretation of the dimensions generated by the MDS output, mean ratings on each of the unidimensional scales were regressed on the speech samples' stimuli coordinates (see Table 2). Because the derived MDS dimensions are orthogonal, the standardized regression coefficients can be thought of as correlations between the mean of the unidimensional rating scales and the stimuli location on each of the dimensions.

After performing regression analyses, two criteria were adopted to assist in selecting unidimensional scales that would best represent the dimensions in the INDSCAL solution. The first criterion required that the correlation between the selected unidimensional scale and the derived dimension be relatively high, and at the same time, the correlation of that scale with the other dimensions be low. The second criterion required that the selected unidimensional scales be mean-ingful and appropriate according to more qualitative speech sample analysis.

Table 2

Outline of statistical analyses

Multidimensional scaling	
Technique	**Data**
Individual differences Scaling (INDSCAL) model	Holistic ratings transformed to three (one for each group) dissimilarity matrices

Multiple regression analyses	
Technique	**Data**
Regression	Mean ratings on each of the unidimensional scales (encompassing intelligibility, linguistic, and personality variables) across all raters

Results

Dimensions of the overall solution

Davison (1983) recommends two criteria to select the most appropriate dimensional representation of the data. The two criteria are: i) fit indices; and ii) interpretability. In the present study the low average stress value of 0.12 and the high R^2 of 0.95 indicate that the nonmetric three-dimensional solution provides a good fit to the data. The three-dimensional stimulus coordinates are presented in Appendix A and the stimulus space plots are presented in Appendix B.

Dimension one

The first dimension to emerge was best defined by the two unidimensional scales 'grammar' and 'pronunciation' (see Table 3). The fact that both grammar and pronunciation represented dimension one was somewhat puzzling at first. Examining the speech samples closely, however, indicated how grammar and pronunciation can and do function jointly, and can be related because of inflectional markers in MSA. MSA has three short vowels /a/, /u/, and /i/ that are represented with diacritical marks placed above or below the letter they follow and function mainly as inflectional markers, i.e., case markers for nouns and mood markers for verbs. A simple inflectional change, therefore, can cause an error in verb tense, gender, etc. As such, the smallest inflectional mispronunciation is not only an error in pronunciation but also an error in grammar.

Table 3

Regression weights

Variable	Dimension One	Dimension Two	Dimension Three
Grammar	–0.56	–0.26	–0.21
Pronunciation	–0.55	–0.38	–0.11
Creativity	–0.02	–0.76	–0.23
Adequacy of information	–0.21	–0.74	–0.07
Providing detail unassisted	–0.25	0.04	–0.82
Length of subject's responses	0.48	–0.22	–0.94

(The directionality of the regression weights is of no consequence. Of importance, however, is that the unidimensional scales defining the derived dimensions are both either positive or negative.)

Furthermore, in order to help interpret dimension one, the speech samples across the three test methods were examined. In the present paper, analysis of subject one's performance is reported. The location of subject one's stimuli along the 'grammar-pronunciation' dimension indicated that her performance on the interview had the highest dimensional value, then the narration, and lastly the read-aloud test. The magnitude of difference between her narration and read-aloud locations was, however, small (see Appendix A).

Examining her interview sample first, it was clear that subject one showed native-like pronunciation and made few grammatical errors. Her performance on the narration was not as good. Although her pronunciation of the sounds was still quite good, her speech was grammatically flawed. In order to illustrate the mistakes that demonstrate the association between grammar and pronunciation, a sentence from subject one's speech sample is analyzed below. The sentence is 'qarrara an yarkabu darrajatuhu', meaning 'he decided to ride his bicycle'.

English	Arabic	Subject one	Correctness
He decided	qarrara	qarrara	correct
to ride	an yarkab<u>a</u>	an yarkab<u>u</u>	incorrect
his bicycle	darrajat<u>a</u>hu	darrajat<u>u</u>hu	incorrect

(he rides=yarkabu) (bicycle=darrajatu; his=hu)

The first phrase is correct, but the second is incorrect. In the second phrase, the subject failed to make the appropriate inflectional change and said 'an yarkabu' instead of 'an yarkaba'. The inflectional marker 'u' at the end of the utterance 'yarkabu', meaning 'he rides', indicates that the verb is in the present tense. When a present tense verb, however, is preceded by the particle 'an', as in this example, the inflectional marker 'u' should change to 'a'.

In the third phrase, the subject mispronounced 'darajatahu' as 'darajatuhu'. When the word 'darrajatu' is in a nominal position it takes the nominal case marker 'u'. When, however, it is in the accusative, as in the present example, then the ending changes to 'a', and is pronounced 'darajata', The above is one example of the type of mistakes that subject one made. This type of mistake in her speech explains the drop in her ranking on the 'grammar-pronunciation' dimension.

Subject one's performance on the read-aloud test was not very different from the narration test. The subject made mistakes similar to those encountered in the narration. To illustrate, the utterance "Limtu ... anna lisSan SaTa ...', meaning 'I found out that a thief broke into', is analyzed similar to the previous example.

English	Arabic	Subject one	Correctness
1 I found out	'limtu	'limtu	correct
2 that	ann<u>a</u>	an_	incorrect
3 a thief	lisSan	lisSan	correct
4 broke into	SaT<u>a</u>	SaTa<u>n</u>	incorrect

The first and third phrases are correct. In the second phrase, however, subject one mispronounced 'anna' as 'an'. 'Anna' means 'that' and 'an', as explained earlier, is a particle that precedes a present tense verb. In the fourth phrase, the subject mispronounced 'SaTa' as 'SaTan', i.e., subject one supplied the wrong mood marker for the verb. In short, subject one's rating dropped considerably on the narration and the read-aloud tests because she made a number of inflectional mistakes.

Dimension two

Dimension two was best represented by the unidimensional scales 'creativity' and 'adequacy of information in subject's narration' (see Table 3). For ease of communication, dimension two was labelled 'creativity in presenting information'. 'Creativity in presenting information' is not meaningful to the read-aloud test. The following discussion, therefore, will focus on the narration and interview tests.

Analysis of subjects' speech samples corroborated the location of those samples on the dimension 'creativity in presenting information' (see Appendix A). Subjects who were creative and engaging in presenting information scored higher on dimension two. For example, subject two's narration included descriptions about the setting and how the characters felt, all of which enlivened the account and provided the listener with a feel for the story. Subject four's narration, on the other hand, was dull and without any embellishment that would capture the listener's attention. Subject two, consequently, scored higher than subject four.

Subjects two's and four's dimensional scores were reversed on the interview. Subject four's performance on the interview in terms of 'creativity in presenting information', was better than subject two's. This was also reflected in their location along dimension two where subject four received a higher dimensional value than subject two (see Appendix A). Analysis of the interview speech samples showed that subject four's interview was quite engaging. Her responses to the interviewer's questions were interesting and varied, and even humorous at times. For example, when asked whether she would like to get married, she responded saying 'hopefully one day, although this is more difficult than studying'. Subject two's interview, on the other hand, was dry and more monotonous. He carried on about his father's profession saying 'he used to work like a director. He was working in a place where he was going to take pictures of people and students and others also'. In summary, analyses indicated that creativity and ability to engage the listener meaningfully were deemed important to raters' judgements of the interview and narration tests.

Dimension three

Based on regression weights and speech sample analyses, dimension three was identified as 'amount of detail provided'. Dimension three was best represented by the unidimensional scales 'the ability of the subject to give detail unassisted' and 'length of subject's responses' (see Table 3). With regard to the read-aloud test, giving detail was not applicable in a meaningful manner. The following discussion focuses, therefore, on the narration and interview tests.

Analysis of the interview speech samples verified the location of the stimuli on the 'amount of detail provided' dimension. To illustrate, subject one's performance on the interview was compared to the performance of subject three.

Subject one, although one of the better speakers, repeatedly responded with short answers and only after much probing on the part of the interviewer. The following is a sample of subject one's interview:

Interviewer:	Have you visited a European country?
subject one:	Yes, France.
Interviewer:	How long did you stay in France?
subject one:	Two months.
Interviewer:	In what city?
subject one:	Toulouse'.
Interviewer:	Is it pretty?
subject one:	Yes, very pretty.
Interviewer:	Is it prettier than Paris?
subject one:	No, Paris is prettier.

As evidenced here, although subject one was providing responses to the questions, she was not volunteering any additional information. She did not elaborate or explain what she meant. Subject three, on the other hand, elaborated in his description of his travels. He described with detail why he liked Cairo, (busy streets, hot weather, great pyramids, etc.). When asked whether he worked while studying, he provided his work schedule and described his duties at the restaurant and the adolescence centre. The difference, therefore, in the 'amount of detail provided' by each of these two subjects explained their respective locations on dimension three, i.e., subject one received lower scores than subject three (see Appendix A).

With respect to the narration, examining the amount of detail presented in subject one's and subject three's narrations again explicated their respective rankings on the dimension 'amount of detail provided', i.e., subject one received a lower score than subject three (see Appendix A). In narrating, subject one presented a more summarized account of the visuals whereas subject three discussed every picture individually, stating the number of the picture and describing it. In describing the bicycle accident, for example, subject one said 'the young man saw the beautiful girl and did not see the road and he broke his leg'. Subject three, on the other hand, said 'the man looked at a girl wearing short pants and he got into an accident with a big tree and thus got off the road ... the man has a broken leg and arm'. In short, subject one, similar to her performance on the interview, was very brief and provided no detail. Subject three, however, elaborated and provided more detail on both the interview and the narration tests.

Rater group differences

In addition to the multidimensional solution, INDSCAL provided weights that depicted the extent to which each of the three rater groups relied on each of the dimensions in their holistic rating of subjects' L2 oral ability. Subject weights, presented in Table 4, indicate that the three rater groups were emphasizing the three dimensions differentially when judging subjects' overall L2 oral ability. The group of non-teaching Arabs in the US emphasized all three dimensions in their ratings, although dimension three, 'amount of detail provided', had the most salience. Raters in the teaching group seemed to be relying most heavily on dimension two, 'creativity in presenting information'. The group of non-teaching Arabs residing in Lebanon, however, emphasized almost solely the 'grammar-pronunciation' dimension, i.e., dimension one.

Table 4

Rater group weights

	Dimension		
Rater group	**One**	**Two**	**Three**
US residents	0.49	0.35	0.76
Teachers	0.01	0.94	0.29
Lebanese	0.98	0.01	0.04

Results of the present study are not consistent with research (Galloway 1980; Hadden 1991) indicating that teachers tend to emphasize grammar in their assessment of students' proficiency and non-teachers tend to be concerned with the more communicative aspects of the language. Results reported in the literature, however, were based on studies using languages other than MSA. More specifically, results in the present study could have been due to diglossia in Arabic.

In a diglossic situation, two varieties of the same language exist side-by-side, each variety having a specialized function. Two forms of the Arabic language co-exist in the Arab World: MSA and the colloquial variations of Arabic. MSA is a written and a spoken language used for formal instruction, general lectures, official correspondence, administrative announcements, and in mass media. MSA is readily understood by educated Arabs. Colloquial Arabic is used for everyday activities. It comprises the local spoken dialects, which are acquired natively by Arabs and is not readily understood by all Arabs.

The salience of the dimension 'creativity in presenting information' to the teaching rater group may be due to the combined effect of two factors. Specifically, because MSA is the form used in most AFL classes in the US and because AFL classes increasingly emphasize communicative language teaching and learning, the teaching rater group is probably accustomed to using MSA not only in its typical domains but also for everyday activities, which may explain why teachers emphasized the more communicative aspects when rating the speech samples.

On the other hand, the non-teaching Arabs in Lebanon probably use MSA in its more formal contexts where accuracy plays a central role. Thus, in judging learners' L2 oral ability, this group relied to a large extent on the 'grammar-pronunciation' dimension.

Two factors may explain why the group of non-teaching raters in the US differed from the non-teaching Lebanese group. First, those in the US may be aware of the communicative-based AFL classroom situation; and/or second, they have been increasingly using MSA to communicate with other Arabs around them, because, as mentioned earlier, MSA is readily understood by educated Arabs.

Conclusion

L2 research has documented variability in language performance across different tests. This phenomenon was also evident in the present study. Performance variability may be attributed to some extent to the difference in the demands that the test places on the linguistic and cognitive processes of the subjects, thus influencing their performance. For example, with regard to the interview, the interviewer was present to interact with the subjects and to direct their efforts in constructing their speech. In the read-aloud, subjects were provided with a text that obviously constrained their language production. Also, unlike the interview and the narration, the read-aloud did not allow for interaction with another speaker or for immediate feedback. In the narration, subjects were not as constrained with a selected text or set of questions. They were required, however, to interpret and present the visuals without access to any linguistic support or feedback.

Variability, however, was not evident on all three dimensions. Whereas subjects' performances varied somewhat from test method to test method when examined in terms of the 'grammar-pronunciation' and 'creativity in presenting information' dimensions, subjects' performance remained relatively unchanged when analyzed in terms of the third dimension, 'amount of detail provided'. In summary, some aspects in learners' performance may be relatively stable from test to test and others may vary. More research is needed that investigates those dimensions in L2 oral production that are stable across test methods in contrast to those that vary.

In addition to variation in subjects' language products due to test method, results of the present study indicate that rater groups also vary in their expectations and evaluations. The teaching rater group considered those dimensions important that are more in line with the profession's shift in focus to more communicative assessment. The non-teaching rater groups, who do not have professional training, were operating with a different set of criteria. The Lebanese rater group differed from those residing in the US. Whereas the rater group in Lebanon seemed to emphasize the grammar-pronunciation dimension, the US rater group was more diversified in terms of the dimensions they employed when rating subjects' L2 oral performance. An obvious question at this point is who should be used as the rater criterion in L2 oral assessment? Should different rater groups be employed depending on the purpose of the test? Further research needs to investigate these issues as they influence the use and interpretation of L2 oral scores.

Finally, because both test methods and raters affect learners' L2 oral scores, researchers might need to reconsider employing generic, component scales. The present study argues for a research approach that derives scales empirically according to the given test methods and audiences. Such an empirical research approach provides educators with a rigorous understanding of the kind of trait that L2 oral test scores represent and can lead to improvement in the assessment of the L2 oral ability. Moreover, the empirical approach adopted in this study can verify the plausibility of a priori posited claims regarding the nature of L2 oral ability.

In the context of the present paper, further analyses need to be performed on each of the three test methods separately. It would be interesting to discover whether the dimensions that emerged when investigating all three tests together would still come out when analyses are performed on each of these tests separately. It would also be interesting to investigate whether the same pattern of subject weights would be generated. Additionally, it is important to note that findings reported in the present paper need to be validated with other languages, L2 oral ability levels, test methods, and rater groups.

Appendix A: Stimulus coordinates

Subject Symbol	Subject Number	Task	Dimension One	Two	Three
1I	1	interview	-2.7195	-1.3321	-0.6265
3N	3	narration	0.4162	-0.1890	-0.8231
1R	1	read-aloud	0.3488	-0.4242	0.6128
2N	2	narration	-1.0726	-1.1865	-1.0055
3I	3	interview	-0.1833	-0.7407	-0.8921
4N	4	narration	-0.1935	-0.0187	0.3845
5I	5	interview	1.1935	0.4986	0.1926
6N	6	narration	1.5620	2.2126	2.0428
3R	3	read-aloud	-0.0488	0.5425	-0.6050
6I	6	interview	0.5951	1.0199	1.2956
2R	2	read-aloud	-0.7881	-0.4951	-1.3251
4I	4	interview	-0.9086	-1.3202	-0.5692
6R	6	read-aloud	1.1601	1.3881	1.8205
5N	5	narration	0.7273	1.0481	0.8269
2I	2	interview	-0.9881	-0.6638	-1.2442
4R	4	read-aloud	-0.0999	-0.7474	-0.2603
1N	1	narration	0.3263	-0.6559	-0.4762
5R	5	read-aloud	0.6731	1.0636	0.6515

(The dimensions are reversed, i.e., higher ratings
indicating better performance aggregate at the negative
ends of the dimensions.)

Appendix B: Stimulus space plots

DIMENSION ONE

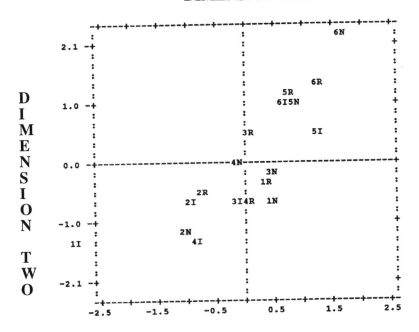

DIMENSION ONE

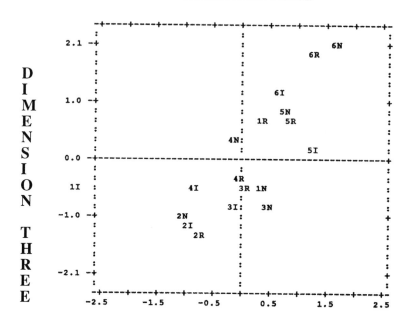

DIMENSION TWO

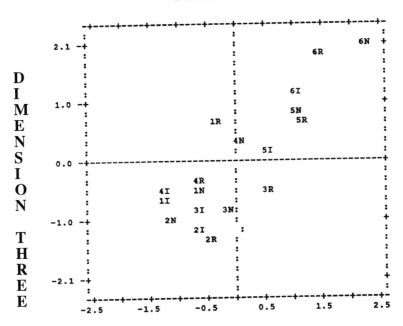

References

Albrechtsen, D., B. Henriksen and C. Faerch. 1980. Native speaker reactions to learners' spoken interlanguage. *Language Learning* 30: 2.

American Council on the Teaching of Foreign Languages. 1986. *ACTFL/ETS Oral Proficiency Guidelines*. Hastings-on-Hudson, NY: ACTFL.

Bachman, L. F. 1990. *Fundamental Considerations in Language Testing*. Oxford: Oxford University Press.

Bachman, L. F. and A. S. Palmer. 1981. A multitrait-multimethod investigation into the construct validity for six tests of speaking and reading. In A. S. Palmer, P. J. M. Groot and G. A. Trosper (eds.), *The Construct Validation of Tests of Communicative Competence*. Washington, D.C.: TESOL.

Barnwell, D. 1989. 'Naive' native speakers and judgements of oral proficiency in Spanish. *Language Testing* 6.

Brown, G., A. Anderson, R. Shillcock and G. Yule 1984. *Teaching Talk: Strategies for Production and Assessment*. New York: Cambridge University Press.

Canale, M. 1983. On some dimensions of language proficiency. In J. W. Oller Jr. (ed.), *Issues in Language Testing Research*. Rowley, MA: Newbury House.

Canale, M. and M. Swain 1980. Theoretical bases of communicative approaches to second language teaching and testing. *Applied Linguistics* 1,1.

Clifford, R. T. 1981. Convergent and discriminant validation of integrated and unitary language skills: The need for a research model. In A. S. Palmer, P. J. M. Groot and G.A. Trosper (eds.), *The Construct Validation of Tests of Communicative Competence*, Washington, D.C.: TESOL.

Davison, M. 1983. Introduction to multidimensional scaling and its applications. *Applied Psychological Measurement* 7.

Ellis, R. 1985. *Understanding Second Language Acquisition*. Oxford: Oxford University Press.

Ellis, R. 1987. *Second Language Acquisition in Context*. Englewood Cliffs, NJ: Prentice-Hall International.

Engber, C. 1987. Summary of the discussion session. In A. Valdman (ed.), *Proceedings of the Symposium on the Evaluation of Foreign Language Proficiency*. Bloomington. Indiana: Committee for Research and Development in Language Instruction.

Fayer, J. M. and E. Krasinski. 1987. Native and non-native judgments of intelligibility and irritation. *Language Learning* 37 (3).

Galloway, V. B. 1980. Perceptions of the communicative efforts of American students of Spanish. *Modern Language Journal* 64.

Hadden, B. 1991. Teacher and nonteacher perceptions of second-language communication. *Language Learning* 41 (1).

Harlow, L. and M. Caminero. 1990. Oral testing of beginning language students at large universities: Is it worth the trouble? *Foreign Language Annals* 23 (6).

Henning, G. 1983. Oral proficiency testing: Comparative validities of interview, imitation, and completion methods. *Language Learning.*

Lambert, W. E. 1967. The social psychology of bilingualism. *Journal of Social Issues* 23.

Larsen-Freeman, D. and M. H. Long. 1991. *An Introduction to Second Language Acquisition Research.* London: Longman.

Messick, S. 1993. Trait equivalence as construct validity of score interpretation across multiple methods of measurement. In R. E. Bennett and W. C. Ward (eds.), *Construction Versus Choice in Cognitive Measurement: Issues in Constructed Response, Performance Testing, and Portfolio Assessment.* Hillsdale, NJ: Lawrence Erlbaum Associates.

Moss, P. A. 1992. Shifting conceptions of validity in educational measurement: Implications for performance assessment. *Review of Educational Research* 62.

Omaggio, A. C. 1986. *Teaching Language in Context: Proficiency-oriented Instruction.* Boston, MA: Heinle and Heinle Publishers, Inc.

Shohamy, E. 1983. Rater reliability of the oral interview speaking test. *Foreign Language Annals* 16.

Shohamy, E. 1984. Does the testing method make a difference? The case of reading comprehension. *Language Testing* 1.

Shohamy, E., C. M. Gordon and R. Kraemer. 1992. The effect of raters' background and training on the reliability of direct writing tests. *Modern Language Journal* 76 (1).

Shohamy, E., T. Reves and Y. Bejerano. 1986. Introducing a new comprehensive test of oral proficiency. *English Language Teaching Journal* 40 (3).

Tarone, E. 1983. On the variability of interlanguage systems. *Applied Linguistics* 4 (2).

Tarone, E. 1989. Accounting for style-shifting in interlanguage. In S. Gass, C. Madden, D. Preston and L. Selinker (eds.), *Variation in Second Language Acquisition volume II: Psycholinguistic Issues.*

Underhill, N. 1987. *Testing Spoken Language: A Handbook of Oral Testing Techniques.* New York: Cambridge University Press.

Young, F. W. and D. F. Harris. 1990. Multidimensional scaling: Procedure ALSCAL. In *SPSS User's Guide.* Chicago, IL: SPSS Inc.

4 What raters *really* pay attention to

Alastair Pollitt
Neil L. Murray
Research Centre for English and
Applied Linguistics
University of Cambridge

Introduction

Assessing quantity and quality

Assessment in language, as in other fields of endeavour, involves quantitative and qualitative decisions about students' abilities, and it is probably true to say that no assessment is ever purely one or the other. At one extreme, Pilliner (1968) made it clear that so-called objective tests are subjective in most respects, including the qualitative decisions about what to include, and how to subdivide the subject being assessed. At the other, it is well nigh impossible for any teacher or tester to describe a student's performance without simultaneously evaluating it, and evaluation is necessarily quantitative. Yet testers seem to try to keep these aspects of their work separate, and nowhere more so than in the assessment of oral proficiency. This paper reports an attempt to recombine these two aspects of assessment, by finding a more natural scale for judging students' performance in oral tests.

The role of rating scales in language proficiency assessment

There are different kinds of rating scale used in language testing. Alderson (1991) described three types, distinguished by their function:

user-oriented (UO) scales aim to describe to potential employers and others outside the education system the sorts of circumstances, in work or social life, in which the student will be able to operate adequately;

constructor-oriented (CO) scales aim to describe the sorts of tasks that the student can do at each level, and so describe potential test items that might make up a discrete test for each level;

assessor-oriented (AO) scales aim to describe the sort of performance that is typically observed in performance by a student at each level.

The three types are clearly distinguishable by inspection, for they contain different kinds of statement about students' abilities. This study will suggest that 'AO' scales are not always what they seem, and should sometimes be called DO scales.

Pollitt (1991) made a related distinction between *counting* and *judging*, the two fundamental strategies that we choose between in assessment. AO rating scales use the judging strategy (the paradigmatic analogy is the judging of competitive ice dance): the assessor focuses on the quality of the performance, the response, how well the task was done, and ignores any possibility that some tasks may be more difficult than others. UO and CO rating scales appear to use the counting strategy, where measurement consists of counting the number of successfully completed tasks (the paradigmatic analogy is a high jump competition): this approach focuses on the ordering of the tasks by difficulty, the stimuli, and ignores how well each task was done.

The types of scale differ too in their relationship to the test. UO scales are quite unconnected to the process of assessment; somehow each candidate is assigned to a level, and then the corresponding grade descriptor is attached, but the circumstances described in the descriptor could not have occurred during the test. In the case of CO scales the grade descriptors describe possible test tasks but, as Alderson notes, very few of the tasks could actually have been presented in any single test. The similarity between tests using CO scales and the high jump is illusory; in practice, CO scales seem to be used like UO ones. Of the three types, only AO scales are directly linked to the assessment process, as the descriptors describe the qualities that are actually observed during the test performance itself. This surely must be the starting point of any assessment, as the performance is the only evidence we have to work from. On the other hand, the kinds of description that AO scales offer, of how well the speaker handles syntax, or how accurate the pronunciation, give the outside user little help with interpretation.

Two solutions to this problem seem possible. In one, carefully specified tasks, which therefore have definable difficulties, could be calibrated using an extended latent trait model for polytomous data (e.g. Andrich 1978; Wright and Masters 1982), so that ability estimates could be derived that take account of task difficulty. This has been demonstrated successfully for writing tasks by Pollitt and Hutchinson (1987), but it would be difficult to specify many of the most common oral tasks sufficiently tightly for this to work well. A second approach would be to take a single test or set of tests through a sequence of development from assessment orientation to user orientation. There is, after all, no reason why a single test should not employ more than one scale, perhaps one for use by assessors in assessing, and another to be published for users in interpretation.

Consider how this second approach corresponds to the development of a traditional standard test. First, a test is devised that demands the skills that are to be assessed: traditionally this mostly meant writing good questions, but here it mostly means writing good performance descriptors that correspond closely to the performances the raters see. The aim is to maximise reliability without sacrificing validity. Then, when the test is ready, attention turns to developing an interpretation system for the test, through the collection of normative data, or of standards of expectation, or through linking levels of performance on the test to specifiable criteria taken from the world outside the classroom. The first part of this procedure is driven by the normal demands of measurement theory, and produces scores that have no intrinsic meaning; the second part calibrates on to this measurement scale real world information relating to standards, expectations and tasks. The separating of these two parts of the test development is intended to make clear that satisfactory empirical evidence is *essential* if a scale of task performance is to be linked to a set of real world descriptors. It is not clear that such evidence has ever been collected to underpin any UO or CO rating scales.

The source of rating scale descriptors

This study, however, is concerned with the first part of the process. It has been argued that during the assessment process raters must be easily able to match the performance they see to the set of AO descriptors they have to use. This has implications for the nature of the descriptors.

Most AO rating scales are analytic; each student's performance is rated on each of several components of performance. In the Cambridge Assessment of Spoken English (UCLES 1991), for example, there are seven such components, together with an 'Overall' scale, and considerable effort has been put into studying how raters use each of them, in order to maximise their reliability. Most tests use fewer than seven components, but this often means that several different aspects of performance are confounded in a single scale. The general model is of a rectangular grid, component by level, every cell of which is filled with a descriptor; the argument behind this model, though, seems to be predominantly logical rather than empirical. Fulcher (1993) argues that many of the descriptors in current rating scales are thought up by the scale designers for the sake of creating consistent looking scales that have little empirical basis. He argues for, and demonstrates, a method for developing rating scales in *fluency* and *accuracy* from a recorded corpus of student talk.

The emphasis on empirical evidence in Fulcher's approach is laudable. But why these two components? Or why CASE's seven? And is the filled rectangular grid the most appropriate approach to oral assessment? How is the construct of speaking proficiency to be best represented in a set of descriptors? The point has already been made that the set of descriptors should closely match *what the raters perceive* in the performances they have to grade. The starting point for scale development should surely therefore be a study of the perceptions of proficiency by raters in the act of judging proficiency.

Two analytical techniques for investigating perceptions

This study attempts to measure and analyse what are essentially private or subjective experiences by bringing together two methods or techniques whose commonality seems not to have been recognised before: Kelly's 'Repertory Grid' procedure and Thurstone's 'Method of Paired Comparisons'.

Repertory grid procedure

Repertory grid technique is an application of personal construct psychology. The creation of George Kelly (1955), personal construct psychology has been defined as:

> ... *an attempt to understand the way in which each of us experiences the world, to understand our 'behaviour' in terms of what it is designed to signify and to explore how we negotiate our realities with others.*
> (Bannister and Fransella 1971: 27)

According to Kelly, the reality for each individual person is the universe as they perceive it; reality is subjective rather than objective. As they go through life, they actively build up a system of constructs for making sense of the world which is constantly undergoing modification as they experience new events or different outcomes for familiar events. The ability to construe implies the ability to predict (not necessarily always correctly) future events, and so, perhaps, to control one's fate.

Each individual has their own repertory of constructs, and repertory grid analysis is a procedure designed to elicit from an individual how they construe the world. This is the key for our purpose: the repertory of constructs tells us what a subject sees in the world, what is salient, and so offers an insight into the thinking processes in a procedure like assessment.

Depending on the purpose of the analysis, data may be gathered either by eliciting subjects' personal constructs; or by supplying them with typical constructs to which they are required to respond. The former approach is necessarily used in psychotherapy, where the concern is for the individual client, and often in the early stages of research, while the latter may be used when the subjects can be assumed typical of some population, often in later stages of research. In our context, we feel that the more basic method is necessary, as we do not want to impose our, or anyone else's, construals of proficiency on the subjects. How then do we get at individuals' constructs?

A construct is, says Kelly (1955: 111–12), 'a way in which some things are alike and yet different from others'. As a simple example, he gives the statement 'Mary and Alice are gentle; Jane is not', which would (probably) be interpreted as indicating that *gentleness* is a construct that the speaker uses to organise experiences of people. 'The minimum context for a construct is *three* things,' he points out: here these are Mary, Alice and Jane. Kelly's main concern was with human personality, and particularly with deviant personality, and his therapeutic technique involved asking clients to consider the similarities and differences amongst three people who were significant elements in their lives. But it is not always necessary that all three are mentioned explicitly: 'To say that Mary and Alice are 'gentle' and not imply that somewhere in the world there is someone who is 'not gentle' is illogical. More than that, it is unpsychological.' Since in our context the 'elements' would be examination candidates not well known to the subjects, comparisons of three would be difficult for them to cope with, and we chose to depend on the presence of the implied third member in each construct elicitation statement.

Repertory grid analysis was originally used in psychotherapy as a means of understanding and thus helping combat patients' psychiatric disorders. More recently, the technique has been applied in various fields including economics (Earl 1983), anthropology (Orley 1976) and education (Beard 1978; Pope 1978; Shaw 1978). To our knowledge, its only application to understanding rater behaviour in foreign language proficiency was in a study carried out by Lee (no date), who sought to find out which constructs were used by their lecturers in evaluating EFL writing of Hong Kong students. Lee chose to provide a set of constructs for the lecturers to use, but we felt that this would be premature in our context.

The method of paired comparisons

The method of paired comparisons operationalises Thurstone's Law of Comparative Judgement (Thurstone 1959). It constitutes a methodological response to the question of how to scale *complex attitudes* toward stimuli, and, in the words of its founder, illustrates that 'psychophysical experimentation is no longer limited to those stimuli whose physical magnitudes can be objectively measured' (ibid, p. 5). Its focus is therefore *psychological* measurement; its aim, the creation of *psychological* continua upon which such stimuli may be mapped, thereby providing a means of measuring their relative values according to the degree to which subjects perceive them as encapsulating whatever attribute the researcher is concerned with. 'The ordering of ... objects *upon the basis of judgements*' (Edwards 1957: 19; our italics) – i.e. perceived stimulus dominance – is therefore what underlies psychological continua, and those attributes that form the focus of such judgements may, for example, be aesthetic, ethical, or, as in the case of the present study, linguistic in nature.

The method of paired comparisons is, then, the process underlying this scaling technique. The location of each stimulus on the continuum is derived from the pattern of its dominance in repeated comparisons with all of the other stimuli, and the more stimuli there are to be scaled the more paired comparisons or judgements are required. Each stimulus is paired with every other one; thus, given n stimuli, there will be $n(n-1)/2$ pairs. Subjects are presented with each pair and asked to decide which of the two appears greater or more dominant with respect to the attribute to be scaled. No equality judgements are allowed, for as Torgerson notes, 'This is consistent with the derivation of the law, wherein the probability of a zero discriminal difference is vanishingly small' (1958: 167).

Summary

Both Kelly's and Thurstone's methods exploit features of the *context of comparison*. They each simplify the universe by narrowing the subject's focus to just two or three similar objects in that universe. Comparison of similar elements means that 'most other things are equal', in each description or judgement. In each method, the sharpening of focus seems to produce more precision than could otherwise be obtained. However, they are different in that Kelly focuses on quality, and Thurstone on quantity; repertory grid technique tries to discern the salient features of objects, whereas the method of paired comparisons determines which of them has most of whatever feature is most salient.

In this study, Thurstone's method was employed to monitor consistency within individual raters and between raters, to see that they were using a scale which was essentially unidimensional. Those grading consistencies (similarities) and inconsistencies (differences) that appeared were analysed according to Kelly's technique in order to ascertain which constructs of performance were used by raters during the assessment procedure, and to seek correlations between these constructs and the relative proficiency levels that emerged.

Methodology

Since the 'subjects' in this study were asked to behave first as quantitative *raters* and then as qualitative *describers*, the term *judge* will normally be used to refer to them, except where it is intended particularly to imply one or other orientation.

The judges

Six volunteers took part in the project, four native speakers of English and two non-native speakers with native-like proficiency. All the judges had experience of between one and 14 years in TESOL. Two had acquired the RSA TEFL diploma and three others were studying for an M. Phil in English and Applied Linguistics. They were told in general terms what the study was designed to achieve, but given no detailed information about the two techniques involved. Pseudonyms are used to identify them in the report.

Procedure

Both techniques require comparison between pairs of students. The necessary control over stimulus presentation was achieved by using video recordings. Five interviews were selected for analysis, taken from the speaking component of the Cambridge Certificate of Proficiency in English (CPE) examination. A reasonable range of proficiency was deemed necessary to make sure a scale would emerge from the Thurstonian judgements, but it was predicted that comparisons at a similar ability level would elicit more insights into the less obvious aspects of rater behaviour. The five chosen recordings had no particularly unusual features that might unduly influence the judges: we were investigating normal rating behaviour, not sources of bias. The basic plan was to have each judge watch a pair of performances and make an immediate Thurstonian decision about relative proficiency, before switching to a qualitative Kellyan description of the two performances.

The candidates:

All candidates were young adults:

Candidate	Nationality	Sex	Interviewer's Sex
1	French	Female	Female
2	Taiwanese	Male	Male
3	Turkish	Male	Female
4	Brazilian	Male	Female
5	French-Italian	Female	Male

Thurstone's method of paired comparisons

For Thurstone's method of paired comparisons, each of the performances was paired against every other one, enabling judges to evaluate each of them with respect to all others of the selection. There were ten comparisons to be made, and they were permuted as follows:

(i)	**1** versus **2**			(vi)	**1** versus **3**		
(ii)	**3** " **4**			(vii)	**5** " **2**		
(iii)	**5** " **1**			(viii)	**4** " **1**		
(iv)	**2** " **3**			(ix)	**3** " **5**		
(v)	**4** " **5**			(x)	**2** " **4**		

Since each performance was to be viewed four times, four extracts each of two to three minutes were selected from the complete 13–14 minute interview. This should enhance the representativeness of the recordings, as well as minimising tedium for the judges. Of course Thurstone's method assumes comparison of the *same* stimulus in *all* comparisons, but it was predicted that this change would not add very much inconsistency to the ratings. The consistency seen in the results tends to bear this out. Any sequence effects in interviews, such as 'warming up' or 'fatigue', were controlled by trying as far as possible to pair up equivalent extracts of each interview.

The performance pairs were transferred from the original tapes on to a single master tape in the order given above, for convenience. It should be noted that convenience is a vital feature of this method. Judges should be taken as smoothly as possible from one comparison to the next, without being given time to revise their views, or to internalise their impressions of the candidates. Nor should they be allowed time to rationalise their comments into a proto-scale which they could begin to use in later judgements; it is difficult, but essential, to force them to keep comparing one candidate with the other rather than with any internalised rating scale.

Immediately after observing each pair of performances, judges were required to make a comparative judgement, stating *only* which of the two performances was 'better', without elaborating further in any way. Experience in piloting the technique showed that this point had to be stressed repeatedly.

Kelly's personal construct elicitation

Immediately following each comparative judgement, judges were told simply to talk about how they felt the two performances were similar and different. Experience from piloting showed the need to stress to them that the discussion should focus as far as possible on *qualitative* comparisons rather than *evaluative*; i.e. on saying how the two performance extracts were similar/different rather than on stating which was superior/inferior and describing them independently of one another. Occasionally too it seemed as if a judge was comparing one student to an internalised scale, rather than to the other. Where necessary, prepared prompts were used to control these effects, and to elicit as much information as possible about the constructs underlying judgements. All the discussions were recorded for subsequent analysis.

Results and discussion: Thurstone

Data

The results obtained from the six judges on the comparative judgement task were as follows (the names are pseudonyms):

Table 1

JUDGE: Irene	1	2	3	4	5
1	–	1	1	–	–
2	–	–	2	4	–
3	–	–	–	3	5
4	1	–	–	–	5
5	1	5	–	–	–

JUDGE: Mona	1	2	3	4	5
1	–	1	1	–	–
2	–	–	2	4	–
3	–	–	–	3	5
4	1	–	–	–	5
5	1	5	–	–	–

JUDGE: Susan	1	2	3	4	5
1	–	2	1	–	–
2	–	–	2	2	–
3	–	–	–	4	5
4	1	–	–	–	5
5	1	2	–	–	–

JUDGE: Anne	1	2	3	4	5
1	–	1	1	–	–
2	–	–	2	4	–
3	–	–	–	4	5
4	1	–	–	–	5
5	1	5	–	–	–

JUDGE: David	1	2	3	4	5
1	–	1	1	–	–
2	–	–	2	2	–
3	–	–	–	4	5
4	1	–	–	–	5
5	1	2	–	–	–

JUDGE: Valeh	1	2	3	4	5
1	–	1	1	–	–
2	–	–	3	4	–
3	–	–	–	4	5
4	1	–	–	–	5
5	1	5	–	–	–

Rank orderings

These translate to the following rank orderings for the five candidates as seen by each judge:

Table 2

JUDGE:	Irene	Mona	Susan	Anne	David	Valeh
Better	1	1	2	1	1	1
	5	5	1	5	2	5
			5	4	5	4
	2-3-4	2-3-4	4	2	4	3
Worse			3	3	3	2

The results in Table 2 show that of the six judges, four were internally wholly consistent in their judgements. The other two produce identical rank orderings and share the same inconsistency: In both cases, candidate 2 is judged better than 3; 3 is judged better than 4; yet 4 is judged better than 2. This issue will be explored in the next section.

The Thurstone scale

Taken together, these six sets of rank orderings produce the scale shown in Figure 1. Due to the small sample size and the fact that the data exhibited few inconsistencies, it was not necessary to use the full Thurstonian 'dominance matrix' of relative probabilities for each performance dominating each other one. As a result, the placement of the performances on the scale represents only the order of their proficiency and does accurately quantify it.

Given the overall inter-rater consistency evident in the results, the paired comparisons method does appear to be a reliable way of achieving a rank ordering of proficiency. The only striking inconsistency in the results is the judges' widely differing perceptions of performance 2 and the consequent difficulty in placing it on the scale.

Figure 1

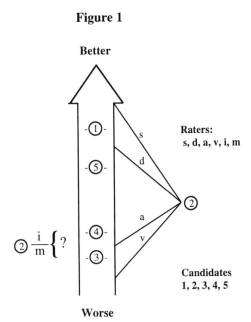

The inconsistencies involving 2, 3 and 4 suggest that the performances were quite similar and led – at least in the cases of Irene and Mona – to some difficulty in decision-making. These considerations are reflected in the close proximity of the three performances on the scale.

In defining the scale, performance 5 is of particular interest, for by emerging between performance 1 and performances 2, 3 and 4 on the scale, we can conclude that it has more of the trait than 2, 3 or 4, and less of it than 1. What that trait might be is the focus of analysis in the next section.

Results and discussion: Kelly

The study produced 60 recorded comparisons; some system was needed to organise them for detailed analysis. Three types of comparison were defined in terms of the Thurstone procedure – *scale defining* comparisons that 'fitted' the overall pattern of scaling, *misfitting* comparisons where the judge's decision conflicted with those made of the same candidates by the other judges, and *inconsistent* comparisons where a set of three or more decisions by one judge failed to define a unique rank order. Comparisons were assigned to these three groups and the groups studied in turn.

Scale defining comparisons

Every comparison involving candidate 5, except Susan and David's comparisons of 5 with 2.
All comparisons including candidate 1 except Susan's of 1 with 2.
Attention was focused on the consistent comparisons involving 5.

Misfitting comparisons

The only misfitting comparisons were those made by Susan and David involving candidate 2.

Inconsistent comparisons

The six comparisons involving 2, 3 and 4 by Irene and Mona.

Remaining comparisons

The remaining ten comparisons are less clear. Susan, Anne, David and Valeh between 2, 3 and 4: *intra*-rater consistency, but not *inter*-rater consistency.

Comparison of 4 with 5: a scale defining comparison

The theme common to most of the discussions could be called 'fluency'.
Also evident is the salience of structure and vocabulary.
Willingness to respond/initiate (i.e. candidates' attitudes) and accuracy of response.
Judges were perhaps as concerned with their *interpretation* of what they observed as with those objective features in the performances.

Irene and Mona on 2, 3 and 4: inconsistent comparisons

The most likely cause of the inconsistency found in Irene and Mona's ratings is their perception of comprehension.

i) In her discussion of comparison 2/4 – the comparison where the inconsistency appeared – Mona made reference to 2's comprehension problems before any other feature of the performance, suggesting its greater salience for her and clearly its importance to her decision.

ii) In discussing comparison 3/4, all Mona's comments except one refer to the superiority of performance 4, yet she opts for performance 3 as the better of the two. The one exception – which must therefore have carried her decision – was a comment that 4 had comprehension problems whereas 3 had none; again the comment which emerged first in the discussion.

iii) Irene also made the observation that unlike candidate 3, candidate 4 failed to comprehend a question.

iv) Mona explicitly stated of comparison 2/4 that had candidate 4 *not* made the comprehension errors he did, she would have chosen his performance as the better.

Irene's statement that she was 'shocked' at the comprehension errors made by 2 strongly suggests a great mismatch between the candidate's oral production and his comprehension skills.

How judges perform: Some conclusions

Defining sections of the proficiency scale

Although not all the discussions included in the study have been reported here, the picture that emerges throughout is that certain performance characteristics appear to be strongly associated with particular sections of the proficiency scale. These are summarised in Figure 2. A correspondence with three of Canale and Swain's (1980) four components of communicative competence is also suggested. (*Note*: 'Stilted Speech' refers to formal, rigid, uncreative speech – a feature of the content – whereas 'Hesitant/Staccato' refers to the lack of smoothness of delivery – an acoustic property.)

Figure 2

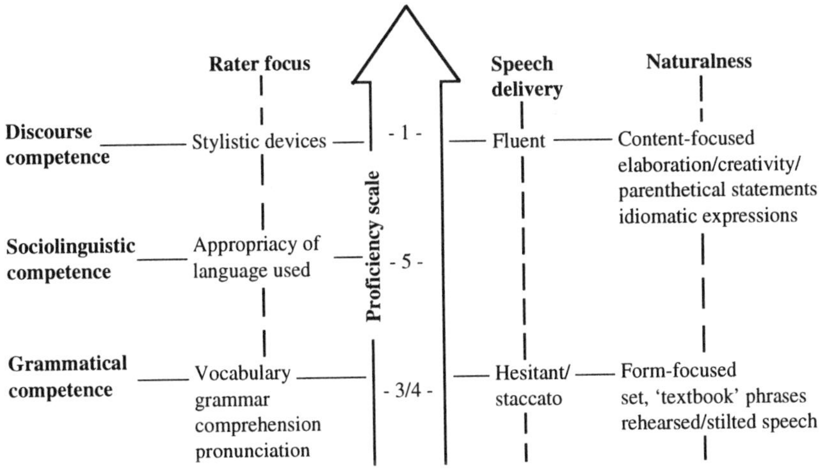

It seems likely that those performance characteristics associated by judges with the lower end of the scale become increasingly less evident at the higher end because they are less problematical for candidates and therefore less salient; instead, other characteristics more representative of sophisticated speech are used as criteria at the higher end of the scale. Although performance 5 appeared to be a fairly clear 'dividing line' with regard to these characteristics one has to assume that this is an artefact of the small data set, and that in general variability in candidates' performances – and therefore judges' focus – is more gradual in nature. Thus the dashed lines in Figure 2 represent continua: learner speech does not suddenly change from being form-focused to content-focused, or from hesitant and staccato to fluent. Any increase in form-focus will be proportional to decreases in content-focus.

These findings raise a number of interesting points:

Choosing assessment criteria

In the discussions of comparisons involving the higher-proficiency candidates (i.e. 5/1), the almost total lack of reference to traits from the bottom of the scale suggests that judges were selecting their judgement criteria according to the joint level of the candidates involved. A similar trend involving comparisons of candidates of lower proficiency reinforces this hypothesis. As we have seen, where candidates in a pair are of 'mixed' abilities – representing the high *and* low ends of the scale – the criteria judges focused on were generally those associated with the lower-level candidate of the pair. The only obvious instance where this pattern was not followed was in Susan's discussion of comparison 1/2 which produced the most exceptional judgement of any (one she was later to regret!). It is perhaps significant that with the exception of David, who was singular anyway in his almost exclusive focus on sociolinguistic traits, the others judged performance 2 much inferior and, like Susan, made reference to the lower-end traits of the scale. It may be that Susan also saw 2's weaknesses but these were 'hidden' by her very tangible preoccupation with 2's 'wonderful' comprehension, a trait all other judges associated with *lower* proficiency.

Two contrastive approaches to assessment

Mona, Valeh and David at times appeared to be utilising a *synthetic* process in which a holistic image of the speaker is formed derived primarily from the individual's preconceived, that is preconstructed, understanding of language learners. In other words, just as in meeting a stranger at a social event, a comprehensive image of the person is evoked by a few first impressions. Some aspect of the performance serves as a primary indicator of level, and the observed performance is then compared with the judge's memory of a person at that level; if it fits reasonably then all of the traits in the judge's repertoire become part of the description of the individual. Evidence for this process lies in the strong tendency for Mona and Valeh to group the traits of comprehension, grammar, vocabulary and pronunciation together and for David to group together humanistic traits, even when there were no performance data to support it. Mona, for example, spoke of candidate 4's weaker grammar, vocabulary and comprehension in two cases where there was clearly no evidence of any comprehension problems in the extracts.

Judges Irene, Anne and Susan tended not to take this synthetic approach. They limited their comments to observed behaviour; a more objective, less natural mode signalling perhaps a greater effort to think within a strictly assessment-oriented framework. The impression is that they 'scored' the candidates intuitively for each observed utterance, and somehow added these up. The puzzle with them is to see how they were able to form holistic Thurstonian judgements if they did not form holistic models of the candidates in their minds.

Other issues

The forced comparison procedure is designed to elicit underlying constructs, and it was no surprise to find evidence that the judges were influenced to some extent by the candidates' personalities, physical attractiveness, nationalities and cultural backgrounds. We were, however, made very aware of two issues where the judges' personal constructs challenge the nature of the 'official' construct of oral proficiency.

The problem of comprehension

'Comprehension' was clearly prevalent in judges' discussions of the comparisons at the lower end, frequently raised in the guise of the 'appropriacy' of responses. This raises the question of whether or not comprehension should be an issue in oral proficiency tests. There is a strong case for saying that comprehension problems should be recognised as a cause of inappropriate responses, and that candidates should not be penalised in such a case; Paper 4 in the CPE examination is designed to assess candidates' comprehension ability, and this Paper 5 is supposed to assess oral *production* skills. If we do not take this line, then we should recognise that Paper 5 is a test of *oral interaction ability*, not oral production ability.

The sort of interview used in CPE and many other proficiency batteries seems, on this evidence, to lie uneasily between a test of oral production in which the interlocutor's function would be merely to elicit speech, and a test of oral interaction in a social context in which the two participants would be more or less equivalent in function and status. Perhaps both are needed in a comprehensive assessment of proficiency, but perhaps a blend of the two – formal questions and answers pretending to be informal conversation – is not a good idea.

The question of paralinguistic features

A similar issue arises with regard to the paralinguistic features that accompany speech. Should personality, manner, facial expression or the impression of friendliness be considered a valid part of oral proficiency? If a test of oral proficiency is taken to mean a test of the ability to communicate in a face-to-face setting, then this must surely include appropriate attitudes etc., for 'communicativeness' is for the audience as well as the speaker. If this stance is taken, another problem is solved along the way: personality is frequently tied up with culture – generally considered to be a bias that should be controlled – but a distinction between the two will generally not be apparent to the assessor who is not thoroughly familiar with the candidate's culture. In treating personality – and on the same grounds cultural traits such as appropriate gesture – as valid criteria of proficiency, this whole issue is circumvented.

On the other hand, it seems rather unfair if the attractive candidate always gets better marks. Perhaps we should narrow the construct down to being simply a test of the ability to produce grammatically well formed and meaningful utterances under a real time constraint?

Implications

Methodology

The combination of the Thurstone and Kelly procedures does seem to have generated insights very efficiently. Setting up a set of video recordings for such a study is not simple, but both approaches proved successful. The consistency amongst raters, none of whom had any experience of, or training in, formal oral assessment was impressive; it would be worth repeating the study with experienced raters, to see if they could match the consistency of these amateurs. The study again shows the ability of Thurstone's method to generate a scale for reliable assessment.

The comparison format also seems to have facilitated the expression by the judges of the aspects that seemed salient to them. Although it is clear that the judges found it difficult to be non-evaluative in their comparisons, this is probably not too serious when our aim is to elicit the constructs used in the live assessment process. It was necessary to ask for Thurstonian choices in order to be able to classify the choices as shown in section 5, and this may have set up an unshakeable context of testing in the judges' minds. In a future study, perhaps some of the judges could skip the forced choice part; the choices of the others would still indicate the scale and which were the scale-defining comparisons.

Oral proficiency

Several conclusions are offered. Should comprehension be assessed as part of oral proficiency? Should a proficiency battery test language production or language interaction, or both? Should the oral test be one of communicative success or linguistic ability?

Should proficiency be assessed as a rectangular set of components, in what seems to be the dominant model nowadays? One clear implication of this study is that the trait of 'proficiency' is understood in different terms at different levels; high proficiency speakers are judged against criteria of native-like behaviour, and in terms of what they say, while at a lower level the emphasis is more on correctness, or how they say it. The implication is two-fold: first, that the matching of performances to grade descriptors will be easier and so more accurate if the descriptors deal only with constructs that are normally salient at each level, and second, that it is pointless and even counter-productive to write, for example, descriptors for pronunciation at high levels of proficiency.

The problem here is, perhaps, that Alderson's trichotomous scheme for rating scales misses one important distinction. When assessment is intended to provide 'diagnostic' information to teachers and students the idea of a profile seems to dominate all other considerations. The rectangular grid of descriptors that is so common today is a verbal profile; in practice it is not ideal for assessment, since some of its components will always be irrelevant. A truly *assessor orientated* scale will make the rater's job as easy as possible, but these *diagnosis orientated* scales do not. They seem to be AO scales, but their true function, the one that determines their form, is the transmitting of diagnostic information to teachers and students: that is, they are DO scales.

In this study the judges were teachers, and familiar with the terminology of linguistics. But the skill being assessed will be reported to a world of certificate users who are not so trained; the next phase of research should perhaps be to repeat this study using naive judges, that is judges who are not trained in linguistics, to see if the order of proficiency they produce is similar to that produced by teachers. Without that confirmation we will not know that 'proficiency' as judged by teachers is the same thing as the world knows by that name, and the validity of the test will be compromised accordingly.

References

Alderson, J. C. 1991. Bands and scores. In J.C. Alderson and B. North (eds.), *Language Testing in the 1990s: The Communicative Legacy.* Review of English Language Teaching Volume 1. Number 1. Modern English Publications. London: Macmillan

Andrich, D. 1978. A rating formulation for ordered response categories. *Psychometrika* 43: 357–74.

Bannister, D. and F. Fransella. 1971. *Inquiring Man: The Psychology of Personal Constructs.* London: Croom Helm Ltd.

Beard, R. 1978. Teacher's and pupil's construing of reading. In F. Fransella (ed.), *Personal Construct Psychology 1977.* London: Academic Press.

Canale, M. and M. Swain. 1980. Theoretical bases of communicative approaches to second language teaching and testing. *Applied Linguistics* 11: 1–47.

Earl, P. 1983. *The Economic Imagination.* New York, NY: Sharpe.

Edwards, A. L. 1957. *Techniques of Attitude Scale Construction.* Englewood Cliffs, NJ: Prentice-Hall.

Fulcher, G. N. 1993. *The Construction and Validation of Rating Scales for Oral Tests in English as a Foreign Language.* Unpublished PhD dissertation. Lancaster University.

Kelly, G. A. 1955. *The Psychology of Personal Constructs,* vols. I and II. New York, NY: Norton.

Kelly, G. A. 1977. The psychology of the unknown. In D. Bannister (ed.), *New Perspectives in Personal Construct Theory.* London: Academic Press.

Orley, J. 1976. The use of grid technique in social anthropology. In P. Slater (ed.), *Explorations of Intrapersonal Space,* vol. 1: *The Measurement of Intrapersonal Space by Grid Technique.* New York, NY: Wiley (John Wiley and Sons).

Lee, Y.P. In preparation, no date. Where markers of essays agree and where they don't – An application of repertory grid analysis.

Pilliner, A. E. G. 1968. Subjective and objective testing. In A. Davies., *Language Testing Symposium. A Psycholinguistic Perspective.* Oxford: Oxford University Press.

Pollitt, A. 1991. Giving students a sporting chance. In J. C. Alderson, and B. North (eds.), *Language Testing in the 1990s: The Communicative Legacy,* Review of English Language Teaching Volume 1, Number 1. London: Macmillan: Modern English Publications.

Pollitt, A. and L. Hutchinson. 1987. Calibrating graded assessments: Rasch partial credit analysis of performance in writing. *Language Testing* 4: 72–92.

Pope, M. 1978. Monitoring and reflecting in teacher-training. In F. Fransella (ed.), *Personal Construct Psychology 1977.* London: Academic Press.

Shaw, M. L. 1978. Interactive computer programmes for eliciting personal models of the world. In F. Fransella (ed.), *Personal Construct Psychology 1977.*

London: Academic Press.

Thurstone, L. L. 1959. *The Measurement of Values*. Chicago: The University of Chicago Press.

Torgerson, W. S. 1958. *Theory and Methods of Scaling*. New York: John Wiley and Sons.

UCLES. 1991. *Cambridge Assessment of Spoken English*. Cambridge: University of Cambridge Local Examinations Syndicate.

Wright, B.D. and G.N. Masters. 1982. *Rating Scale Analysis*. Chicago: MESA Press.

5 A study of the decision-making behaviour of composition markers

Michael Milanovic
Nick Saville
Shen Shuhong

Introduction

Direct tests of writing in Cambridge examinations and the concern for the reliability problems

Direct tests of writing have always been standard practice in Cambridge examinations for the assessment of both first (L1) and second language (L2) writing abilities. Even when the value of direct tests of writing was disputed and then fell into disfavour in some countries, being replaced in many places by multiple choice tests, the position in direct tests of writing remained central to Cambridge examinations. Faith in their validity and good impact on teaching convinced examiners and educators at Cambridge and elsewhere in Britain of the advantages of direct tests of writing ability over indirect ones.

The fact that all its stages are a wholly human endeavour (Hamp-Lyons 1990) makes the direct test of writing open to sources of error than can be detrimental to the accuracy of the assessment of writing ability. This intrinsic weakness, related to reliability, has long been a concern at Cambridge. In the early 1970s, a 'good deal of research' on reliability was conducted (Wood 1989). The work of Nuttall and Willmott (1972), Willmott and Nuttall (1975) and Willmott and Hall (1975) looked at some 150 Certificate of Secondary Education (CSE) examinations and 29 General Certificate of Education (GCE) examinations*. They were scrutinised for technical soundness, and much of the research concentrated on the reliability of marking examinations, which was considered to be one of the main sources of measurement error in assessing a candidate's performance.

As a result of these studies, Cambridge set out in its 1976 paper 'School examinations and their function' some 'stringent conditions which were thought to be necessary if an examination was to provide a qualification which might affect the career of a candidate' (Cambridge 1976:8). One of the four conditions stated that 'The marking of answers has to be as reliable as possible'. Accordingly,

*These two schemes were designed to assess secondary school performance at age 16 on a national level. They were replaced in 1988 by the General Certificate of Secondary Education (GCSE).

researchers at that time focused on improvements to marker standardisation. Although reliability was given primacy above everything else, estimates of reliability of marking under the enhanced conditions proved 'hard to come by' (Wood 1989:182).

The marker – one of the three basic sources of measurement error

Reliability studies on composition tests have not only addressed the issue of marking procedure but also opened other problematic issues like the marker. The marker is a recognised source of measurement error in direct assessment of writing ability. Reliability of composition tests is very much 'affected by variations in the perceptions and attitudes of those who read the essays, and the kind of training they receive for reading writing assessment' (Hamp-Lyons 1991).

Various studies have found that 'different markers responded to different facets of writing' (Diederich, French and Carlton 1961). Indeed, Vaughan (1991) notes that 'despite their similar training, different markers focus on different essay elements and perhaps have individual approaches to reading essays'. In attempts to understand what it is that markers are judging, differing results have been obtained. Grobe (1981) found that markers were primarily influenced by vocabulary diversity, while Freedman (1979) showed that content was the most significant single factor in the final judgement of an essay. Stewart and Grobe (1979) concluded that markers were influenced by length and accuracy. Vaughan (1991) found that 'raters are not adhering to a single, internalised method for judging essays', but were influenced by 'the environment of the essays – the effect of the papers'. These findings indicate that markers do not seem to measure one common construct that might be termed writing ability while carrying out an assessment. It seems clear then that marking is not simply a matter of reliability, but also concerned with the issue of construct validity.

Results from previous studies have also shown that marker behaviour varies in ways that can be partially attributed to variables such as sex, experiential background, profession, amount of exposure to L2 writing, etc. (Hamp-Lyons 1990).

Aims and objectives of the study

Clearly the marker is an important variable in the assessment of writing ability. An understanding of the values, decision-making behaviour and even the idiosyncratic nature of the judgements markers make is of primary importance for both reliability and construct validity. Yet very little is known about the decision-making processes which are employed by the markers in making an assessment. Lack of knowledge in this area makes it more difficult to train markers to make valid and reliable assessments.

This paper reports on the first phase of a study designed to explore the thought processes of examiners for Cambridge EFL compositions. This phase investigated:

1 markers' decision-making behaviour in terms of the approaches they employed while marking EFL compositions;
2 the elements markers focused on while marking compositions.

A model of the decision-making process in holistic marking

Holistic marking is a technique that rests on the assumption that trained markers will respond to a composition in the same way if they are given a set of characteristics to guide them (Vaughan 1991). Sets of composition characteristics are generally laid down in marking schemes to guide markers in assessing writing ability at different levels. These, however, tend not to be empirically validated. In addition, they are only concerned with the composition elements markers are required to focus on in marking rather than the marking processes. To investigate markers' decision-making processes in holistic marking, a model of this process is required. This model should reflect a hypothesis for the decision-making process in holistic marking, and serve as the basis for data collection.

The model used in the present study was based on a model of the decision-making process developed for the purposes of marker training in this and other studies carried out by the researchers (Milanovic, Saville and Shen 1992). The model, illustrated in Figure 1, draws on the findings in Cumming's study (1990) of the decision-making behaviour in analytic marking where 28 common decision-making behaviours were revealed in markers' introspective verbal reports.

After a careful study of Cumming's 28 decision-making behaviours, a tentative model was developed for holistic marking. The model attempted to capture both the process of decision-making behaviour in holistic marking, and the composition characteristics markers are supposed to focus on. Several changes were made in the model, after many discussions with experienced markers. The model is tentative, and it was hoped that the present study would provide some empirical basis for further research which would be of value in developing a better validated model of the decision-making process.

Figure 1

A model of the decision-making process in composition marking

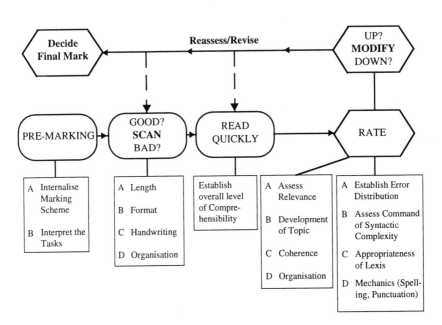

Method and procedure

Design of the study

Both writing assessment and writing itself are cognitive activities. They involve complex thought processes, which call on many components of expectation, attitude, perception, value, etc. In planning this study, it was felt that no single research method was wholly adequate to capture markers' thought processes while marking compositions. Verbal reports, for example, might not give a very accurate picture of exactly what goes on in a marker's mind; on the other hand, in writing down one's thoughts, some material might get lost in the actual writing process. The complex nature of the issue under investigation encouraged us to make use of multiple methods. It was anticipated that different methods would compensate for each other's inadequacies. The following methods were employed for data collection in this study: the retrospective written report, the introspective verbal report and the group interview.

A   The retrospective written report

Markers were asked to note down what was going on in their minds while marking compositions: how they had reached their final decision as to what mark to give to the composition. The number of reports carried out by examiners varied greatly. They were asked to carry out the retrospective report after they finished marking each composition. In this study, no prompts or checklists were offered as guidance.

B   The introspective verbal report

Markers were asked to give a verbal report on marking a limited number of compositions. It was made explicit that the report should consist of think-aloud, stream-of-consciousness disclosure of thought processes while marking, and should be unedited, and unanalysed. The verbal reports were tape-recorded and transcribed.

C   The group interview

A 30-minute group interview was scheduled after markers finished completing the questionnaire. Markers were put into four groups according to their professional backgrounds. The interviews were highly structured. They were conducted according to a pre-designed interview questionnaire which focused on their marking processes, factors affecting their decisions, and comments on the research methods employed. The group interviews were tape-recorded and transcribed.

Subjects

Sixteen markers participated in this study, eight male and eight female. In selecting the markers, consideration was given to their professional background, experience in marking FCE/CPE compositions, and gender. Thirteen of the examiners had participated in earlier projects, and had gained some experience in this context. Three of them had no such experience.

The 16 markers fell into four groups.

Group 1   4 experienced FCE Paper 2 markers
Group 2   4 experienced CPE Paper 2 markers
Group 3   4 EFL teachers with little experience in marking compositions
Group 4   4 experienced teachers of English as a mother tongue

Instrumentation

Scripts

FCE (First Certificate in English) is an intermediate level EFL examination. The candidates are required to write two compositions in 90 minutes, from a choice of five topics (a letter, a speech, a description, an argumentation and a topic based on optional reading specified in the examination regulations), each of which should be between 120–180 words.

CPE (Certificate of Proficiency in English) is an advanced level EFL examination. Candidates are required to write two compositions from a choice of five topics. Descriptive, situational or discursive topics including one topic based on optional reading of background texts are offered. (See Appendix A for an illustration of the UCLES EFL Five Level Examination System).

Forty compositions were prepared, 20 of them were selected from FCE, June 1990, and the other 20 from CPE, June 1990. Examples of this kind of script taken from the examination Handbooks for users are presented in Appendix C.

Sixteen photocopies of the 40 selected compositions were made (one set for each marker). The 40 compositions in each set (16 sets) were arranged in exactly the same order, as it was believed that sequencing might introduce inconsistency into the marking criteria themselves, and affect marking behaviour.

These scripts covered the full range of topics, and represented all five points of the marking scale.

The marking schemes and the level guide

The marking schemes used in this study had been adapted from those used in previous studies on FCE/CPE Paper 2. The same level guide was also adopted for training purposes (see Appendix B).

Procedure

Marker training

Marker training was conducted in two stages: self-access training through marking practice at home, and pre-marking training on site. The purposes of the training were:
1 to help establish and maintain consistency in marking;
2 to demonstrate how to report on thought processes in the written and verbal form.

Data collection

After the training session, each marker was asked to mark the same 20 CPE compositions, which were arranged in exactly the same order. They recorded the marks on a separate mark sheet, and noted down immediately after marking the thought processes they had employed.

The collection of introspective verbal reports was in two separate small rooms. Shortly after the marking session started, individual markers (two at a time) were asked to go and give introspective verbal reports on two compositions (one FCE and the other CPE). All the markers had done the written report before they were asked to do the verbal report. All the verbal reports were tape-recorded, and transcribed in full.

Data analysis

Data from the retrospective written reports, audio-taped verbal reports and group interviews was transcribed in full, and then reviewed impressionistically to develop a coding scheme.

Two distinct aspects of the marking strategies emerged in the markers' various reports. The first aspect related to the broad approaches to the process of marking. The second aspect concerned the details of that approach, reflecting the particular composition elements markers claimed to be focusing on and, where possible, making some assessment of differences in weight attributed to these elements. To a certain extent, this twofold division is artificial – not least because the markers themselves did not report according to it, generally presenting their reports as more 'dynamic' and less 'systematic'. Nevertheless, it is suggested that this separation reveals more than it obscures, and may serve as a basis for further investigation.

Findings

1. The four broad approaches to the process of assessment

Analysis of the data revealed that four identifiable marking approaches had been used. We refer to these as:
1 principled two-scan/read;
2 pragmatic two-scan/read;
3 read through;
4 provisional mark.
Each approach is discussed below.

Principled two-scan/read

Markers adopting the principled two-scan/read approach scan or read the script twice before deciding on the final mark. The second reading was 'principled', being undertaken indiscriminately with all scripts, hence the term 'principled two-scan/read'. This approach was used by six markers for the FCE scripts and four for the CPE .

There were variations between the markers. Some markers gave their attention only to specific elements in the paper on the first scan. Others were interested in more general aspects, and still others just looked at the layout and paragraphing.

For Ex. 1 (belonging to the first group), during the first scan attention was paid to quite specific elements in the paper. These included length (in 12 out of 14 of the papers marked), interest of the paper (whether it was lively or dull), task realisation, that is, whether it achieved the task set in the question (eight out of 14), or organisation, that is, whether it contained a good 'plot' or structure (five out of 14). Data from her group interview suggested content was 'very much' included in this first scan. Her second scan focused on similar categories but, according to her report, was yet more detailed in its analysis.

By contrast, Ex. 9's first reading picked up on the more general aspects of communication – what she called 'clarity and vitality' – and it was only on the second reading that the 'mechanics' of language use were examined.

Ex. 13's approach (for nine out of the 13 FCE papers), although subsumable within the general principled two-scan/read category, was different again. Her approach was to first make what she described as a 'visual scan' of a script, which picked up on layout and, more specifically, paragraphing, before then reading it once through.

Pragmatic two-scan/read

Markers adopting the pragmatic two-scan/read approach to the process of marking also read the scripts twice before assigning a mark to the script. What distinguishes this marking approach from the principled two-scan/read approach is the motivation behind the second reading of the composition. The pragmatic two-scan/read occurred only when the marker encountered difficulties in the script or in the marking environment and had to re-read to determine a mark. That is to say, markers only had recourse to this approach in the event of the failure of another method to generate a confident mark.

Ex. 4 offered some indication of the circumstances in which it was used: she reported reading an FCE script again when she was distracted (in one paper out of the 20 she marked) and when she was unsure of the mark to award (three out of 20). As another illustration, Ex. 8 re-read a total of 13 of her 20 FCE papers. Six of these second readings could be placed in the 'principled' two-scan/read category while the remaining second readings could be classified as attempts to grade papers which resisted easy grading. She indicated in her FCE written reports that on one occasion, the re-reading was intended to find 'something positive'. On another, she consulted the marking scheme before re-reading .

Ex. 6's written reports for both the FCE and CPE papers suggest a marker who is quite satisfied with reading each script only once. In his verbal report, however, there was an indication that having read one of the scripts once, he sometimes 'gives it a quick skim' just 'to confirm' the initial impression.

The pragmatic two-scan/read was used by a similar number of markers to the previous 'principled' version.

Not all the markers, however, appreciated the usefulness of this approach. Ex. 5 in her written report on the CPE marking included the statement that 're-reading ... sometimes causes me to feel confused and irritated, depending on how alert and fresh I am feeling.'

Read through

This approach, used by 13 markers in all, is the least sophisticated of the marking approaches. It consists of reading a script through once to pick up its good and bad points.

One good illustration of this technique can be obtained from Ex. 15's retrospective written reports which indicate he made no exceptions to the use of the read through technique. A typical, and entire, response to a script follows: 'Read through – very heavy error incidence. Communication affected – too short to develop fully'.

Provisional mark

The provisional mark approach is also characterised by a single reading of the script, but with a break in the marking flow, usually imposed towards the start of a candidate's effort, which prompts an initial assessment of its merits before reading is resumed to discover whether the rest of the answer confirms or denies that assessment.

This approach appeared in the written reports of three markers for the FCE scripts and of eight of the CPE papers. The initial break normally coincided with a convenient halt in the script. Ex. 2, who used this approach every time, sometimes read ten lines, sometimes a paragraph, sometimes half a page and, other times still, the whole first page before assigning a provisional mark. The reports of Ex. 11 and Ex. 3 showed they followed a very similar approach.

In the group interviews the number of markers who reported arriving at an initial impression of a candidate's grade before the script was read in its entirety increases dramatically. Only four markers claimed to reach a mark after at least one reading. The status of the initial grade produced by the remaining 11 markers was said to range from 'tentative' to 'rough' to 'pretty sure' to 'final'.

Ex. 8 recorded her fear that a marker could be 'caught out' by finalising a mark too early in a script which then 'just deteriorates'. It would seem reasonable to suppose that assessment of writing ability relying on the earlier part of the candidates' scripts – which may be just the section which candidates devote most of their energies to – could generate higher marks than they deserve.

Some of the responses suggested that the provisional mark approach should not be regarded as a separate category but rather as a technique which all examiners have recourse to as part of their usual marking procedure.

2. Composition elements markers focused on in marking

Summary of composition elements markers focused on in marking

What is most striking about the composition elements which the markers focused on is their diversity. The relatively modest number of characteristics catalogued by the markers in their written and verbal reports on each paper suggests that they only remarked upon the elements which distinguished a paper. Some markers concentrated almost exclusively on a paper's bad points while others were equally prepared to mention those aspects which credited a candidate.

Analysis of data revealed 11 composition elements which markers focused on in marking FCE/CPE compositions. These elements are listed below.

Length
Legibility
Grammar
Structure
Communicative effectiveness
Tone
Vocabulary
Spelling
Content
Task realisation
Punctuation

Length

This refers to the number of words in an essay. It is assessed by counting the number of words on a chosen line and then multiplying this figure by the exact number of lines or by taking a 'quick glance'.

Legibility

This refers to both the handwriting of the compositions, and the readability of the photocopies of the scripts.

Grammar

This refers to grammatical mistakes, or what the markers referred to as 'errors' in their reports.

Structure

This is used as a broad term which covers grammatical structure (at sentence level), paragraph structure (sequencing and linking) and narrative structure (the way candidates present the development of ideas).

Communicative effectiveness

This refers to the degree of success with which the candidates put across the meaning in the written language, or the extent of effectiveness of the compositions in conveying the candidates' meaning in English. This criterion is obviously related to grammar, vocabulary and structure, all factors which assist coherence and comprehension.

Tone

This can be regarded as synonymous with the style, fluency or naturalness of a candidate's expression. The tone of a candidate's language could be seen to affect communication.

Vocabulary

This refers to the accurate and proper use of the words (using the right word for the right occasion) and variety of the words used.

Spelling

Spelling refers to the accuracy of the spelling of the words in the composition.

Content

This refers to the content of the compositions. This element embraces a number of different qualities, from demonstrations of 'individuality' to whether a piece was 'lively or dull'. It is one of the more visibly 'subjective' essay elements, the point where markers' personal responses may most influence a candidate's final score.

Task realisation

This refers to the extent to which the candidates' scripts meet the criteria set in the questions. When the content of a script was considered 'irrelevant' this was principally a reflection on the candidate's task realisation. Task realisation cannot be measured in entirely absolute terms, and examiners often responded positively to a candidate's 'serious attempts' to fulfil the demands of the question.

Task realisation is often balanced against linguistic attributes. Some examiners split a candidate's final mark between these two criteria, and some appeared to consider language ability and task realisation to be more closely related: 'Competence in writing makes the task reasonably realised.'

Punctuation

This refers to the accuracy of the use of mechanisms, such as comma, full stop, etc. in a composition.

A discussion of the possible weight markers attributed to the composition elements in marking

Markers' decision-making behaviour with regard to the final scores they assigned to the scripts was influenced to a varying degree by the weight they attributed to the composition elements. Although it is impossible to obtain any exact information regarding the effect of these elements on the final scores, data in this study offers some insight into the possible weight markers attributed to each element in marking.

Length

To some extent, all the examiners' initial impressions were influenced by the length of the composition although they did not seem to regard the length of a script as something which should overly determine the mark they award.

A rather heterogeneous treatment of this essay element by markers from different groups was apparent. Some markers simply ignored this element in marking. Ex. 7, an experienced CPE marker, awarded a 3 to a CPE script which two of the inexperienced markers isolated as too short to mark. Another marker (Ex. 10) awarded 5s to two FCE papers which he noted have 'just two paragraphs!' and 'only one paragraph.' Similarly, Ex. 3 decided to 'disregard' what he admitted as the excessive length of two FCE pieces.

Legibility

Two-thirds of the markers seemed to be affected to a varying degree by the handwriting of a script. One of the markers (Ex. 5) wrote in his written reports 'Large, clear writing cheered me up.' 'Illogically, I felt that the handwriting looked intelligent, and this biased my first impression.' Ex. 12 (jokingly) remarked that had a CPE paper she felt justified in giving a 2 been typed, she 'may have given it a 4'.

Grammar

The weight attributed to this element was difficult to estimate. In the written reports the markers were often talking about mistakes 'impeding meaning' and 'affecting communication'. It seems that the majority of the examiners sought to balance grammatical accuracy with communicative competence, giving the latter a slight priority. For example, Ex. 6 awarded a 5 to an ambitious essay with errors, and a 4 to one which was error-free but simpler. Similarly, Ex. 9 awarded a 2 to one paper with 'serious errors' and one with 'gross errors' because 'overall the communication succeeds'.

Structure

It is difficult again to determine what emphasis was placed on this element. On one occasion, one marker (Ex. 6) considered poor structure affected task realisation. On another, lack of paragraphing did not prevent the candidate receiving a 4. Ex. 14 reported that one composition was 'definitely a 5 because of structure, few errors'.

Communicative effectiveness

Some markers' comments revealed the importance this element was understood to have. For Ex. 10 the distinction between a single candidate's two papers was that one 'communicates something, so not a 1,' while the other is 'almost gibberish' so 'I think a 1'. For several other examiners, good communication of meaning may apparently take primacy over grammatical points, while errors were seen to 'impair communication'. In one CPE report, this idea was expressed: 'ultimately ... the content will override language beyond the point where the language is judged adequate for that content'.

Tone

The reports contained some clues to the weight markers attributed to this element. Some FCE essays which received high marks used 'idiomatic' expression, and some were credited with fluent use of English. Conversely, use of 'non-native' expression (Ex. 12) or 'translations of mother tongue' (Ex. 11) were penalised by markers. In the verbal report, the motivation behind focusing on this element is expressed (Ex. 12) 'non-native problems ... would upset a reader in the real world and ... I am always concerned with that'. One marker, however, voiced the opinion that a candidate's native tongue should be taken into account when assessing their performance.

Vocabulary

Examiners seemed to attribute different weight to this element. Some did not seem to rely too heavily on this element, as is seen in the statement that a script with 'fairly basic' vocabulary 'might go up to 5.'

Others seemed to be much affected by vocabulary in their marking behaviour. Ex. 3 reported that 'one or two vocabulary errors repeated throughout' contributed to a paper's mark being reduced to 2. Another marker said in the verbal report that 'I think sometimes my reaction to [impressive] vocabulary can sort of tip the scales towards the higher bands.'

Spelling

Although most of the markers checked spelling in the scripts they were marking, it is difficult to specify what emphasis was placed on accurate spelling. A hint may be found in one of the FCE reports. Experiencing difficulty deciding whether a script was worth a 4 or 5, the marker reported 'it has many spelling errors so I give it a 4'. In the experienced CPE examiners' group interview, one marker declared 'if people ... drop the "d" off the end of the word "and", they are not going to be penalised for that'.

Content

This is one of the most subjective composition elements. Markers' personal responses to a script, which can vary greatly, may most influence a candidate's final score. This can be seen in one marker's comment, 'I am always favourably inclined to a candidate who can interest, surprise, inform or ... amuse me.'

The extent of the subjectiveness can be illustrated by briefly sampling the variety of reactions markers reported to the same quality in some scripts. One marker (Ex. 2) awarded some of his lower marks to candidates whose efforts were 'anecdotal' or 'autobiographical', understanding this attribute in a negative way. Another marker (Ex. 7), on the other hand, singled out the 'anecdotal' aspect of a paper as its 'good quality'. To illustrate this further, one paper which was considered as having an 'interesting approach' by one marker, and which was 'thoroughly enjoyed' by another, was described as 'almost gibberish' by a third marker, and a fourth marker decided it was 'too "bizarre" to deserve a 3'.

The personalisation of marker response can seem excessive at times. One marker (Ex. 12), for example, marked the content of a candidate's script down as 'trivial – maybe because I know and love the Impressionists'. Another candidate's attempt showed, according to the marker, 'knowledge about art' and this 'might be an indicator to my grading'. In one verbal report the candidate's definition of poverty as an 'evil' provoked the marker's magisterial comment 'No, not necessarily, young lady, not necessarily. There are several well known theories dealing with this.'

Some markers, conscious of the prejudice their subjective response to this element might cause, seemed to be very cautious in their marking. Ex. 9 remarked that she may 'overmark' a 'congenial subject', while Ex. 5 cautiously reminded herself that 'I mustn't let my own views intrude'. Similarly, Ex. 10 claimed that 'annoyance always prejudices an examiner against a candidate, so must try to be objective.'

Many markers, believing marking should not be unduly influenced by content, were very cautious in their response to the content of a candidate's scripts. However, this is still a very difficult area to control because of the different standards for the various issues involved. This is shown in one written FCE report which expressed uncertainty whether a candidate's 'lack of intelligence' should be penalised in the absence of any faults in their language.

Task realisation

This element was specifically mentioned many times in both FCE and CPE reports. A typical example is 'scan the text to assess the task realisation'. Regarding this as a very important element, most markers contended they attempted to interpret and get familiar with the tasks, and that they 'always' prepared themselves for marking in this way. However, the exact weight markers attributed to this element is difficult to determine.

Punctuation

This did not seem to carry much weight in the marking of FCE papers, as it was referred to only twice. For the CPE papers, on the other hand, it featured in over half of the written reports. Three markers were particularly concerned about one candidate's tendency to use 'annoying' and 'irritating' underlining for emphasis. Again, the exact weight is difficult to determine.

Conclusion

In this paper, two aspects of the research findings have been reported in some detail, namely the four broad approaches to rating compositions and the linguistic elements which markers focus on. Although not reported here, two other variables were also investigated in relation to marking behaviour; these are:

1 the effect of the proficiency level of the scripts (FCE or CPE in this case);
2 the effect of examiner background (across the four marker groups in the study).

With regard to proficiency level, it was noted that, with higher level scripts (CPE), markers focused more on vocabulary and content, whereas with the intermediate level scripts (FCE), markers focused more on communicative effectiveness and task realisation.

In relation to background, it seemed to be the case that different experiential backgrounds can influence how markers assess compositions, even if special training has taken place for a specific marking exercise. FCE markers frequently noted *length* when marking both FCE and CPE scripts, whereas CPE markers more often noted *content* in the FCE scripts and mother-tongue teachers were more concerned with *tone*.

Rater effects which are well documented elsewhere in the literature were also observed in this data. Sequencing of scripts seemed to have an influence on some markers who appeared to be judging the level by comparing it to the previous one marked. Layout also seemed to lead to prejudices in some markers before they had even considered the content. This also applies to the recognition of handwriting across national group (e.g. French or Italian which have common features across writers) which lead to comments which may suggest some effect on judgement.

As this phase of the work was designed to be exploratory, the general conclusions must be seen as tentative. These results, however, enabled the researchers to develop a more focused research design for the next phase of the work.

Having reviewed both the findings themselves and other aspects of the study, such as the data collection methods, the following objectives were set:

1 to investigate the extent to which approaches used by markers to evaluate compositions confirm findings from the exploratory study especially in relation to the proposed model of marking behaviour (Figure 1);
2 to compare marking behaviour in relation to rater consistency;
3 to investigate the extent to which different categories of marker adjust their marking behaviour according to the level of the script.

In order to reduce the variables in the follow-up study[1], it was decided that a range of compositions across a single examination level should be selected and that the markers should all be experienced in marking for that particular examination. Introspective verbal report were used as the main data collection method (i.e. think aloud while marking).

It is hoped that the results of this next phase will contribute to our understanding of how markers make decisions about compositions and that this in turn will lead to ways of identifying 'good' markers and of providing better training for specific marking requirements.

Notes

1 A presentation of the follow-up study was given by Milanovic and Saville at the 28th TESOL Convention, Baltimore. 1994

Appendix A: The UCLES EFL main suite – A five level system

UCLES has developed a series of examinations with similar characteristics which span five levels.

Cambridge Level Five Good User	Certificate of Proficiency in English CPE	High level examination
Cambridge Level Four Competent User	Certificate in Advanced English CAE	
Cambridge Level Three Independent User	First Certificate in English FCE	Intermediate level examination
Cambridge Level Two *Threshold Level* User	Preliminary English Test PET	
Cambridge Level One *Waystage Level* User	Key English Test KET	Low level examination

Appendix B: Assessor-oriented rating scale

FCE Composition marking scheme used in the project

The writing test is designed to assess the candidate's ability *to write at an intermediate level*. He/she must complete two separate tasks in free composition based on a variety of stimuli. The tasks are of the following kind:

(a) a letter
(b) a description
(c) a discursive composition
(d) a narrative

Band	Writing Ability	Task Realisation
5	Demonstrates intermediate competence in writing with few errors	Task fully realised Credit given for organisation
4	Demonstrates intermediate competence in writing although there may be some errors of various types	Task well attempted and realised
3	Demonstrates some intermediate competence in writing but with a number of major errors	Task reasonably attempted and realised
2	Demonstrates only limited intermediate competence in writing, some communication established despite many errors of various types	Task attempted but only partially realised
1	Suggests incompetence in writing	Task only partially attempted and realised or grossly irrelevant
0	Total incompetence in writing or no evidence of writing ability	Task not attempted or too short for assessment

Writing ability

Writing ability in the context of FCE Composition must be assessed on the basis of a clear understanding of the level.

Examples of an intermediate level of competence (ie. Band 5) should have most of the following characteristics:

– evidence of simple rhetorical structure
– generally unambiguous and coherent expressions
– evidence of grammatical control
– evidence of appropriate use of vocabulary (for the level)
– generally accurate spelling and punctuation

The tasks which the candidate chooses must be appropriately attempted and

realised as this forms part of the test.
* Sensitivity to register is not tested at this level
* Creativity in the artistic sense is not a criterion

Length

In order to fulfil the tasks, compositions should be between 130 and 180 words. It is unlikely that the task will have been adequately dealt with if the composition is much below the lower limit: this should be reflected in the assessment.

If the candidate only writes one or two lines, the composition will be deemed *too short for assessment* (therefore 0).

Spelling, punctuation, format and handwriting

Errors and weaknesses in any of these areas should be taken into account in the overall assessment, bearing in mind, however, that some errors would normally be expected from students at this level. Handwriting *per se* should not be judged. If the handwriting is unintelligible, it will mean that the writer's intentions are not communicated to the reader. Then of course it will affect the marker's judgement.

American usage

Appropriate colloquialisms, spelling and other American usage should be accepted as correct.

Appendix C: Example FCE and CPE scripts

Example FCE script – Average candidate

Some jobs are more suitable for men and others more suitable for women. Do you think this is still true?

> *Nowadays, things are not like before. Indeed, there has been a great evolution for the last forty years and in many subjects: technology, way of living, and the most important: the way of thinking. In fact there is less and less prejudices about sexual segregation in everyday life, in work.*
>
> *So, little by little, women have been able to challenge and finally replace men in a lot of works. For instance, a women can be a doctor, a journalist or a director, things that would never have happened before. Some women have chosen to do a job that are only supposed to be for men. In a newspaper there was an article about Lisa, a woman who has chosen working in Alaska; she's installing pipe-line, and she's the only woman of the crew.*
>
> *However, both men and woman can't really do all the sorts of jobs that exist, even if there is some exception like Lisa. Moreover she was explaining the it was not so easy to be the only woman of the whole crew.*
>
> *So, I would say that nowadays both men and women can have more and more choice in the job they want to do. And even if there is some exceptions, some jobs are more for men and some, more for women.*

Comments: This is a well-planned answer which communicates some interesting ideas. It is ambitious in tackling the topic with a fairly abstract introduction and then bringing in a concrete example to prove the point. The last part is rather less cohesive (*So, I would say.... And even*).

There are some good items of vocabulary – *prejudices, segregation, exception* – and structure – *women have been able to challenge and finally replace* – but some fairly basic errors, especially in the singular/plural confusions. Some expressions are rather awkward.

Example CPE Script – Average candidate

Nowadays people live longer than they did in the past. Discuss the advantages of living longer and the problems created by this situation.

Thanks to the progress made by medicine and the improvement of lifestyles, nowadays people have a much longer life expectation than their ancestors. Moreover the length of life is still progressing. Reaching the age of 120 will not be exeptional by the end of the next century.

Already, people can enjoy a better life than their parents. They can choose to have children later, in order to make the most of their youth. When life was shorter, people did not have time to travel and develop their personality. Life was entirely devoted to working and building a family.

Nowadays, at the age of retirement, people do not feel so tired as they used to. They are no longer considered as old. Indeed, recently retired people often get involved in voluntary work. For example they can make others benefit from their experience and skills by becoming teachers. More often, a hobby acquired during active lifetime is developed to a high degree of expertise. Therefore it is commonly accepted that retirement must be prepared several years in advance. The more active people are while working, the more likely they are to enjoy a fulfilling retirement.

For that reason, people prepare more actively for their future. This attitude has given use to a dramatic change in people's attitude towards life. leisure is taking an increasing importance. Having a successful career is still regarded as vital, but achieving personal balance has become a general expectation. In doing so, active people intend to prepare themselves for a period of retirement during which they will still be fit and capable of enjoying their former activities.

This radical change is bound to generate a growing problem in western societies. the age of the population is rising. Therefore the number of pensioners per worker is growing. This trend faces modern societies with an increasing problem of funding. The issue is made even more acute by the fact that older people cost more in terms of health expenditure. Each year, developped countries allow an increasing part of their national products to health.

For fear of letting general dissatisfaction install, governments will have to address the problem, and it will probably imply drastic steps and changes.

Comments: The language used in this essay is generally competent and assured. There are some natural and appropriately used expressions (*'the more active people are while working the more likely they are...'*; *'this attitude has given rise to...'*; *'this radical change is bound to generate...'*), but also some lexical confusion, particularly with verbs (*'they can <u>make</u> others benefit'*; *'this trend <u>faces</u> modern societies with ...'*; *'developped countries <u>allow</u> an increasing part'*; *'it will probably <u>imply</u> drastic steps'* etc.).

The task is recognised and dealt with. The strengths of this essay are organisation; relevance to the topic chosen; appropriate vocabulary and expression; clarity of ideas and of the ways in which they have been ordered and set down. The errors are occasional rather than pervasive and, perhaps, arise more from the candidate's desire to set out thoughtful and extensive observations on the topic than to an inability to construct more mundane but very correct statements/observations which would be the mark of a less well-developed composition. The number of words misused does, however, bring the mark down.

References

Cumming, A. 1990. Expertise in evaluating second language compositions. *Language Testing* 7: 31–51.

Diederich, P. B., J. W. French and S. T. Carlton. 1961. *Factors in Judgements of Writing Ability*. ETS Research Bulletin RB-61-15. Princeton, N.J.: Educational Testing Service.

Freedman, S. 1979. How characteristics of student essays influence teachers' evaluation. *Journal of Educational Psychology* 71: 328–38.

Grobe, C. 1981. Syntactic maturity, mechanics and vocabulary as predictors of quality ratings. *Research in the Teaching of English* 15: 75–86.

Hamp-Lyons, L. 1990. Second language writing: assessment issues. In Kroll B. (ed.) 1990. *Second Language Writing*. Cambridge: Cambridge University Press.

Hamp-Lyons, L. (ed.) 1991. *Assessing Second Language Writing in Academic Contexts*. Norwood, N.J.: Ablex Publishing Corporation.

Milanovic, M., N. Saville and S. Shen. 1992. *Studies on direct assessment of writing and speaking*. Cambridge: UCLES internal research reports.

Nuttall, D. L. and A. S. Willmot. 1972. *British examinations: Techniques of analysis*. Slough: NFER Publishing Company.

Stewart, M. and C. Grobe. 1979. Syntactic maturity, mechanics of writing and teachers' quality ratings. *Research in the Teaching of English* 13: 207–15.

University of Cambridge Local Examinations Syndicate. 1976. *School Examinations and their Function*. Cambridge: UCLES.

Vaughan, C. 1991. Holistic assessment: What goes on in the rater's mind? In L. Hamp-Lyons (ed.), *Second language writing in academic contexts*. Norwood, N.J.: Ablex Publishing Corporation.

Willmott, A. S. and C. G. W. Hall. 1975. *O-level Examined: The Effects of Question Choice*. London: Schools Council.

Willmott, A. S. and D. L. Nuttall. 1975. *The Reliability of Examinations at 16+*. London: Macmillan.

Wood, R. 1991. *Assessment and testing: A survey of research*. Cambridge: Cambridge University Press.

6 A study of writing tasks assigned in academic de programs: a report on st... ... the project

Carol Taylor
Educational Testing Service

Theoretical background and rationale

The identification of writing tasks typically required of college and university students is a key issue in the development of a writing test intended to measure the kinds of writing skills students are expected to demonstrate in their academic studies. Therefore, it is essential to know what types of writing students are assigned in their classes, as a framework for developing valid essay topics for an academic writing test.

Most of the research on types of writing tasks has employed a survey method, usually with a questionnaire, wherein faculty members are questioned about the kinds of writing tasks and/or the purpose or form of the writing that they assign. Eblen (1983) identified several situations in which writing was required, including essay tests, analytical papers, documented papers, abstracts of readings, laboratory reports, technical reports, book reports, essays and others. West and Byrd (1982) found that, in engineering departments, the most common situations involving writing were examinations, quantitative problems and reports; homework and papers were somewhat less common; and progress reports and proposals were least common.

Bernhardt (1985) found that faculty across several departments reported giving the following types of assignments, in decreasing order of frequency: expository writing, problem descriptions, procedural-instructional pieces, creative pieces, letters, case studies, laboratory reports, and legal briefs. Donlan (1980), surveying science and mathematics teachers, found that writing assignments more often involved reporting information and rehearsing facts and details than exploring ideas. Other surveys involving several disciplines (Bridgeman and Carlson 1983; Sharton 1983) observed considerable diversity among disciplines as to the types of writing tasks that were assigned.

There are some limitations in a faculty survey approach, in that survey respondents may not accurately describe their practices. As Anson (1988) notes, '[teachers] may simply believe in certain principles of teaching and learning, responding to a questionnaire under the assumption that their choices accurately eflect what they do in practice' (p. 13). Horowitz (1986), agreeing with Johns (1981) and Zemelman (1978), comments that 'the use of a questionnaire or interview leaves open the question of whether the data reflect what the respondents do, what they think they do, or what they want the researcher to think they do' (p. 448).

Canseco and Byrd (1989) employed a more open-ended approach to the identification of academic writing tasks by examining course syllabi in graduate business classes. Focusing initially on writing situations, these authors found that writing was assigned in the following situations, in decreasing order of frequency: examinations, problems and assignments, projects and papers and reports. However, they found that only a limited number of syllabi actually specified the content of writing assignments.

Horowitz (1986) examined actual university writing assignments in academic disciplines. He asked faculty members from several disciplines to provide writing assignment handouts and essay examinations. The types of assignments observed included synthesis of multiple sources, connection of theory and data, summary of/reaction to a reading, report on a specified participatory experience, research project and annotated bibliography. However, the study was based on undergraduate classes at a single institution, and the response rate was extremely low (5%), thus limiting the generalizability of conclusions.

Purposes of the research

There were several considerations motivating the current research, including the limited scope of data available and the recognition that writing demands may differ considerably across institutions and disciplines at the undergraduate and graduate levels. The purpose of the current study was to collect and examine writing assignments given by faculty members and instructors at several institutions in the US and Canada in order to expand the understanding of the types of writing tasks that are actually required in undergraduate and graduate academic studies and to provide a basis for developing valid essay topics and tasks for inclusion in an academic writing test. Writing assignments given in many types of situations were included to provide a relatively comprehensive picture of the kinds of academic writing demands that students encounter.

On the basis of a sample of the collected assignments, the development of a classification scheme was planned to characterize the different types of writing tasks represented in the data. The objective was to develop a classification scheme that was stimulated by examination of the collected assignments and captured the essential differences among them, rather than to begin with a predetermined set of categories to classify the assignments.

Research design and method

Data were obtained about writing tasks assigned in various disciplines at the undergraduate and graduate level, via examination of the actual assignments given to the students, not the students' written products. In classifying the writing tasks, the major objectives were to identify those categories that best characterize the writing assignments according to aspects of their form or purpose (e.g., description, persuasion, etc.) and situation (e.g., laboratory reports, term papers). An ultimate goal was to determine the frequency with which different forms of writing were observed in each situation, separately by discipline and by undergraduate and graduate status.

Sample

The participants included faculty members and instructors from one Canadian and seven US institutions that enroll large numbers of international students (at least 400 at both the undergraduate and graduate levels). The selected institutions varied with respect to geographic location, size and control (i.e., public vs. private). Represented among the selected institutions was one with a 'writing across the curriculum' emphasis. See Appendix 1 for enrollment data for contributing institutions in the research sample.

Within each institution, eight disciplines were chosen at the undergraduate level and five at the graduate level. In most cases, the disciplines selected represented those fields of study with the highest foreign student enrollment as reported by the Institute of International Education (1990). At the undergraduate level the disciplines included business, chemistry, civil engineering, computer science, economics, English, history and psychology. Undergraduate history and economics were included because they represent courses that are most often considered core requirements for all undergraduate majors in the College of Arts and Sciences and the College of Business. Graduate-level disciplines included business, chemistry, civil engineering, computer science and psychology.

Within each discipline, the goal was to obtain course materials from three key courses that included large enrollments of students in the first year at the undergraduate level and three key courses with first-year students at the graduate level. A few special considerations were given; in English, the freshman composition course was included in the sample. In the case of a lecture course with an accompanying lab, the lab was included where possible, and for a large course with several sections, only one section was included. Also, courses were excluded that involved essentially no writing, where writing was defined as requiring a response of more than one or two sentences to any given question. The teachers of the selected courses comprised the sample of participants.

Procedure for obtaining writing assignments

The participating faculty members and teaching assistants were asked to provide copies of assignments that involved writing of any kind (i.e., the tasks assigned, not the students' products). This included parts of tests, work in class or at home that was to be turned in, term papers, or any other relevant assignments. In the case of a test that included a writing section and an objective section, instructors were asked to provide a copy of the entire test or to provide a copy of the writing portion. For a writing assignment given frequently during the term, teachers were asked to provide five examples of that type of assignment and to indicate how many assignments of that type were given during the term. For the assignments of the type just described, in which the students were referred to a book or other source for the questions to answer, the teachers were asked to submit copies of the book pages containing the questions. All assignments that resulted in products to be turned in, whether graded or not, qualified for inclusion among the materials collected. Teachers were also asked to provide copies of written instructions and the course syllabus, partly to verify whether all assignments listed in the syllabus had been supplied for the research. Finally, each participant was asked to complete a brief questionnaire regarding the course and assignments (see Appendix 2).

An on-site coordinator at each institution was enlisted to facilitate the collection of materials. Coordinators and participating faculty members were offered honoraria for their efforts in providing writing assignments.

Classification of writing assignments

After the writing assignments were collected, they were examined by a group of consultants, consisting of three people prominent in the writing-assessment community and the three project staff members. The consultants were asked to work with project staff to develop a classification scheme on the basis of examination of the writing assignments. It was anticipated that this activity would result in categories that differentiated among assignments along more than a single dimension – for example, not only the nature of the writing task (e.g., description, persuasion, etc.), but also the genre, the locus of writing, the specificity of the prompt (e.g., amount of directions given regarding organization), and so forth. The team members were free to draw on their knowledge of existing typologies; no system of categories was imposed *a priori*.

After the classification scheme was developed, each of the writing assignments that had been collected was categorized according to this scheme, in order to determine the frequency with which each category in the scheme was represented. This categorization was done separately for writing assignments representing various situations – e.g., laboratory reports, term papers, etc. – to determine the prevalence of various types of writing requirements per situation.

Furthermore, categorization was done for each discipline, separately at the undergraduate and graduate levels.

Results

Sample description

At the undergraduate level 363 faculty members or teaching assistants were invited and 115 (31.7%) participated in the study. At the graduate level 178 were invited and 61 (34.3%) participated for a total of 176 (32.5%) participants. In some cases, a faculty member represented two different courses within a discipline.

A total of 184 sets of materials were submitted for examination. In the end, not every discipline was represented at each institution and in some cases only one course within a discipline was represented from a given institution. In a limited number of cases as many as four to six sets of course materials were submitted for a single discipline within an institution. Table 1 provides a description of responses to invitations sent to participate in the study. The invitations represent the number of courses identified and teachers contacted. In many cases a single faculty member taught more than one of the critical courses identified for sampling. Of the 760 courses initially thought to be eligible for participation in the study, 186 were withdrawn because they involved essentially no writing. In the final analyses of the data certain sets of course materials that represent duplicate courses may also be eliminated.

Development and validation of classification scheme

The initial classification scheme was developed during two, three-day working sessions with a team consisting of the three writing consultants and the three project staff members. Prior to the first session, the consultants reviewed the purpose of the project, the instructions sent to teachers, and a sample of course materials from 16 participating teachers. The consultants were also asked to think about other classification efforts with which they were familiar, either from the literature or their own work.

The team then worked with a sample of 110 teachers' materials to develop the classification scheme. During the first session, the group began examining sets of course materials from across disciplines at the undergraduate level and recorded, by discipline, observations regarding the types of writing tasks required of students. This process was repeated for graduate courses across disciplines. At the end of the first session, the team began discussing existing classification schemes (Bloom 1956; Horowitz 1986; Purves et al. 1984) and how these schemes fit the initial observations from examined samples.

Table 1

Description of Responses*

| | Undergraduate | | | | | |
	NV	Dec	NR	NW	Sub	Inst
Business	55	1	26	18	6	4
Chemistry	124	7	33	30	20	7
Civil Engineering	45	3	14	22	4	4
Computer Science	59	5	24	18	12	6
Economics	68	7	31	18	15	7
English	40	3	16	–	20	7
History	63	8	30	2	24	7
Psychology	71	4	27	21	18	6
Total Undergraduate	525	38	201	129	119	

| | Graduate | | | | | |
	NV	Dec	NR	NW	Sub	Inst
Business	40	3	15	3	16	6
Chemistry	62	3	18	25	12	5
Civil Engineering	43	6	11	17	6	4
Computer Science	44	1	21	8	11	5
Psychology	46	4	18	4	16	6
Total Graduate	235	17	83	57	61	
TOTAL	760	55	284	186	184**	

* NV = number of courses invited (or course components, where both lecturer and laboratory/discussion teacher were invited); Dec = number of teachers who declined; NR = number of teachers who did not respond to invitation; NW = number of teachers who indicated that their course involved no writing; Sub = number of teachers who submitted materials; Inst = number of institutions represented in a row

** Includes 4 teachers from 3 institutions who submitted materials for special writing classes

In preparation for the second session, each team member took the re1 of materials for a specific discipline for closer examination. Some te2 also began reviewing a number of additional sources (Auerbach 1983; Bachelor and Haley 1947; Bain 1866; Bloom 1956; Brooks and Warren 1949; Connors 1981; Fulton 1912; McCrimmon 1950; Naylor 1942; Rorabacher 1946; Scott 1894; Smalley and Ruetten 1990) in order to develop and refine working definitions for the categories and subcategories emerging in the classification scheme. By the end of the second session an initial classification scheme had been developed. It contained six general categories: locus of writing, length of product, purpose, cognitive demand, genre, and rhetorical task.

A stratified random sample of 17 sets of course materials representing all disciplines and both undergraduate and graduate courses was selected for initial application of the classification scheme. The three project staff members, working independently, applied the classification scheme to the 17 sets of materials and then met to review their ratings. The completed questionnaires and entire set of materials provided by instructors were also examined as part of the rating process.

The purpose and cognitive demand categories were most problematic in application in that a high degree of inference was required to classify assignments in these categories. The purpose category, which was intended to reflect what the teacher wanted the student to do (i.e., learn, demonstrate, or participate), was eventually eliminated because the lack of specificity encountered in the majority of assignments reduced the classification process for this category to guessing. Although ratings for the four subcategories of cognitive demand (i.e., retrieve/organize/relate, apply, analyse/synthesize, and evaluate) lacked consistency, there was fairly consistent agreement on whether an assignment reflected lower or higher cognitive demand. Therefore, the four subcategories were collapsed into two general subcategories consisting of retrieve/organize and apply/analyse/synthesize/evaluate.

The subcategories under genre (i.e., essay, summary, lab report, research report, case analysis, plan/proposal) were expanded to reflect further distinctions that were not captured in the original classification scheme. The additional categories included library research, report of an experiment or observation with and without interpretation, and documented computer program. Other minor revisions were made to the classification scheme and the training sets were again independently rated, this time with two of the consultants participating in the rating process.

After thorough discussion of the ratings three final additions were made to the scheme. A further distinction in length of product was made to reflect the differences between written responses of up to one page in length and those of between one to five pages in length. Also, for several assignments the locus of writing and level of cognitive demand could not be determined from the assignment or accompanying materials; therefore, categories of indeterminant and uncertain were added. After further refinements to the scheme and elaboration of instructions for application of the scheme, the team agreed on the following classification scheme:

Classification scheme

A   Locus of writing (indicate one)
   1   In class (up to 8 hours)
   2   Out of class
   3   Indeterminant
B   Length of product (indicate one)
   1   NED (Nonextended discourse) < 1/2 page; (around 75 words)
   2   SED (Short extended discourse) 1/2 page to 1 page
   3   ED (Extended discourse) >1 page; (up to 5 pages)
   4   LED (Longer extended discourse) 6 to 10 pages
   5   VED (Very extended discourse) more than 10 pages
C   Genres (What does the product look like?) (indicate one)
   1   Essay
   2   Library research (review several references and prepare analysis)
   3   Report of experiment/observation without interpretation
   4   Report of experiment/observation with interpretation
   5   Summary (includes annotated bibliography without comment)
   6   Case study
   7   Plan/proposal
   8   Documented computer program
   9   Other (note nature of assignment; includes annotated bibliography with comment)
D   Cognitive demands (What does writer have to do to accomplish task?) (indicate one)
   1   Retrieve, organize
   2   Apply/Analyse/Synthesize/Evaluate
   3   Uncertain
E   Rhetorical specifications. (How does the instructor define the form?)
   1   Rhetorical tasks (indicate all that apply)
      a)   Narration
      b)   Description
      c)   Exposition
      d)   Argument
   2   Patterns of exposition (indicate all that apply)
      a)   Process
      b)   Classification/enumeration
      c)   Exemplification/illustration

    d) Comparison/contrast
    e) Cause-effect/problem solution
    f) Definition
    g) Analysis
    h) Unspecified

Efforts in progress

Once consensus had been reached on the ratings and classification scheme to be used, the remaining sets of course materials and accompanying tally sheets were prepared for the full rating sessions. In order to quantify types of assignments accurately in the final analyses, all materials were first examined and assignments coded in terms of the number of tasks of a given type that were assigned and the number provided for examination. The tally sheets also contained notations for writing assignments, such as book reports or term papers, mentioned in the syllabus or elsewhere but not included among the sample assignments. Assignments to be classified (i.e., individual questions as well as larger writing projects such as term papers or documented computer programs) were then identified and numbered.

   The application of the classification scheme to all sets of course materials has taken place. Each set of materials was rated by two independent raters and by a third for any category in which a disagreement in classification occurred. Analyses of the ratings and questionnaire data are now underway. Once the writing assignments have been categorized separately for each type of writing situation, additional analyses will be performed. The principal set of analyses will involve combination of data across all situations in which writing was assigned, to determine, for each discipline, the frequency with which each category in the classification scheme was represented. The objective is to determine the prevalence of various writing requirements per discipline, computed across the range of situations in which writing was assigned in each discipline. A final report of stage II activities is expected in the spring of 1994.

Notes

The study of academic writing tasks was conducted by Gordon Hale, Carol Taylor and Brent Bridgeman of Educational Testing Service. Consultants on the project were Barbara Kroll of California State University at Northridge, Joan Carson of Georgia State University, and Robert Kantor formerly of Ohio State University and currently of Educational Testing Service.

Carol Taylor

Appendix 1

Enrollment data for contributing institutions in the research sample*

* Figures obtained from *Open Doors:* 1989/90 (IIE 1990); enrollment data from University of Toronto not available.
** 1 = Private, 2 = Public

Institution	Public/ Private**	No. of Foreign Students	% of Foreign Students	Total Enrollment
Columbia University, NY	1	2,849	14.8	19,231
Harvard University, MA	1	2,246	13.2	16,985
Iowa State University, IA	2	2,160	8.5	25,489
Texas A & M University,	2	2,156	5.3	40,492
University of California, Berkeley, CA	2	2,143	6.9	31,121
University of Hawaii at Manoa, HI	2	1,850	10.2	18,049
University of Missouri, MO	2	1,712	7.1	24,220
University of Toronto, Ontario, Canada	2			

Appendix 2

Questionnaire for writing task study

We would appreciate your answering the following questions. (If you feel uncomfortable about a particular question, you may leave it blank.)

1   Department name and course number

2   This entire course (including parts taught by others, if any) is: (check one)
   ___ seminar only
   ___ lecture only
   ___ laboratory only
   ___ lecture plus laboratory section(s)
   ___ lecture plus discussion or recitation section(s)
   ___ other (please specify)

3   What is your role in this course? (check one)
   ___ teacher of seminar (for course that is seminar only)
   ___ teacher of lecture
   ___ teacher of laboratory
   ___ teacher of discussion or recitation section
   ___ other (please specify)

4   What is your position? (check one)
   ___ faculty member
   ___ graduate assistant
   ___ other (please specify)

5   How is this course defined? (check one)
   ___ lower-division undergraduate course (i.e., for freshmen/ sophomores)
   ___ upper-division undergraduate course (i.e., for juniors/seniors)
   ___ graduate-level course
   ___ other (please specify)

6   If you answered 'lower-division undergraduate course' to Questions 5, roughly what percentage of students you taught in this course were freshmen?
   ___ 75% or more
   ___ 50% to 75%
   ___ less than 50%
   ___ don't know

7   Is this course required for majors in your department? (check one)
    ___ yes
    ___ no
    ___ don't know

8   Is this course often taken by majors in other departments to fulfill a
    general requirement? (check one)
    ___ yes
    ___ no
    ___ don't know

9   Approximately how many students did you teach in this course (during
    the term in question)?

    ___

10 Approximately how many international (foreign) students did you teach
    in this course? (If you are not sure of the number but can give a range
    within which you think the number fell, please do so.)

    ___

11 The nature of the writing assignments for this course was determined
    primarily by: (check one)
    ___ departmental policy
    ___ a course supervisor
    ___ individual instructor
    ___ other (please specify)

12 Did you sometimes require students to write in teams? (check one)
    ___ yes
    ___ no

13 If you answered 'yes' to Question 12, approximately what percentage of
    your writing assignments were team assignments?
    ___ %

14 Did you have help in grading your students' writing?
    ___ yes
    ___ no

15 If you answered 'yes' to Question 14, what type of person or persons
    provided help?
    ___ graduate assistant(s)
    ___ undergraduate assistant(s)
    ___ fellow team teacher(s)
    ___ other (please specify)

16 Approximately what percentage of a student's course grade was based on: (Entries should total 100.)

___ out-of-class writing

___ in-class writing, including test questions that involved writing (i.e., more than one or two sentences)

___ objective (e.g., multiple-choice, true-false) or short-answer questions

___ problem sets with essentially no writing (e.g., numerical problems or drawn figures)

___ other (please specify)

17 To what extent were your writing assignments influenced by apparent limitations in the writing ability of students in your course?

___ not at all

___ some

___ a lot

18 To what extent were your writing assignments influenced by the special needs of international students in your course?

___ not at all

___ some

___ a lot

19 If you answered 'some' or 'a lot' to Question 17 or 18, please describe briefly the ways in which your writing assignments were affected.

20 We have asked you to provide copies of printed writing assignments. How often were those assignments accompanied by verbal instruction that further specified what a student's written product should contain?

___ often

___ occasionally

___ never

NOTE: If your files contain notes with the verbal instructions that accompanied a particular assignment, we would like you to attach a copy of those instructions to the assignment. (See cover letter.)

If you are unable to provide copies of verbal instructions, can you briefly describe the kinds of verbal specifications you typically gave? (Use space below.)

21 If you wish, please feel free to offer additional comments – (a) to expand upon responses made above, (b) to help in interpreting the results of the study, or (c) for any other reason. (For example, we would be interested in knowing what factors affected the type and extent of writing you assigned, and in what ways those factors affected your assignments.) (Continue on the back of this sheet if necessary.)

References

Anson, C.M. 1988. Toward a multidimensional model of writing in the academic disciplines. In D.A. Jolliffe (ed.), *Advances in Writing Research:* Vol 2. *Writing in Academic Disciplines*. Norwood, NJ: Ablex.

Auerbach, B. and B. Snyder. 1983. *Paragraph Patterns*. New York, NY: Harcourt, Brace, Jovanovich.

Bachelor J. and H. Haley. 1947. *The Practice of Exposition*. New York, NY: D. Appleton-Century.

Bain, A. 1866. *English composition and rhetoric: A manual*. New York, NY: Appleton.

Berlin, J. A. 1984. *Writing Instruction in Nineteenth-century American Colleges*. Carbondale, IL: Southern Illinois University Press.

Bernhardt, S.A. 1985. Writing across the curriculum at one university: A survey of faculty members and students. *ADE Bulletin* 82.

Bloom, B.S. (ed.) 1956. *Taxonomy of Educational Objectives*. New York, NY: Longmans, Green and Company.

Bridgeman, B. and S. Carlson. 1983. Survey of academic writing tasks required of graduate and undergraduate foreign students, *TOEFL Research Report No. 15, ETS Research Report No. 83-18*. Princeton, NJ: Educational Testing Service.

Brooks, C. and R. P. Warren. 1949. *Modern Rhetoric*. New York, NY: Harcourt, Brace & Company.

Canseco, G. and P. Byrd. 1989. Writing required in graduate courses in business administration. *TESOL Quarterly* 23: 305–16.

Connors, R.J. 1981. The rise and fall of the modes of discourse. *College Composition and Communication* 32: 444–55.

Donlan, D. 1980. Teaching models, experience, and locus of control: Analysis of a summer in-service program for composition teachers. *Research in the Teaching of English* 14: 319–30.

Eblen, C. 1983. Writing across-the-curriculum: A survey of a university faculty's views and classroom practices. *Research in the Teaching of English* 17: 343–8.

Fulton, M.G. 1912. *Expository Writing: Materials for the College Course in Composition*. New York: The Macmillan Company.

Horowitz, D. 1986. What professors actually require: Academic tasks for the ESL classroom. *TESOL Quarterly* 20: 445–82.

Institute of International Education. 1990. Open Doors: 1989–1990. *Report on International Educational Exchange*. New York, NY: Institute of International Education.

Johns, A. M. 1981. Necessary English: A faculty survey. *TESOL Quarterly* 15: 51–7.

McCrimmon, J. M. 1950. *Writing with a Purpose.* New York, NY: Houghton Mifflin.

Naylor, J. S. 1942. *Informative Writing.* New York, NY: The Macmillan Company.

Purves, A. C., A. Soter, S. Takala and A. Vahapassi. 1984. Towards a domain-referenced system for classifying composition assignments. *Research in the Teaching of English* 18: 385–416.

Rorabacher, L. E. 1946. *Assignments in Exposition.* New York, NY: Harper and Brothers.

Scott, F. N. 1894. *Paragraph-writing.* Boston, MA: Allyn and Bacon.

Sharton, M. 1983. Composition at Illinois State University: A preliminary assessment. *Illinois English Bulletin* 71: 11-12.

Smalley, R. L. and M. K. Ruetten 1990. *Refining Composition Skills: Rhetoric and Grammar for ESL Students.* New York, NY: Maxwell Macmillan International Publishing Group.

West, G. K. and P. Byrd 1982. Technical writing required of graduate and engineering students. *Journal of Technical Writing and Communication* 14: 1–6.

Zemelman, S. 1978. Writing in other disciplines: A questionnaire for teachers. *Conference on Language Attitudes and Composition Newsletter* 5: 12–16.

7 Linguistic accuracy versus coherence in assessing examination answers in content subjects

Yasmeen Lukmani
Research Centre for English and Applied Linguistics,
University of Cambridge/University of Bombay

Introduction

A question that interests all educationists is the identification of factors which lead to academic success. This success is usually judged by means of the written examination in the field of study concerned. It is possible for some teachers to feel that reading and listening skills are what is most essential to academic success for non-native speakers, as revealed in a study by Johns (1981). But this was related to success in the classroom. Success, as judged by the wider community, is normally based on the final mark that is assigned to the student's work (usually a written examination). In judging success, then, student performance on the examination has to be assessed by the subject examiner, though it must be borne in mind that this performance is affected by the nature of the test items, and the criteria by which they are assessed. In this paper, the concern is with the nature of the criteria subject examiners employ and the manner in which these differ from those employed by English examiners when looking at the same student scripts.

Academic writing, particularly by non-native speakers of English, but increasingly even by native speakers, has come under attack from university faculty. Often, as Ballard and Clanchy (1990) point out, the problems are shrugged off as relating to surface structure errors in English. However, they feel these are more often caused by poor structuring and presentation of ideas. This view is shared by many other researchers and teachers in recent years (e.g. Spack 1988; Johns 1991). Spack, dealing with the expression of subject content, speaks of the need for English teachers to deal with rhetorical and academic skills, summarising, paraphrasing, etc., which would necessarily vary from discipline to discipline and even within disciplines. The areas of weakness in student writing identified by Johns (1991) are similar, relating to the interpretation of content, conceptualisation, organisation and expression.

Ballard and Clanchy (1990) also suggest that the real, but unacknowledged, problem with student writing is the disjunction between culturally shaped attitudes to knowledge and their rhetorical expression, as held by non-native students and their assessors. The issue of cultural differences in rhetorical patterning (Kaplan 1966) is, however, not taken into consideration in this study as that leads us away from the practical situation, namely, that Western models of academic writing are accepted as the norm in India, to which students would be expected to conform by their Indian assessors.

Attempts to overcome problems in student writing have led to an emphasis on rhetoric, particularly in the US, and to the Writing Across the Curriculum movement which gained prominence in L1 writing instruction at the same time as the ESP movement took hold of the field in L2 learning. In both, the attempt was to combine the teaching of English with content subjects, and the rhetorical patterning these required, focusing particularly on reading and writing skills. The current debt to ESP is that it spawned the field of English for Academic Purposes, and also that it gave rise to newer manifestations of the intermesh between subject content and the specific rhetorical patterns required to express this (e.g. Henderson, Dudley-Evans and Blackhouse 1993), bringing together the concerns of ESP and EAP. Academic writing in content subjects has, thus, become an exciting new area with considerable potential for practical application.

The study

In considering student performance in the subject examination answer, therefore, as content has to be expressed in language, the central question is, does language play a role in determining the marks that students get in their individual fields of study?

A study was conducted earlier by this researcher (Lukmani 1985) on students at the University of Bombay in their first year at college in three different subjects, namely, Economics, Logic and Zoology, to investigate this issue. It must be borne in mind that while English is the medium of instruction at these colleges, it is a second language for most of the students. The results indicated that language was important in assessing the students' mastery over their subjects in the examination, though the significance of the language factor varied from field to field. It was found to be most important for Economics, less so for Logic, and least important of all for Zoology.

In addition, two aspects of language were isolated for attention in that study, namely, intelligibility and acceptability, and their relative importance in determining success at the subject examination. It was found that acceptability was considered more important in assessing Economics papers than intelligibility, both acceptability and intelligibility were equally important in Logic, while intelligibility was more important in Zoology.

The earlier study was concerned with analysing the effect of linguistic factors on assessment (done by subject teachers, English teachers and native speakers). The emphasis was on assessor reaction rather than on features of text.

The next logical step seemed to be the analysis of specific linguistic components in student scripts and their relative importance in assessment. This became the subject of the present investigation. Grammatical well-formedness was first isolated as one of the key components in writing. The sphere of grammar, however, is the sentence, and as writing samples consist of running text, it was necessary to bring in a framework larger than the sentence. The discourse perspective was therefore introduced, with its concomitant notions of cohesion and coherence.

Cohesion was considered to be the relationship between adjacent sentences, following the framework outlined by Halliday and Hasan (1976), while coherence was taken to be text-based, relating to the rhetorical patterning of the examination answer, as well as the demands of readership which arose from this organisation of subject content.

When applied to the scripts, cohesion in terms of cross-reference and economy proved to be sometimes a matter of syntactic well-formedness and sometimes of coherence, but the features of grammaticality and coherence remained distinct. So, only two linguistic components were isolated, namely, i) well-formedness of language, relating to syntax, lexis, and spelling; and ii) coherence of discourse, relating to linguistically signalled organisation and rhetorical patterning, along with audience demands, such as the appropriate academic register and level of abstraction. It was expected to be distinct from features of content, but closely related to it. Cohesion sometimes fell into one category and sometimes into the other.

These linguistic components of text were isolated in order to look at aspects of student performance in the academic context. The questions addressed were:
1 How much do well-formed sentences contribute to academic achievement?
2 How much, in comparison, do coherent texts contribute to it?
Answers to these questions were to be based on the view points of different assessors, the relevant groups being subject teachers (who normally assess these scripts), English teachers (who teach the language which is then used to express subject content), and native speakers (to provide an added dimension, namely, to judge how far student writing had deviated from native speaker norms of correctness and coherence). Two other questions arose in this context:
3 Is it true that the subject teacher's judgement from the point of view of subject matter disregards language ability? More importantly, what kinds of language ability does it disregard, e.g., grammatical correctness? What other kinds does it include, e.g. coherent statement?
4 Is it true that the language teacher's judgement is based on evidence of language ability? What kinds of language ability does it tend to be based on, and what kinds does it exclude?

It seemed important to determine how far the criteria employed by subject teachers match those of English teachers. Should considerable disparity become evident, it would appear that English teacher criteria, and thereby, by implication, the focus of English teaching, lacked relevance for academic success.

There is another way of looking at the relationship between subject matter and language. Although one commonly assumes that an understanding of the content is distinct from the ability to write about it, it is possible that the two are indistinguishable at a certain level (Widdowson 1978; Fathman and Whalley 1990): that a clearer or more coherent statement shows not just better language ability but a clearer understanding of the subject itself, and conversely, that an inadequate command of basic writing skills limits the depth of one's understanding of the subject. To the extent that there is a real connection between understanding and expression, the subject teacher's judgement of what shows a good understanding of the subject will correlate with the language teacher's judgement of what indicates a developed ability to handle discourse structure. The problem here is that the language teacher's judgement, in the Indian tradition, is likely to be influenced much more (if not exclusively) by sentential correctness, thus negating the expected correlation.

By attempting to elicit assessor criteria, this study aims at throwing light on what should be the focus of student attention in English, and by implication, the teaching emphasis in the General English class, whether the focus should be on correct sentence production, or the coherent presentation of content.

It was considered unlikely that assessment criteria would be precisely formulated by teachers or reflect the actual considerations at work. This is corroborated by Johns (1981) who points out that the use of a questionnaire or interview leaves open the question of whether the data reflect what the respondents do, what they think they do, or what they want the researcher to think they do. In keeping with these views, instead of eliciting conscious statements on criteria, an indirect means of tapping underlying processes was sought. Raters were asked to assess samples of student writing representing different degrees of discourse ability. As the level of actual student writing in the corpus was almost uniformly low in coherence, it was not possible to select, from among the available scripts, sets that represented sufficient variation in rhetorical patterning. In such selection, there would have also been problems of subject-matter equivalence between the different scripts.

Editing the original scripts in order to produce versions which were distinct from each other seemed a suitable alternative procedure. Correction, revision or manipulation of compositions written by non-native speakers had already been attempted by Johansson (1978). While agreeing in general with views like that of Santos (1988), that artificially prepared passages, though providing maximum control of variables, sacrifice the natural quality of unaltered connected discourse, thus preventing assessors from deciding for themselves which errors are the most glaring, this procedure was considered necessary for the above-

mentioned reasons. Accordingly, the scripts were suitably edited for:
1 grammar alone (+G),
2 coherence alone (+C),
3 both grammar and coherence (+G+C).

It is also argued that while it is true that only the original script is authentic in the true sense, the 'ideal' (edited for both grammar and coherence) reads naturally enough, and to a large extent, so also does the version corrected for grammar. The only problem is with the version edited for coherence. The degree of coherence achieved without grammatical support does seem a bit unnatural. However, since the object of the study was to specifically contrast the value of grammar versus coherence, since interview data is even more suspect (Johns 1981), and since the exercise of seeking assessor ratings on original student scripts on the criteria of overall rating, intelligibility, acceptability and content had already been done in a previous experiment on the same data, this was considered a suitable procedure.

The same scripts were used as in the previous experiment (Lukmani 1985), in order to be able to compare the findings from two different types of elicitation, briefly reported later in Table 2. Three fields of study were chosen, namely, Economics, Logic and Zoology, which were considered to be varied enough to cover a wide range of rhetorical and linguistic functioning.

Based on this reasoning, an experiment was designed to test the following hypotheses:
1 Version (+G+C) would be rated higher than all other versions by all assessors for all three fields of study.
2 Version (+C) would be rated higher than version (+G) by subject teachers for all three fields of study.
3 Version (+G) would be rated higher than version (+C) by English teachers and native speakers for all three fields of study.

Method

Data

Scripts of six Economics students, six Logic students and four Zoology students were selected from the randomly selected students of three representative colleges of the University of Bombay (used in the experiment referred to earlier), and four versions of each were made. This yielded 24 Economics scripts, 24 Logic scripts and 16 Zoology scripts. Economics and Logic were the focus of interest in the relationship between language and subject matter. Zoology scripts were fewer in number for they were used only as a point of contrast.

The original scripts were selected from the corpus in the following manner. In the first stage, the scripts were divided by the investigator into three groups – 'intelligible', 'somewhat intelligible' and 'completely unintelligible'. Only those falling into the first two groups were retained. Those scripts dealing with one common topic were then further selected from this group. As this number was found to be inadequate, scripts dealing with related topics were also included. After this preliminary selection, subject specialists in each of the fields were consulted. Only those scripts which they judged as deserving 35%–50% marks were finally retained. These criteria were adopted because the study attempted to i) focus on the average student who neither failed nor got first class marks (in Bombay University's marking scheme), and ii) prevent wide variability in the content factor of the students' answers in terms of the relevance and adequacy of treatment of the subject matter. With adequacy of treatment of content on a similar level for all students, it was felt that any variation in the marks received in further assessment would be due to non-content factors, i.e. mainly language.

Only two or three paragraphs of student writing per script were taken, as this length was considered sufficient for assessing ability in the field concerned. No answers, however, were cut short in the middle of a topic or sub-topic. In some cases, the question itself was modified by restricting it to the topic covered in the answer so that the answers were a complete response to the question asked.

Three versions of these original scripts were then made, to yield the four versions referred to. The originals are henceforth referred to as Version 1 (-C-G). Version 2 (+G) was edited for sentential grammar alone, with the addition or replacement of a few cohesive markers, whenever these were considered essential for the well-formedness of a sentence. Version 3 (+C) was rewritten in the most coherent form possible. The changes made in Version 3 related to

1 the use of the appropriate conventions of register;
2 the organisation of individual sentences in terms of their topic-comment relations;
3 the rhetorical ordering of these sentences in the answer; elimination of redundancy and contradiction; and the cohesive devices affecting cross-references within the text. In this version, syntactic deviation was left unchanged.

Version 4 (+C+G) was edited for both syntactic well-formedness and coherence. Care was taken to ensure that this version did not become a model of correct and coherent utterances, but that it represented a level of well-formedness and coherence which the student could reasonably have been expected to achieve.

The different versions were produced by the investigator in consultation with subject specialists as well as with other linguists specialising in English. The content of the answers was left untouched in all the versions. Also, whenever the original script included a figure, it was reproduced in identical form in all the versions. All answers were typed to eliminate handwriting bias.

Assessors

Seven Economics teachers and six teachers each of Logic and Zoology (19 in all) and six English teachers, the same for all the fields, were selected as the assessors. They were all experienced examiners and reputed to be good in their field. Native speakers of English (three in all), who were British or American, were also chosen to assess the scripts. None of the native speakers were subject specialists. Only two had visited India but even these had spent little time in the country, and so none of them was familiar with the way in which Indian students wrote English. It was expected that they would have greater difficulty in decoding these answer papers than Indian teachers.

Materials and procedures

The three sets of assessors, subject teachers, English teachers and native speakers, had to assess every version of the scripts in the subjects concerned, giving an overall mark out of a total of 20. Each set of assessors was asked to look at the scripts from the point of view of its own group, namely, that of subject teachers, English teachers or native speakers. No criteria for assessment were specified, deliberately, to ensure normal evaluation procedures, that is, subjective, impressionistic marking. It was expected that subject teachers would look for relevance in the ideas presented and for coverage and adequacy of treatment. English teachers and native speakers, on the other hand, being non-subject specialists, were expected to be more concerned with the linguistic and rhetorical aspects of the scripts.

The scripts were presented in jumbled order to the assessors so that each had his/her own individually assembled set of scripts. This was done in order to i) prevent different versions of the same script being dismissed as copies of one another (jumbled ordering separated the different versions); and ii) avoid having some scripts marked higher than others because of the order in which they were presented. The assessors were told that these were scripts produced under regular examination conditions. They were asked to evaluate each individually and not be concerned about any evidence of copying.

Analysis

The analysis was mainly descriptive as the sample size was somewhat limited for meaningful statistical analysis. The statistical tests were performed mainly to ratify the descriptive analysis. The statistical measures employed were:

1 Analysis of Variance tests to determine whether the mean scores of the variables, script type (versions), individual student scripts and assessors differed significantly from each other.
2 Multiple Classification Analysis to provide individual scores on the deviation of each of the categories from the others within the variables.

Results

Statistical analysis

1 Analysis of Variance
The data are presented in Tables 3, 4, and 5 in Appendix A.
The results indicated that;
  i)   the different versions of the scripts were distinct from each other;
  ii)   the difference between the students was highly significant in Economics and Logic, but not in Zoology;
  iii)   the differences between the three types of assessors were highly significant for all three fields, indicating that the criteria used were, in each case, markedly different.

2 Multiple Classification Analysis
The data are given in Table 6 in Appendix A. The results are presented in terms of script type, students and assessors.

Script Type

In Economics, version 2 (edited for grammar) and version 4 (edited for grammar and coherence) were both marked much higher than version 1 (the original) and version 3 (edited for coherence).

In Logic, there were less gains in scores from the original (version 1) to the version edited for coherence (version 3) than in Economics. The version edited for grammar (version 2) also got lower scores in Logic than in Economics. However, the scores for versions 2 and 4 (edited for grammar, and for both grammar and coherence, respectively) were still overwhelmingly higher than for versions 1 and 3.

In comparison with Economics and Logic, in Zoology, the grammatically edited version (+G) was closest to version 4 (+C+G). Version 3 (+C) got higher scores in Zoology than in either Economics or Logic. However, even so, the rank ordering of the categories for Zoology remained the same as for Economics and Logic, the order being versions 4, 2, 3, 1. The scores for version 3 (+C) fell midway between those for the original and Version 2 (+G).

Students

In Economics, there was wide variation in the abilities of the six students under investigation. The differentiation was less in Logic and even less in Zoology.

Assessors

In Economics, there was a wide gap between the evaluation criteria of the subject teachers and native speakers, with English teachers falling in between the two. In Logic, there was less variation within groups of assessors. However, English teacher scores in Logic, as in Economics, fell half-way between subject teacher and native speaker scores. In Zoology, like Economics, there were wide variations within assessors. However, English teacher scores in Zoology came much closer to subject teacher scores than in either Economics or Logic.

Descriptive Analysis

Having established, through the statistical analysis, that the four versions were distinct, as also assessor criteria, it was possible to proceed with a descriptive analysis of the mean scores of the ratings of each set of assessors in the three fields of study.

This indicates that the scores for version (+C+G) were the highest for all groups of assessors in each subject. It was also found that the rank ordering of scores for the different versions, by all assessors combined, for each subject, was versions 4,2,3 and 1, though specific differences in the ordering did occur in individual assessor groups.

The results are presented in Table 1 below.

Table 1

Mean scores of scripts according to assessors in Economics, Logic and Zoology

Groups	–C–G	–C	–G	+C+G	Means
Economics					
STs	6.5	7.5	7.6	8.3	
ETs	5.7	12.3	7.1	13.2	
NSs	7.8	13.7	9.9	15.5	
Means					
Logic					
STs	9.3	9.8	8.8	10.4	
ETs	8.0	11.5	8.9	13.0	
NSs	9.8	13.7	9.6	16.9	
Means					
Zoology					
STs	10.8	11.0	11.1	11.1	
ETs	8.1	12.0	11.0	13.1	
NSs	9.0	17.2	14.3	18.7	
Means					

STs = Subject teachers; ETs = English teachers; NSs = Native speakers

It is possible to look at the results from another perspective, that of what students stand to lose through inadequate command of grammar and/or coherence in their examination answers. Figures 1, 2 and 3 present the results for Economics, Logic and Zoology respectively, as assessed by subject teachers, English teachers and native speakers. For clarity of focus, the "ideal" version 1 (+C+G) is taken as the starting point and the "ideals" in each field of study have been merged into single starting points by correcting for actual scores observed.

Figure 1

Graph showing loss of marks for Economics students for lack of i) coherence (C), ii) grammaticality (G), iii) both coherence and grammaticality (CG) as rated by subject teachers (S), English teachers (E) and native speakers (N)

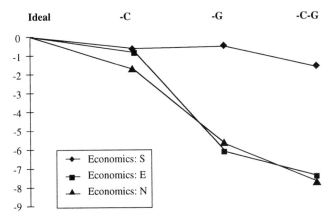

Figure 2

Graph showing loss of marks for Logic students for lack of i) coherence (C), ii) grammaticality (G), iii) both coherence and grammaticality (CG) as rated by subject teachers (S), English teachers (E) and native speakers (N)

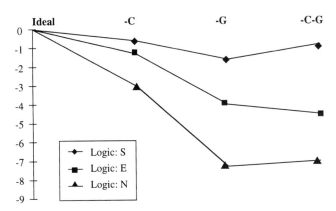

Figure 3

**Graph showing loss of marks for Zoology students for lack of i) coherence
(C), ii) grammaticality (G), iii) both coherence and grammaticality (CG) as
rated by subject teachers (S), English teachers (E) and native speakers (N)**

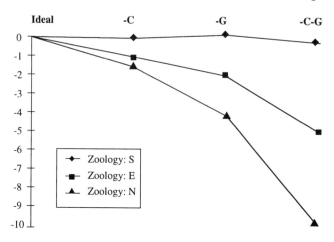

Assessor performance across fields can also be seen at a glance in Figure 4, where
a profile emerges of the marking patterns of subject teachers, English teachers
and native speakers and the extent to which they penalise students for poor
grammar, coherence, and grammar and coherence together. Subject teachers
seem to be the most lenient about grammar and coherence, English teachers less
so, while native speakers have the highest standards. This is contrary to the
evidence provided by Santos (1988) who found that non-native speaking
teachers were more severe in their judgements than native speakers. The contexts
in which the judgements were made might have something to do with the results:
the NNS teachers used by Santos were operating in the US, and therefore,
perhaps on their mettle to maintain standards; whereas, in the present study, the
NNS were experienced examiners operating on home ground, in full knowledge
of prevailing standards in English, while the native speakers (who were not
teachers at all) reflected normal, educated, native speaker standards of English.

A field-specific picture also emerges in Figure 5, where the ratings for
Economics, Logic and Zoology across assessors are presented.

Figure 4

Graph showing loss of marks for lack of i) coherence (C), ii) grammaticality (G), iii) both coherence and grammmaticality (CG) by subject teachers (S), English teachers (E) and native speakers (N) for all three subjects.

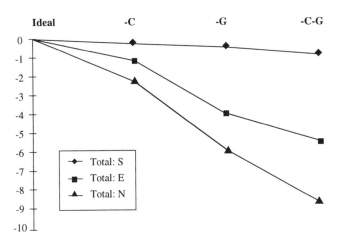

Figure 5

Graph showing loss of marks for lack of i) coherence (C), ii) grammaticality (G), iii) both coherence and grammaticality (CG) for all three subjects across the three groups of raters

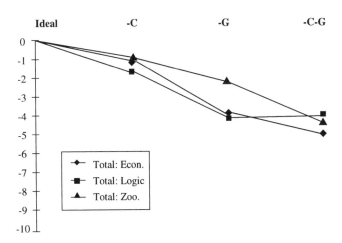

The results indicate that in terms of the actual student scripts, lacking C and G, it is easiest to get higher scores in Logic, then comes Zoology, then Economics. In spite of this, perhaps for reasons discussed earlier, the greatest penalisation for lack of grammar (-G) is in Logic, with Economics scores being almost the same, while the greatest penalisation for lack of coherence (-C) is also in Logic. Economics and Zoology scores differ from Logic almost to the same extent.

Discussion

As these findings emerged in both the statistical and descriptive analyses in each of the fields selected, hypothesis 1 seems to have been borne out. It therefore appears that both the aspects of writing ability under consideration, grammatical correctness and coherence, are important for subject teachers, English teachers and native speakers, for the scripts containing these are rated higher than the original versions. Moreover, this finding applies not only to Arts subjects like Economics and Logic, but also to a Science subject like Zoology.

The version edited for coherence alone (+C) does not get the unequivocally higher ratings expected for it by subject teachers in comparison with the ratings for the original. Hypothesis 2 is, thus, not borne out in any clear manner. In Economics and Zoology, it is found that subject teacher ratings for the versions edited for grammar (+G) and for coherence (+C) are almost identical, showing a rise from the original scores. This shows that both grammatical well-formedness and coherence, when isolated, carry equal weight in subject teacher assessment in these two fields, with coherence being slightly more important. The presence of either feature can raise scores. Ratings by Logic teachers for added grammaticality are, however, considerably higher than those for added coherence – the scores, in fact, fall with added coherence. Thus, hypothesis 2 as it stands, namely, that (+C) would be rated higher than (+G) by all subject teachers, is not entirely borne out.

Nevertheless, in spite of this, coherence is seen to be important. Firstly, as seen above, version (+C+G) was marked higher by all groups of assessors – higher than version (+G) – which indicates the importance of the role played by coherence over and above purely grammatical well-formedness.

Secondly, two out of the three groups of subject teachers indicate that coherence is at least as important as grammaticality, if not more important.

Thirdly, substantial gains in scores from the original to the coherence-edited version are seen in ratings by all assessors (except in Logic, by subject teachers and native speakers). It appears that in Logic, a basic level of grammatical well-formedness is required before the coherence of the scripts can be fully appreciated. (This condition exists in version (+G+C) but not in version (+C)) In Zoology, on the other hand, subject teacher assessment indicates that there is no difference between versions (+C) and (+C+G). That is to say, once a basic level of coherence is reached, further grammaticality has no value.

The ratings also show that with higher grammaticality, the need for coherence is less in Economics and Zoology. In Logic, subject teachers and native speakers indicate, however, that it is with lower grammaticality that the need for coherence is less.

English teachers and native speakers, without exception, rated version (+G) much higher than version (+C), in all three fields. This is in accordance with hypothesis 3. These two types of assessors were expected to give much more weight to linguistic well-formedness than to the adequacy of statement of subject content. Their scores on the grammatically edited version are found to be closest to those on version (+C+G).

Subject teacher scores show low gains from the original to the version edited for grammar, in comparison with English teacher and native speaker scores. The major leap in subject teacher scores occurs from version (+G) to version (+G+C). This is in contrast with the major leap in English teacher and native speaker scores from the original to version (+G). The relationship that emerges between coherence and grammaticality in these three subjects is, thus, of interest.

Answers in Economics can be said to be normally concerned with the development of an argument, from the statement of the basic thesis to the various stages for proving the claims of that thesis. The linguistic demands of the subject relate to the connection between different points in the argument, the expression of opposing opinions, of modification and restriction in views, the drawing of a conclusion, and so on. Economics also involves temporal, spatial and consequential relations between ideas.

The findings of the experiment indicate that the basic requirement in Economics is that the answer should present its argument with clarity. This clarity, it seems, can be achieved either through a more coherent organisation of ideas and explicit statement, or through grammatically well-formed language which does not deflect the reader's attention from the argument. Thus, both coherence and grammaticality, independently, help in getting the answer good marks, with either factor carrying approximately equal weight with the assessor. Coherence is, thus, not inseparably linked with grammatical well-formedness, for both are independently effective. However, the highest marks are awarded to scripts with high coherence in addition to high grammaticality.

Zoology, being concerned with the description of parts of organisms and the functions of these parts, seems mainly to require the expression of the spatial relationships between the parts. This is chiefly in terms of where these are situated and the changes they undergo in relation to other parts of the organism in the execution of their allotted functions. Spatial relations can be indicated fairly clearly by diagrammatic representation and by linking statements through the simple device of sequence without necessarily stating the nature of the connection. It is perhaps for this reason that the demands of coherence are greater than grammaticality in Zoology. However, there is a demand for either feature when the other is in short supply. Thus, the addition of either coherence or grammaticality can lead to higher scores.

All assessors of Logic indicate that coherence is not appreciated on its own without grammaticality. However, an increase in both grammaticality and coherence is rewarded highly. Thus, the two factors, coherence and grammaticality, have to occur simultaneously in order for the student to perform well. Perhaps the reason for this might lie in the fact that Logic is in essence a meta-subject, concerned with matters such as the nature of categorisation and classification. These factors are in themselves aspects of coherence, and so, in the expression of logical principles, language and thought are seen to be inextricably linked. By extension, grammatical well-formedness and coherence in this subject are two sides of the same coin. Perhaps this is why these two features are so closely connected in the assessment of Logic scripts. A rise in coherence has to be accompanied by a corresponding rise in grammar.

However, in spite of this, grammatical correctness and coherence do not carry exactly the same weight in the assessment of Logic answers. Subject teachers as well as English teachers and native speakers give higher ratings in Logic for grammaticality. Thus, somewhat paradoxically, where the content of the subject is coherence itself, grammatical well-formedness seems to overtake it in importance, even in the eyes of the subject teacher. Perhaps linguistic coherence draws attention to logical incoherence: this might explain the fall in scores for coherence-edited scripts.

The relative importance of grammaticality and coherence in the three fields for subject teachers is presented in summary form in Table 2 below. This is presented along with the ratings for acceptability and intelligibility for original student scripts in the previous study referred to earlier.

Table 2

The relative importance of i) grammaticality (G) and coherence (C) and ii) acceptability (A) and intelligibility (I) for Economics, Logic and Zoology, for subject teachers

	Experimental mode for arriving at language aspect	
Field	**Reader's analysis of unaltered texts along dimensions**	**Reader's assessment of reconstituted text**
Economics	A	Either G or C sufficient; both G and C in conjunction better
Logic	A and I	Both G and C in conjunction only
Zoology	I	Either G or C sufficient

Major leap in scores for Subject Teachers: –C–G to +C+G
Major leap in scores for English Teachers: –C–G to +G

Conclusions and implications

The experiment has provided some insights into the nature of the English required by the different subject areas, as seen by the demands of the three assessor groups. This relates to:

1 The value of grammaticality

English teachers and native speakers find grammatical correctness, relatively speaking, most important for Economics, less so for Zoology, and even less for Logic. On the other hand, grammar is valued highly by subject teachers of Economics, less so by their counterparts in Logic, and least of all in Zoology.

2 The value of coherence

In Economics and Zoology, while coherence is valued, grammaticality is considered more important. However in Logic, coherence is valued only when it coexists with grammaticality.

It appears that the major difference between the criteria of English teachers and subject teachers is the extent of their preference for grammaticality and coherence. Both factors are required by each. However, English teachers value grammaticality more than subject teachers do, while in general, subject teachers rate coherence higher than English teachers. So, while well-formed sentences do contribute to academic success (based on subject teacher ratings), coherent texts would appear to be more valued than they are by English teachers. It would, then, seem reasonable for English teachers to pay greater attention to features of discourse structure in teaching and testing than they do at present in General English courses. This would imply extending their notions of academic excellence, which in turn would lead to a revision of existing teaching and testing techniques.

Appendix A

Table 3

Analysis of variance of script type, students and assessors in Economics

Source of variation	Sum of squares	df	Mean square	F	Signif of F
Main effects	75033.0	10	7503.3	73.379	0.000
Script type	37833.06	3	12611.2	123.331	0.000
Students	15954.2	5	3190.8	31.205	0.000
Assessors	21245.2	2	10622.6	103.884	0.000
2-way interactions	18056.3	31	582.5	5.696	0.000
Explained	93089.4	41	22270.5	22.204	0.000
Residual	3067.7	30	102.3		
Total	96156.9	71	1354.3		

Table 4

Analysis of variance of script type, students and assessors in Logic

Source of variation	Sum of squares	df	Mean square	F	Signif of F
Main effects	33938.9	10	3393.9	26.327	0.000
Script type	23093.8	3	7697.9	59.715	0.000
Students	3380.5	5	676.1	5.245	0.000
Assessors	7464.5	2	3732.3	28.952	0.000
2-way interactions	11276.0	31	363.8	2.822	0.000
Explained	45215.0	41	1102.8	8.555	0.000
Residual	3867.0	31	128.9		
Total	48082.0	71	692.3		

Table 5

Analysis of variance of script type, students and assessors in Zoology

Source of variation	Sum of squares	df	Mean square	F	Signif of F
Main effects	31149.8	8	3893.7	13.907	0.000
Script type	13360.3	3	4453.4	15.906	0.000
Students	2287.7	3	762.6	2.724	0.075
Assessors	13225.4	2	6612.7	23.619	0.000
2-way interactions	12088.6	21	575.6	2.056	0.000
Explained	43238.3	29	1490.9	5.325	0.000
Residual	5039.6	18	279.9		
Total	48277.9	47	1027.2		

Table 6

Multiple classification analysis of mean scores by all assessors in Economics, Logic and Zoology

Variable + category			I Economics Grand mean = 99.99		II Logic Grand mean = 105.07		III Zoology Grand mean = 124.04	
			N	Dev'n	N	Dev'n	N	Dev'n
Script type								
Version 1			18	−25.99	18	−19.13	12	−25.71
Version 2			18	15.90	18	8.04	12	15.23
Version 3			18	−18.65	18	−14.35	12	−7.04
Version 4			18	28.74	18	25.13	12	19.37
Students								
ECO	LOG	ZOO						
2	11	22	12	5.85	12	1.60	12	10.12
4	12	23	12	11.68	12	−12.49	12	3.88
5	13	24	12	−10.74	12	−0.15	12	−4.46
7	15	25	12	16.43	12	−3.74	12	−9.54
8	19		12	4.26	12	7.18		
10	21		12	−27.49	12	7.60		
Assessors								
1	1	1	24	−20.07	24	−11.49	16	−14.23
2	2	2	24	−1.82	24	−1.78	16	−10.73
3	3	3	24	21.89	24	13.26	16	24.96
Multiple R squared				.780		.691		.645
Multiple R				.883		.832		.803

Appendix B

Sample set of script versions of one student in Economics

Q. Critically examine Robbins' definition of Economics

Version 1 (original: -C-G) Robbins' definition of Economics:

Robbins' first pointed out that economics is a science which studies human behaviour as a relationship between ends and scarce. Which have alternative uses. As first only Robbins stated that economics is science it is not a pure science as well as physics and Chemistry. But it far better than the sciences namely psychology and other social sciences. Further he pointed out that economics studies human behaviour as a relationship between ends and scarce. It means that man have to face his ends and scarce according to his income. As suppose a man have 5/Rs. He will make use of these 5/Rs. in buying different commodities such as he will buy a picture ticket or sweet-meet or toys. In this way we se that how a man will make use of his 5/Rs. But further we se that human - wants never declined but it goes on increasing and increasing. this is clear that how ends and scarce have alternative uses. On one hand Robins have stated that Economics is a science. But on the other hand he has stated that Economics is an art in science we come to know where ever in art we learn to do. Thus we see that the definition of Robins' is more acceptable definition than the other definition. Whice states that Economics is a science which studies human behaviour as a relationship between ends – and – scarce. and which have alternative uses. This is the definition of Robbns'

Version 2 (+G)

Robbins was the first to point out that Economics is the science which studies human behaviour as a relationship between ends and scarce means which have alternative uses. At first Robbins stated that Economics is a science, yet it is not a pure science like Physics and Chemistry. But it is far better than sciences such as psychology and the other social sciences. Further, he pointed out that Economics studies human behaviour as a relationship between ends and scarce means. It means that man has to relate his ends and scarce means according to his income. Suppose a man has Rs 5/-. He will make use of these five rupees in buying different commodities such as a ticket for the pictures or sweet-meats or toys. In this way we see how a man will make use of his Rs 5/-. But further we see that human wants never decline but go on increasing. From this it is clear that ends and scarce means have alternative uses. On the one hand, Robbins has stated that Economics is a science. But on the other hand he stated that Economics is an art. In science we learn to know whereas in art we learn to do. Thus we see that Robbins' definition is more acceptable than the other definition. It states that

Economics is a science which studies human behaviour as a relationship between ends and scarce means which have alternative uses. This is Robbins' definition.

Version 3 (+C)

Robbins first pointed out that economics is a science which studies human behaviour as a relationship between ends and scarce. Which have alternative uses. He showed on one hand that economics is science it is not a pure science as well as physics and chemistry. But it far better than the sciences namely psychology and other social sciences. On other hand, he pointed out that Economics is an art. In science we come to know whereas in art we learn to do.

Robbins' definition means than man have to face his ends and scarce according to his income. As suppose a man have 5/Rs. He can make use of these 5/Rs in buying any one of different commodities such as he will buy a picture ticket or sweet-meat or toys. This is clear that how ends and scarce means have alternative uses. Moreover we see that human wants never declined but it goes on increasing and increasing.

Version 4 (+C+G)

Robbins was the first to define Economics as a science which studied human behaviour as a relationship between ends and scarce means which have alternative uses. He showed, on the one hand, that Economics was a science. Though not a pure science like Physics and Chemistry, it was far better than other social sciences such as Psychology. On the other hand, he pointed out that Economics was also an art. In science, we learn to know, whereas in art we learn to do. In Economics, we learn both.

Robbins' definition implies that each man has to face the problem of relating his scarce means (i.e. his income) to his ends. Let us suppose that a man has Rs 5/-. He can use this money for buying any one of different commodities, such as a ticket to the pictures, sweet-meats or toys. This shows how scarce means have alternative uses. Moreover, we know that human wants do not decline, even when some of them are satisfied; they go on increasing.

Robbins' definition of Economics is more acceptable than other definitions.

References

Ballard, B. and J. Clanchy. 1990. Assessment by misconception: Cultural influences and intellectual with traditions. In L. Hamp-Lyons (ed.), *Assessing Second Language Writing in Academic Contexts.* Norwood, NJ: Ablex Pub. Corp.

Fathman, A.K. and E. Whalley. 1990. Teacher responses to student writing: focus of form versus content. In B. Kroll (ed.), *Second Language Writing.* Cambridge: Cambridge University Press.

Halliday, M.A.K. and R. Hasan. 1976. *Cohesion in English.* London: Longman.

Henderson, W., T. Dudley-Evans and R. Backhouse (eds.), 1993. *Economics and Language.* London: Routledge.

Johansson, S. 1978. *Native reactions to errors produced by Swedish learners of English.* Gothenburg Studies in English no. 44. Goteborg, Sweden: Acta Universitatis Gothoburgensis.

Johns, A.M. 1981. Necessary English: A faculty survey. *TESOL Quarterly* 15 (1): 51–7.

Johns, A.M. 1991. Faculty assessment of ESL student literacy skills: implications for writing assessment. In L. Hamp-Lyons (ed.), *Assessing Second Language Writing in Academic Contexts.* Norwood, NJ: Ablex Pub. Corp.

Kaplan, R.B. 1966. Cultural thought patterns in intercultural education. *Language Learning* 16: 1–20.

Lukmani, Y. 1985. *A rationale for proficiency testing in English for college entrance.* Unpub. Ph.D thesis, University of Bombay.

Santos, T. 1988. Professors' reactions to the academic writing of non-native speaking students. *TESOL Quarterly* 22 (1): 69–90.

Spack, R. 1988. Initiating ESL students into the academic discourse community: How far should we go? *TESOL Quarterly* 22 (1): 29–51.

Widdowson, H.G. 1978. *Teaching Language as Communication.* Oxford: Oxford University Press.

8 Applying ethical standards to portfolio assessment of writing in English as a second language

Liz Hamp-Lyons
University of Colorado, Denver

Introduction

Portfolio assessment is in the forefront of alternative assessment approaches. Portfolios have been embraced in a variety of contexts, and have become very common in language arts classes in schools and composition programs in colleges (Yancey 1992; Belanoff and Dickson 1991; Hamp-Lyons and Condon, in press). However, there are very few empirical studies of the consequences of portfolio assessment, of the reactions of and impact on learners, teachers and administrators in the assessment context. The *consequential* basis (to borrow Messick's [1989] terms) for portfolio assessment is very slim. Similarly, when we examine the *evidential* basis for portfolio assessment (that is, the psychometric evidence for test validity) we find that the nature, composition and scoring methods typically associated with portfolio assessment make them difficult to judge in the traditional terms of efficiency, reliability and comparability. Some researchers have gone so far as to claim, in the context of authentic assessment more broadly, that 'we must also redraft, if not reinvent, the assumptions and procedures of traditional psychometrics' (Wolf *et al.* 1991).

While the advantages of portfolios as a teaching tool and as an assessment within classrooms can be convincingly argued (Hamp-Lyons, in press), there is as yet little support for claims that program-wide and large-scale portfolio assessments are fairer to minority group members than are standardized tests, or even traditional direct writing tests. In a recent paper (Hamp-Lyons 1993) I reviewed the existing literature on portfolios and minority/ESL writers, and found disquieting indications that:

1 portfolio scoring is less reliable than scoring traditional essay tests;
2 portfolio evaluators may be judging writers as much as writing, opening the potential of discrimination against writers on the basis of perceived gender, race, ethnicity, language background, etc.;
3 little training in judging portfolios is typically given, and many portfolio evaluators feel unsure how to carry out the task;
4 leading from number 3, evaluators may not be attending to the evaluation task

as consistently or effectively as they do the more familiar essay evaluation task.

Numbering myself among those who have extolled the benefits of portfolio writing assessment for the assessment of non-native writers, I felt that it behooved me to consider the ethical ground upon which such claims could, and should be based. In this paper I explore in theoretical terms the conditions under which the use of portfolios in ESL programs (and in programs which include ESL students among a wider population, say of college freshpersons) might be shown to have empirical and consequential validity. Before I enter that theoretical discussion, I provide a brief overview of the principles and practice of portfolio assessment.

What is a portfolio?

At its simplest, a portfolio is a collection of student work. In the sense in which the term is used in writing assessment, a portfolio is a purposive collection of student writing over time, which contains exhibits showing the stages in the writing processes a text has gone through and the stages of the writer's growth as a writer, and evidence of the writer's self-reflection on her/his identity and progress as a writer. Increasingly, portfolios are being compiled in a way that allows the student to provide evidence of self-reflection about her/his writing and her/his writing processes. The contents of portfolios and the conditions for their collection, collation and evaluation are highly sensitive to context and thus, vary considerably.

What is a portfolio writing assessment?

In this paper I confine my discussion to portfolio writing assessments occurring in classroom and program contexts. While at the elementary and high school levels there are moves toward large-scale portfolio assessment of writing (for example, the Vermont Portfolio Project [Koretz 1993], the Rhode Island Portfolio project [Fowles and Gentile 1989]), it is still unclear how such large scale programs and the testing agencies that typically design and conduct the tests will be able to replicate the conditions of portfolio collection and evaluation that are considered fundamental by writing assessment and composition pedagogy specialists. For the purposes of this discussion, then, a portfolio writing assessment is a writing assessment which is based on the instruction that has occurred and the writing that the student has done over the duration of the course. The portfolio assessment takes multiple texts composed by each student as the data for the judgments to be made. It uses teachers (and perhaps others) familiar with the learning context as the judges of the contents of the portfolio. A portfolio assessment should yield artefacts, that is to say, writing samples and judgments of writing, that reflect the instructional and assessment objectives. For this last element to come into play, the instructional setting must be made as transparent to all the interested parties as is possible. Interested parties include, as perhaps the most important group, the students in the learning environment themselves as well as teachers, program administrators, and parents. Interested parties may also include school district officers, local and state government officials and funding agencies. In addition to the portfolios themselves, conventional outcomes such as scores, placements and reports are typically produced: it is these outcomes that are likely to be publicly reported rather than the artefacts themselves and outside the classroom or program itself interpretations of the effectiveness of instruction will probably based on these conventional outcomes.

Why portfolios?

It is argued that assessment tasks which are the same as or closely resemble the tasks to be carried out in actual language-in-use situations will provide more accurate measures of the language learner's abilities. While English as a Foreign/Second Language educators have been arguing for communicative, task-based or performance testing in all language skill areas for the last two decades (Weir 1993), it is only in the US that the same arguments have had to be made for the assessment of writing. In Britain, for instance, the 'essay test' never went out of style, and portfolio assessment began in the mid-1970s with the GCE mode 3 examinations. This argument is made most strongly in the context of writing, where for several decades writing teachers in first language and second language contexts have insisted that multiple choice tests of 'writing' cannot identify a writer's proficiency, let alone her/his strengths and weaknesses as a writer. Since the late 1970s, considerable progress has been made in introducing the direct assessment of writing to colleges and universities.

A frequent complaint about traditional measures of writing ability is that they undermine regular classroom instruction. These days writing teachers like to teach using a 'process approach' in which students spend time inventing the subjects they will write about, deciding on a viewpoint, finding material to put into their essays, drafting and revising before submitting a 'finished' essay. Recently, the time limits inherent in timed writing tests have been an issue for composition scholars: time constraints seriously limit the kinds of tasks that can reasonably be expected of writers, the kinds of content that writers can be asked to consider, and the extent to which natural or learned processes of composing can be applied. In contrast, because portfolios are built up over extended time periods and contain a variety of writing samples, authentic tasks can be set, writers are able to fully engage a content and an appropriate genre and writing processes can be used and can be shown in the completed portfolio. Portfolios, it is argued, reflect the kinds of instruction valued in composition and therefore judgments made of portfolios are claimed to be inherently more meaningful.

In addition, portfolios as teaching tools demand of teachers and students, richer concepts about good writing by acting as a repository and record of good writing and the processes and drafts by which it has been reached. As students and their teachers work together on the development of the portfolio over the term, the teacher is able to assess the student's growth and learning in the course as well as the level of excellence reached by the end of the course. Portfolios, then, are a tool for thoughtful classroom assessment.

Why portfolios for ESL learners?

It has often been claimed that speeded tests disadvantage ESL learners; portfolios usually occur within a process paradigm, and privilege it, thus they offer not only a wider view to the evaluator but a longer time-line for writers. Many ESL writers never really acquire full competence in the conventional grammar of the language, and in speeded writing tests their 'ESL errors' are noticeable to judges. A great deal of evidence has accumulated suggesting that papers marked by 'ESL errors' are graded lower overall by certain judges/judge types than other papers similar to them in most areas of writing proficiency but showing sentence level errors other than those associated with ESL writing (Santos 1988; Vann, Meyer and Lorenz 1984, 1991; Sweedler-Brown 1993a, 1993b; Mendelsohn and Cumming 1987), although a few studies have found conflicting results (McKenna and Carlisle 1991). In portfolio assessment, writers have time to correct their errors (which most of them are perfectly aware of, they are simply unable to identify and correct them unaided) either themselves or by going for help to a Writing Center.

ESL learners may have complex writing skills/needs/strengths/problems relative to their overall language proficiency. Portfolios are particularly good at identifying cases of uneven development, and these cases are especially common in ESL learners: for example, ESL writers often find it easier to learn conventions of organization than the detailed operation of grammar rules. This is strongly related to the fact that it is easy to notice growth in writing in portfolios. ESL learners usually are in a more critical growth phase than NS learners (although we must note the enormous variety of 'ESL-ness' among any ESL population, and remember that the above generalization is not necessarily true of college- or high school-level bilingual students) and in the duration of a writing class many of them will make considerable progress.

Portfolios offer richer options for feedback to the learner both in responses and in evaluations. It is easy to see how important this is in the ESL context, where learners have so much to gain from detailed explanation of an expert reader's perception of their strengths and weaknesses. The process of interpreting a teacher's or peer's response to a written text and building response to that response into a revision of the text requires the writer to reflect on her writing: When portfolio assessment incorporates good reflective practices, portfolios can help students to formulate concepts about good writing.

Portfolios in the teaching relationship

McLaughlin (1991) lists five key points she sees as central to our thinking about the testing-teaching relationship:

1 It matters what you test: 'because today's tests don't measure ... higher-order skills, they discourage classroom practices that are directed toward teaching them.'(249)

2 Do not confuse standards and standardization: 'almost all test-based accountability schemes in use today employ standardized measures that ignore the complexity and individuality of classrooms and constrain teachers' efforts to develop classroom activities appropriate to their students.' (249)

3 Tests constitute a limited lever of reform: 'In the absence of adequate supports for the enterprise, telling teachers to try harder – to achieve 'world class standards' – misperceives the problem.' (250)

4 Test-based accountability plans often misplace trust and protection: 'ironically, accountability schemes that rely on existing testing technology trust the system (the rules, regulations and standardized procedures) more than they trust teachers to make appropriate, educationally sound choices ... and they protect that system ... more than they protect the students served by the system.' (250)

5 The process of setting standards is as important as the standards themselves: 'Almost four decades of experience with planned efforts to reform education have taught us that (1) teachers are not inclined to take responsibility for carrying out goals and objectives about which they have had no say and (2) teachers have important knowledge and expertise to contribute to the enterprise.' (250)

It seems that McLaughlin sees tests as having the potential to affect teaching negatively (1) but not positively (3). Despite this, she argues that appropriate education for students as individuals can only be entrusted to teachers, and not to systems (2), and that appropriate standards will better come from teachers than from systematized accountability measures such as tests (4). Perhaps (5) captures the source of the conflicts in her arguments that I am aware of: teachers as professionals must have a say in both the input (standards setting) and output (judgments) in testing that affects their students. However, McLaughlin claims that teachers have the knowledge and expertise necessary to support such a role while I am not so sure. Many teachers may have the pedagogical skills needed, but do not have the assessment skills. While I am sympathetic to the deficits McLaughlin identifies in traditional testing, I believe that portfolio assessment is an expert system, and that if teachers are to play a central part in designing a portfolio assessment, they must have professional preparation in assessment.

Problems with portfolio assessment

Because of the contextualized nature of portfolio assessment and the essential element of deep commitment by those who engage in it, portfolio assessment seems eminently suited for use in developing assessment issues and skills in teachers. However, there is little evidence to date to suggest that professional preparation for composition teachers includes any form of training in testing, or that portfolio programs provide sufficient background training for portfolio readers to enable them to fully understand either the processes or the implications of assessing writing with portfolios. ESL/EFL teachers, on the other hand, are more likely to have taken coursework in testing and evaluation – but less likely to have had exposure to principles or practice of portfolio assessment.

If lack of teacher education relevant to portfolio assessment is a problem, it is not the only one. I will consider four major, as yet unsolved, problems with portfolio assessment. First, in traditional writing tests, test developers hold control over test tasks and the scoring procedure. While such control is often deplored, one of the ways the test developers and testing agencies use that control is to provide information publicly about task-types to be expected on the test, and the criteria and standards by which test responses are to be judged (see for example, ETS' *Test of Written English Guide*). The public availability of this information ensures that test takers are fully informed about what is expected of them, and can take steps to prepare themselves for success on the test. This same public availability acts as an important component of accountability by the test agency, since their practices are open to scrutiny by the public as well as by other testers. However, the extent to which tasks can be standardized on a portfolio assessment is open to debate. There are portfolio assessment programs which require all writers to carry out the same writing tasks under the same conditions (or at least, as much 'the same' as is possible when test time is extended across a number of days with the writing for the portfolio broken up by time out of the test environment), but these are both rare, and widely considered to be an invalidation of the arguments for portfolio assessment. Thus, the variability of tasks, assignments and procedures within a single portfolio assessment makes it extremely difficult to provide exact or generally applicable information to the public about what students must do to succeed on any particular portfolio assessment. Following from this, it is difficult to establish firm criteria or scoring standards which will be applicable to the many kinds of writing that students may choose to put into their portfolios. These limitations on the openness of a portfolio assessment, caused by its environmental sensitivity, act as counters to some of the major strengths of the portfolio process. In the future, test development efforts will need to confront these issues if portfolios are to be taken seriously by the public and by groups concerned about the accountability of educators for the effectiveness of educational efforts.

A further problem to be considered is the cost of portfolio assessment.

Unquestionably, assessing every student's writing by portfolio is very costly. Cost is always a serious issue in test administration, and is rarely given enough attention by language testers, whose enthusiasm for innovative methods and for an extra edge on accuracy and detail may overcome caution about the problems expensive test methods carry with them in terms of acceptance by the bureaucracies that must fund them. Assessing every student's writing by portfolio is administratively complex. There is more writing; more paper; more time to read the writing, therefore more readers; more types of writing and tasks, therefore more consideration of varied scoring criteria to match the kinds of writing collected; there are more decisions to be made about how student performance over multiple texts and tasks is to be reported, and potentially reporting is more detailed and complex, requiring more complex report forms: the list is a long one. Each of these increases in administrative complexity brings with it increased direct costs as well as increased demands on oversight, and therefore increased expenditure on trained personnel.

While portfolio assessments do have face validity with L2 and L1 writing instructors, there is very little evidence as yet that portfolios have the other validities. Portfolios are said to have construct validity because basing assessments on writing collected over time, on evidence of processes as well as products, fits writing specialists' views of what is importantly learned in the writing class, and therefore, what should be assessed. But it is far from clear that portfolio judges reward portfolios that exhibit rich evidence of application of writing processes more than they reward portfolios that contain strong products and little sign of writing processes. Studies into this question have simply not been done. It is equally true that investigations of the content, predictive or concurrent validity of portfolios remain to be done. Most of the research into and writing about portfolios has focused on their role as a teacher development tool, and more traditional educational measurement questions have been left aside.

The most important of the traditional questions concerns reliability. As Sommers *et al.* (1993) point out, reliability has yet to be established for portfolio assessment – indeed, procedures for establishing reliability over multiple texts and tasks are still in question. Sommers *et al.* found their portfolios at least as reliable as the previous impromptu writing test, 85% of readers agreeing within one point on a six-point scale in both types of assessment. However, this level of agreement would yield a reliability coefficient of, perhaps, .7, which is generally not close enough to our comfort level. Sommers *et al.* point out some of the reasons why it is difficult to work toward higher rater agreement – impossibility of finding 'anchor portfolios', for instance. Few portfolio assessments have spent even this level of effort on reliability, and arguments that reliability should be replaced with a broader basis of validity evidence are beginning to be heard (e.g., Broad 1992). Messick (1989) is often cited as arguing that validity must replace reliability in our concerns: however, Messick's recent work has made it clear that he is not suggesting abandoning empirical validation, but expanding the expectations of validation studies to include both empirical evidence and consequential evidence. If decisions are to be based on judgments of portfolios, then, such judgments must be reliably replicable using criteria and standards that are externally interpretable.

Validating portfolio assessments: an ethical basis

Linn, Baker and Dunbar (1991) suggest eight criteria for evaluating the adequacy of performance assessments such as portfolios. The following summarizes some of the ways these criteria must be considered in the ethical use of portfolios in ESL writing contexts:

Consequences

According to Messick (1989), the consequential basis of test use and interpretation refers to the reactions of the participants (students, teachers, administrators, score users) to the test and the impact of the testing program on participants. As I have discussed above, many positive consequences have been claimed for alternative assessments generally, and for portfolio assessment with ESL learners specifically. Positive effects would include: higher success rates at exit; better student attitudes to writing; improvements in curriculum; greater job satisfaction among teachers; increased acceptance of outcomes by administrators and the wider public. Negative effects would include narrowing of curriculum to fit the assessment, and wasting instructional time on portfolio preparation activities that do not have instructional purposes. Currently, I am aware of no evidence for either the positive or negative consequences of portfolio assessment with ESL learners. There are, for instance, no studies to show the effect on pass rates from writing courses of ESL writers whose final performance is assessed by portfolio rather than by a timed writing test. Such data are almost certainly potentially available in many writing programs in the US, where almost every college has 5–20% ESL writers in the lower levels of composition courses, but they have not been analyzed in that way. Baker (1993), working with a population of college freshpersons (which probably contained some ESL students, although Baker does not report this) found that there was no effect on students' end of course grades according to whether they were taught in a portfolio section or a 'standard process' section where portfolios were not collected. Nor is there any empirical evidence to support the claim that ESL students' attitudes to writing will be more positive after a writing course in which portfolio assessment is used than after a more traditional class. Baker's study (1993) looked at attitudes, using a pre/post writing attitude surveying students' attitudes according to whether they were in a portfolio-based section or a 'standard' section, but once again, her study was not with ESL writers. Equally, there are no studies to suggest narrowing of curriculum in a portfolio-based writing class, or wasting of time in portfolio preparation practices – but neither are there studies to show the opposite. Clearly, a great deal of research remains to be done into the consequential validity of portfolios with ESL writers.

Fairness

The term 'fairness' has come to mean, in the educational measurement community, freedom from racial/ethnic and gender bias (Miller and Legg 1993). Mehrens (1992) has said: 'It would be a mistake to assume that shifting from standardized tests to (portfolio) assessments will obviate concerns about biases against racial/ethnic minorities.' Linn, Baker and Dunbar (1991) suggest that fairness can be rationally determined by judgmental reviews of test materials for bias and offensiveness, but empirical investigation of prior knowledge would still need to be carried out (Valencia *et al.* 1989) and a method of determining bias on statistical evidence across sub-groups, such as DIF (differential item functioning) or FACETS Rasch-type analysis would need to be applied. While as Miller and Legg (1993) point out, 'Few investigations have been completed on fairness in alternative assessment,' Hamp-Lyons (1993) summarized studies which call into question claims that portfolio assessment eliminates such bias.

Transfer and generalizability

A method of assessment which is more costly, as is portfolio assessment of writing, needs to justify the additional expense if it is to be taken seriously. One such justification could be the wider transferability and generalizability of the information resulting from the assessment procedure. To date, however, it is not clear how this is to be achieved with portfolios, whether in the ESL or first language context. Portfolios are often highly context-specific, in their make-up and in their scoring procedures and values. Thus, score interpretations may not transfer into other contexts; scores may be task-specific and not generalizable to other domains of writing skill. Reporting on such task specific writing requires profile reporting (Hamp-Lyons 1991), and multiple scoring instruments for different writing types. To date, most portfolio scoring has occurred through holistic scoring of the entire portfolio (for example, Black *et al.* n.d.) or through holistic scoring of each essay in the portfolio (for example, Graham 1992), although Moss *et al.* (1992) have suggested a beginning for developing strategies for narrative profiling in K-12 portfolios. The close contextualization and task specificity inherent to portfolios not only create problems with cost effectiveness; they also create problems with reliability. If readers do not share a complete understanding of the context, and of the specific task expectations in each teacher's classroom, they will be unlikely to share a view of how to value the student's text-making, and thus their scores will probably disagree (Hamp-

Lyons and Condon, in press). In ESL portfolio assessment, there is at present no indication of a trend toward great emphasis of the kind of shared understanding that I believe is necessary. Inter-rater and task reliability are required of performance assessments such as portfolios just as they are of more traditional tests (Miller and Legg 1993); while generalizability theory may be of use here, there has been little application of generalizability in the portfolio context.

Cognitive complexity

Linn, Baker and Dunbar (1991) point out that a major argument in favor of alternative assessments is that they are better able to assess cognitive complexity. However, if we are to assess the cognitive complexity revealed by a student's writing, it seems to me that criteria for judging this must be developed. Stiggins (1987) has pointed out that the development of explicit performance criteria to assess cognitive complexity, or what is often called 'critical thinking' in the US these days, is very difficult because tasks requiring critical thinking are by definition not limited and constrained, so that a pre-set instrument may not capture all the acceptable variability of responses. The more complex the task, the more essential are clear scoring instruments and good rater training; however, both these forms of explicitness act against the creativity inherent in critical thinking.

Content quality

Anecdotal evidence suggests that standards of content quality may be compromised in locally designed and scored portfolio assessments. That is, in local assessments where teachers are raters, and where teachers have a stake in students' performance, there may a drift in content expectations so that a student's teacher is less demanding than an unknown reader. I found this in a pilot study of the University of Michigan portfolio assessment (Hamp-Lyons 1988), and confirmed a similar pattern in the fledgling portfolio assessment at the University of Colorado, Denver (note, however, that both these latter are mainstream college writing programs and not ESL programs).

Content coverage

Portfolio assessment assesses process, omitted in traditional assessments, but may still assess only a limited part of the mastery of content by comparison with, say, a 40-item MCQ test. If, as usually happens, students choose the texts to put into their portfolios, they may choose not to put effort into those texts they don't plan to include. Over time, this could lead to a de-emphasis on certain writing activities and text types in a program – the reverse of the hoped-for beneficial teaching-testing relationship. However, it is hard to know how to expect portfolio readers to read all the writing produced in a class, when reading a more limited portfolio from a college freshperson (L1 or advanced L2) can take a reader 30 minutes or more, compared to an average of two minutes for a typical timed writing in a college placement program, or 20 seconds in the TWE (Test of Written English) readings.

Meaningfulness

We still have almost no data on students' views of and responses to portfolio assessment of writing, nor on the impact on students' later writing activities as a result of a portfolio-based writing course. We do not, then, know whether this 'authentic' assessment is more meaningful to students than the more traditional and administratively easier forms of writing assessment. Baker's (1993) findings of no difference in students' attitudes about writing whether they were taught in a regular or a portfolio writing class cause us to question the assumption that portfolios lead to improved student attitudes about writing and its assessment.

Cost and efficiency

An assessment instrument should be no more expensive than it has to be to obtain the desired information. We have yet to offer any clear proof that we have to conduct portfolio assessment because it offers any advantage that we cannot obtain in cheaper and more efficient ways. The advantages claimed, all of which generally can be clustered together under the heading of greater consequential validity, remain to be proved, as I have suggested above. The problems that the portfolio assessment movement, and indeed the authentic assessment movement as a whole, will face over justifying their greater cost and lower efficiency, are likely to bring the alternative assessment revolution to a full halt unless they are seriously addressed by its advocates.

Conclusion

On each of Linn, Baker and Dunbar's criteria, I believe, portfolio assessment is in its infancy. Unless a major program of research is begun soon into all of these ethical issues, what has been hailed as an educational revolution will break down and the tide will turn back to traditional standardized testing. Having had our opportunity and failed to grasp it, we will find it harder to justify future movements into more humanistic assessment models a second time around. This danger is most acute in the US, because the enthusiasm for alternative assessment has been so overwhelming here, and the federal imperative for unassailable forms of educational accountability is so strong, so that the push and pull of conflicting educational lobbies is very evident – but the danger exists elsewhere too. As an advocate of portfolio assessment, I feel a strong responsibility for discovering both the questions and the answers about the ethics of portfolio assessment. While the questions are applicable in the mainstream as well as the ESL context, I consider them to be more urgent when we consider ESL students, partly because ESL teachers are less expert in their knowledge of the field of composition, and partly because many ESL/bilingual students are more precariously situated within our schools and colleges. While we can never justify proceeding ill-advisedly, our potential to harm those 'on the margins' in schools and colleges is greater and so too, therefore, is our ethical imperative.

References

Baker, N. W. 1993. The effect of portfolio-based instruction on composition students' final examination scores, course grades, and attitudes. *Research in the Teaching of English.*

Belanoff, P. and M. Dickson (eds.). 1991. *Portfolios: Process and Product.* Portsmouth, VI: Boynton/Cook.

Black, L., D. A. Daiker, J. Sommers and G. Stygal. (n.d.). *Handbook of Writing Portfolio Assessment: A Program for College Placement.* Miami: University of Ohio/FIPSE.

Broad, R. October 1992. *Portfolio scoring: A contradiction in terms.* Paper presented at the Miami Conference on New Directions in Portfolio Assessment, Miami, Ohio.

Fowles, M., and C. Gentile. 1989. *Validity Study of the 1988 Rhode Island Third-Grade Writing Assessment.* Princeton, NJ: Educational Testing Service.

Graham, J. 1992. *Reading sophomores' portfolios: What we can learn from writing done over two university years.* Workshop presented at the Miami Conference on New Directions in Portfolio Assessment, Miami, Ohio.

Hamp-Lyons, L. November 1988. *Moving to portfolios.* Paper presented at the Michigan Educational Research Association, Novi, Michigan.

Hamp-Lyons, L. 1991. *Scoring procedures for ESL contexts.* In L. Hamp-Lyons (Ed.) *Assessing Second Language Writing in Academic Contexts.* pp 241–276. Norwood, NJ:Ablex.

Hamp-Lyons, L. 1993, April. *Components of portfolio evaluation: ESL data.* Paper presented at the Annual Meeting of the American Association of Applied Linguistics.

Hamp-Lyons, L. In press. The challenges of second language writing assessment. In E. White, W. Lutz and S. Kamusikiri, (eds.), *The Practice and Politics of Writing Assessment.* New York: Modern Language Association.

Hamp-Lyons, L. and W. C. Condon. In press. *Portfolios and College Writing.* Hampton Press.

Koretz, D. April 1993. *The evaluation of the Vermont portfolio program: Interpretations of initial findings.* Paper presented at the Annual Meeting of the National Council on Educational Measurement. Atlanta, Georgia.

Linn, R. L., E. L. Baker and S. B. Dunbar 1991. Complex, performance-based assessment: expectations and validation criteria. *Educational Research*, 20 (8).

McKenna, E. and R. Carlisle. 1991. Placement of ESL/EFL Undergraduate Writers in College-level Writing Programs. In L. Hamp-Lyons (Ed.) *Assessing Second Language Writing in Academic Contexts.* pp 197–214. Norwood, NJ:Ablex.

McLaughlin, M. November 1991. *Some basics in the teaching-testing relationship.*

Phi Delta Kappan.

Mehrens, W. A. 1992. Using performance assessment for accountability purposes. *Educational Measurement: Issues and Practice*, 11 (1).

Mendelsohn, D. and A. Cumming 1987. Professors' ratings of language use and rhetorical organizations in ESL compositions. *TESL Canada Journal, 5*.

Messick, S. 1989. Validity. In R.L. Linn (ed.), *Educational Measurement* (3rd edn.). New York: American Council on Education, Macmillan.

Miller, M. D. and S. M. Legg. 1993. Alternative assessment in a high-stakes environment. *Educational Measurement: Issues and Practice 12*.

Moss, P. A., J. S. Beck, C. Ebbs, B. Matson, J. Muchmore, D. Steele, S. Taylor and R. Herter 1992. Portfolios, accountability, and an interpretive approach to validity. *Educational Measurement: Issues and Practice 11*.

Santos, T. 1988. Professors' reactions to the academic writing of non-native-speaking students. *TESOL Quarterly 22*.

Sommers, J., L. Black, D. A. Daiker and G. Stygall. 1993. The challenges of rating portfolios: What WPAs can expect. *WPA: Writing Program Administrator 17*.

Stiggins, R. 1987. *Linking classroom instruction and assessment.* Paper presented at the National Testing Network in Writing, March. Minneapolis, MIV.

Sweedler-Brown, C. O. 1993a. The effects of ESL errors on holistic scores assigned by English composition faculty. *College ESL 3*.

Sweedler-Brown, C.O. 1993b. ESL essay evaluation: The influence of sentence-level and rhetorical features. *Journal of Second Language Writing 2*.

Test of Written English Guide. Produced periodically. Available from Educational Testing Service, Princeton, NJ 08541.

Valencia, S., P. D. Pearson, C. W. Peters and K. K. Wixson. 1989. Theory and practice in statewide reading assessment: Closing the gap. *Educational Leadership 46*.

Vann, R. J., F. O. Lorenz and D. M. Meyer. 1991. Error gravity: faculty response to errors in the written discourse of non-native speakers of English. In L. Hamp-Lyons (ed.), *Assessing Second Language Writing in Academic Contexts*. Norwood, NJ: Ablex.

Vann, R., D. Meyer and F. Lorenz. 1984. Error gravity: A study of faculty opinion of ESL errors. *TESOL Quarterly* 18 (3): 427–40.

Weir, C. J. 1993. *Understanding and Developing Language Tests*. Hemel Hempstead: Prentice Hall International.

Wolf, D., J. Bixby, J. Glenn and H. Gardner. 1991. To use their minds well: Investigating new forms of assessment. In G. Grant (ed.), *Review of Research in Education:* 17. Washington, DC: American Educational Research Association.

Yancey, K. (ed.) 1992. *Portfolios in the Writing Classroom*. Urbana, IL: NCTE.

9 Comparing test difficulty and text readability in the evaluation of an extensive reading programme[1]

Alan Davies, Aileen Irvine
University of Edinburgh

In this paper it is argued that the assumption that the content dependence of achievement tests puts upper limits on the validity of which they are capable may not always be justified. In other words a test's construct validity (Messick 1988) may be closer to 'true validity' than its content validity.

The Edinburgh Project on Extensive Reading (EPER) has been active now for over 12 years (Hill and Reid-Thomas 1988, 1989; Hill 1992). After initial trialling in Malaysia in the 1970s, further work on development was carried out in Tanzania and Zanzibar. The most recent use is in the Hong Kong school system where the number of state secondary schools involved increases each year. In preparation for that goal the project deliberately snowballs, with some 20–25 schools being added to the existing group each year. Each school is provided with samples of the EPER graded and simplified books (often called, somewhat confusingly, readers), over 2000 titles available, enough in each class for there always to be three books per student.

The EPER boxed sets are arranged in eight graded levels with specially prepared activity cards for each title. The books themselves span a vocabulary (frequency) range of about 400 up to 3000+, the usual limit of unsimplified materials. Publishers have been cooperative in the project with ten well-known ones involved (Reid-Thomas and Hill 1993). Each school in Hong Kong now involved in the project is expected to make two or more periods per week in the first three secondary years available to EPER. Students are assigned to one or other level on the basis of a specially prepared cloze test (Test 'B'), which is thought of as more a test of general proficiency than of reading comprehension, and certainly not of extensive reading.

With good reason therefore the Hong Kong authorities require that as part of the EPER project a test of extensive reading should be provided to measure progress within the scheme. It must be the case that the purpose of devoting so much time and energy to the project in the Hong Kong school system is to offer some well-motivated and at the same time expeditious way of increasing English input in a situation where, in spite of the long association with the UK, most

165

interaction in Hong Kong in general and in the schools in particular, even those calling themselves Anglo-Chinese schools, is not in English but in Cantonese. Very few teachers are native speakers of English, a state of affairs unlikely to change: indeed a government funded scheme to bring in large numbers of native speaking teachers of English (two to each secondary school) in the second half of the 1980s, which was moderately successful, was not extended. EPER as a surrogate means of providing massive language input seems to have been seized on as one alternative to that expatriate English teachers' scheme. (This raises of course the whole question of multidimensionality in its assumption that input is neutral as to mode, written or spoken. That is a question we do not intend to pursue further in this paper.)

When the EPER[2] materials were purchased by the Hong Kong Department of Education, it was agreed that tests of the comprehension of extensive reading would be provided by the Institute of Applied Language Studies (IALS) University of Edinburgh; such tests were to offer measures of progress (Davies and Irvine 1992).

To that end a project team[3] started work in January 1992 on test materials which included three types of test:
comprehension tests of extensive reading,
a reading speed test,
a vocabulary test.

It was agreed that reading comprehension tests should be written at each of the eight EPER levels while there should be only one vocabulary test and one reading speed test. One of the chief reasons for this difference of treatment was that the two uniform tests (reading speed and vocabulary) could provide an anchor against which to assess the various levels of the reading comprehension tests. Because of their long and demanding texts, the whole set of reading comprehension tests could not be administered to every student.

By the end of March 1992, the following tests had been constructed:

Reading Comprehension	8 levels	2 versions
Vocabulary	all levels	2 versions
Reading Speed	all levels	2 versions
(Total N of items = 556)		

Preparation of test materials

For the reading comprehension tests two texts were selected from EPER readers not currently in use in Hong Kong at each of the eight levels (from high or unsimplified to low or most simplified: X A B C D E F G). The criteria used in selection were level, subject matter (given the age group of the Hong Kong students) and text length. One effect of this selection was shorter test-texts for the lower levels and longer test-texts for the higher ones.

Items were written by the project group in short-answer questions and gap-fill format, with one or two yes/no items at the two lowest levels and a couple of multi-choice items in the middle levels. At the two highest levels (X and A) only gap summary was used.

The number of items were as follows:

Level G: 18 items
Level F: 22 items
Level E: 18 items
Level D: 20 items
Level C: 20 items
Level B: 20 items
Level A: 30 items
Level X: 40 items

Following the discussion in Duran (1988) an attempt was made to capture the range of 'envisionment levels' in the tests to characterize increasing depth of comprehension required over the sequence of readers. 'Students' ability to comprehend information appropriately at higher envisionment levels requires adequate comprehension of information at lower envisionment levels. Over a collection of items,' Duran suggests, the purpose is 'to come up with a measure of examinees' maximal level of envisionment in a given academic reading domain' (Duran 1988:116). At the lowest envisionment level these are the expectations:

* 'Understands isolated words signalling concepts and is capable of drawing on this knowledge in performing reasoning exercises'

and at the fourth level:

* 'Can derive an envisionment of a specific situation or set of facts referred to by a text. In performing reasoning exercises can draw on knowledge derived from this envisionment as well as from information conveyed by interrelated or isolated sentences.'

In consequence, the tests at the lower EPER levels (F and G) were more word meaning based and at the higher levels (X and A) more inference tapping. Test items were inserted at intervals into the texts, except at level X where all the items were placed at the end of the text.

Time for tests: 30 minutes each
A reading speed test (two versions) was constructed using the intrusive word method, sometimes called cloze elide (Manning 1987; Davies 1989).

Time for test: 10 minutes.
The reading speed test is not further discussed in this paper.
A graded vocabulary test (two versions) was constructed using a multiple choice method. The items were graded according to difficulty.

Time for test: 20 minutes

We return to the Vocabulary test below.

After a preliminary trial, the tests were revised and a further round of testing took place in Hong Kong in June/July 1992. Student allocation to test was by teacher judgement and/or present reading level. The total N for whom complete scores are available, including Test B = 201

Analysis of tests

Reliabilities (raw scores)
Reading comprehension (by level)   0.92-0.99
    (= parallel forms reliability)
Reading comprehension (global)   0.9
    (= KR21)
Vocabulary   0.8
    (= both parallel forms and KR21)

Item analyses

Reading Comprehension

The Reading Comprehension tests were administered to a sample of students drawn from a wide range of English reading levels, such that as far as possible tests were matched to students' existing reading levels. An 'anchor' design was employed, that is that there was sequential overlap across the whole range whereby student 1 sat for tests at G and F, student 2 sat for tests at F and E, student 3 sat for tests at E and D and so on. On the basis of this procedure, it was considered appropriate to present the analysis of the Reading Comprehension items at all levels on a common scale.

Item analysis using the Rasch program 'Quest' (Adams and Khoo 1992) was carried out on all Reading Comprehension test data. Item difficulties were estimated on the normal 10 point logit scale, where +5 = exceptionally difficult and -5 = exceptionally easy and where zero is used as the item difficulty mean.

The 'Ability' program written by Neil Jones (Jones 1993) was then used to convert item difficulties to 'standardised' student scores for the whole Reading Comprehension test. This conversion provides an interpretation on the common scale for scores achieved on each successive pair of the Reading Comprehension test levels.

The test levels were paired for this purpose as follows:
G/F
E/D
C/B
A/X

A separate Scores Guide (Table 6, Appendix 1) for each version was prepared so as to advise on placement of students on the EPER/ERS scheme. It will be noted that each Scores Guide also contains a separate Vocabulary scale which is calibrated against reading levels. For Reading Comprehension a 75%+ correct response on a neighbouring test pair is taken as mastery at the higher level test of the pair, and a 50%+ correct response as adequacy; a 25%+ correct response is taken as mastery and 25%- as non-adequacy at the lower level test of the pair.

As would be expected, the scale is most robust at the upper and lower levels: in the middle range discrimination is less apparent since there is overlap, and care needs to be taken about allocation within the E–B range. Retesting at the next level up or down, as seems appropriate, is recommended.

Vocabulary

Item analysis using the Quest program for Rasch was carried out on all Vocabulary test data. On the basis of this procedure, it was considered appropriate to present the Vocabulary items at all levels on a common scale.

The 'Ability' program written by Neil Jones was then again used to convert item difficulties to 'standardised' student scores for the Vocabulary test. This conversion provides an interpretation on the common scale for scores achieved on the Vocabulary test. The Vocabulary scale is calibrated against reading levels and presented alongside the Scores Guide for the Reading Comprehension test.

The purpose of providing both a Reading Comprehension and a Vocabulary scale, both related to reading levels, is to increase the amount of information available about a student's progress in reading. Both the Vocabulary and the Reading Comprehension tests lack discrimination in the middle levels, the Vocabulary test less so than the Reading Comprehension tests. As we suggest later, this makes possible the discarding of two of the middle Reading Comprehension tests.

Discussion

Scalability across the eight levels is undoubtedly achieved with a case reliability of 0.89 (Version 1) and 0.88 (Version 2). But there is considerable test redundancy in the middle levels, which must in part account for the Case Separation Index of only 2.89 across the Eight EPER levels (and see the Ability map in Table 7, Appendix 1). Several comments are relevant here.

The tests: it may indeed be the case that the four middle level tests fail to provide adequate discrimination and that the fault therefore is in the tests. We return to this point below.

The sample: in spite of our confident claim above about the students being drawn from a wide range of reading levels, there were serious problems with obtaining an adequate sample. It is possible then that the middle level tests were completed by students whose reading skills were too similar to one another. But given the careful overlapping design it is unlikely that the sample was grossly inappropriate.

Are we then forced back to our first explanation: if it is not the samples then it must be the items? There remains a third possibility.

The texts: it should be remembered that the tests were, as we remarked above, deliberately drawn from the EPER materials, with each level test making use of texts from a 'reader' at its own level. Our claim for test validity was therefore that they had built-in content validity since they were 'parasitic' on the materials; and therefore any question regarding the tests' validity must be directed to the validity of the reading scheme itself. To what extent therefore are the eight reading levels discrete? That was not the question the proficiency test project set out to answer, nor could it have been, since EPER is predicated on the separation in terms of simple/difficult of the eight levels. Whether or not that was our research question in the development of the test it became the primary question to examine in the course of our analysis. We compare below the difficulty levels of the test items at each level with the readability index for each of the test texts.

The reading habit

However, before we present that analysis it is worth reflecting on the purpose of the EPER (and similar) materials. Their purpose is to encourage reading for pleasure in order to build up a reading habit in English. Their philosophy is that to reach for newer, more difficult achievement goals all the time is counter-productive. After all that is what students' school experience often is, and if achievement oriented reading were indeed habit building, then there would be no need for a scheme such as EPER. But the students' school experience does not encourage them to read at home for pleasure and thereby build up the habit of reading which in due course can be used to enhance their own school learning. For the reading habit to be developed then it is important, so the argument goes, for there to be no pressure on 'getting on', with the implication of the need for massive over-learning in reading skills.

Such a view could well explain and support a built-in redundancy in the reading levels, a very slow and deliberately spiral movement through the levels. And this is what we seem to find in the middle levels of our tests, precisely after all where discrimination, where separation of levels is most difficult.

Readability

We turn now to the investigation of the readability of the EPER levels. The texts used in Version 1 of the reading comprehension tests were submitted to the readability measure known as the Gunning-Fog Index. This measures average sentence length + N words over one syllable per sentence, on the assumption that sentences that contain many words of more than one syllable are difficult to read. Such a measure is inevitably very crude, given how easily it can be faulted (for example the word 'elephant' is not as difficult as the word 'get' because of the familiarity of the one and the wide range of possible meanings of the other). Nevertheless, unsophisticated measures of this kind (the T-unit is another example) are useful approximations of the ordering of texts in terms of difficulty and complexity.

The results of the readability analysis are presented in Table 1:

Table 1

Gunning-Fog Indices for the texts of the 8 reading comprehension tests

Reading test texts	N words measured	G-F Index
X	2258	7.0
A	2148	5.6
B	2030	4.8
C	1405	6.7
D	1341	3.9
E	1266	4.1
F	934	5.1
G	708	3.8

On the basis of these indices it appears that, contrary to expectation, the text for test C is more difficult than both texts in tests A and B; and that the text for test F is more difficult than the texts in tests D and E.

Correlation of these indices with the actual EPER test ordering from X to G provides a product moment r of 0.63: in other words we might suggest that there is considerable misallocation in the EPER ordering. (We return at the end of the paper to consider possible reasons for this.)

Content validity a limiting factor?

We have already reported that on the basis of the logit item difficulty values the two upper and the two lower tests (X/A and F/G) discriminated as intended, that is, they were the most difficult and the least difficult. On the other hand the four middle tests in the sequence (B, C, D, E) discriminated less well. We posited that this might be the outcome of faulty test construction. The reporting of the lack of relationship between the readability measures for the texts (on which the tests were based) and the actual EPER ordering now however offers the possibility, as we foreshadowed, that it may not be the tests that are at fault: rather that their very faithfulness to their text source may be where the problem lies.

So what is the relationship between rank orders of the difficulty level of the eight tests and the actual EPER test results? Using the mean test item logit difficulties (adding a constant of 10 to make all means positive) we can show the three-way relationship 'incorporating the EPER-readability correlation already reported' in Table 2:

Table 2

Correlation of EPER levels with text readability and test difficulty

	Gunning-Fog	Test difficulty
EPER levels	0.63	0.89
Gunning-Fog	1.00	0.59

What Table 2 shows is that the tests relate much more closely to the original EPER allocation than do the readability levels: it is as though the item difficulties adjust the difficulty of the texts on which they are based: the test items themselves add to or subtract from the difficulty of the texts in order to bring the tests closer than the texts themselves permit to the original scheme grading. It is unclear to what extent this was deliberate in the test construction: but it is not impossible, given the integrated nature of the test design. To that extent (and to that extent only) it can be claimed that tests can improve the validity of the content on which they are based: and it must be remembered that any adjustment in level by these tests does no more than bring the tests into line with what it was already intended the achievement sequence should be.

Table 3 presents the EPER grade allocation from non-simplified to most simplified, alongside the Gunning-Fog Index and the mean difficulty of each reading comprehension test:

Table 3

Comparison of readability indices, test difficulties and EPER grade levels

EPER levels	Gunning-Fog	Mean item difficulty*
(1) X	7.0	12.25
(2) A	5.6	11.65
(3) B	4.8	9.66
(4) C	6.7	10.55
(5) D	3.9	10.44
(6) E	4.1	9.89
(7) F	5.1	9.47
(8) G	3.8	8.33

* Mean item difficulties based on logit incorrect values for each test.

Conclusion and implications

We address two questions in this part of the paper, first, the issue of conflict between EPER allocation and the readability results; second, the (remaining) problem of lack of discriminability among the tests at the mid-levels and what advice to offer to test users.

Allocation of a book or 'reader' to a level for reading purposes is as much subjective as it is objective. In addition to the more formal aspects, such as those summarised in a readability measure, which include: number of different grammatical structures; sentence length; complexity of sentence structure; paragraph length; information density; vocabulary (number of words, both types and tokens), there are other less precise indicators such as: background knowledge; print size; presence of pictorial material including the cover page; amount of reader support provided (e.g. glossaries) and an assessment of the subject matter itself.

So it is not at all surprising that there is such a range of readers at each level nor that there is overlap from one level to another. Indeed, as we have already suggested, this may well be desirable even if not a deliberate motivating device. If we accept this view, then we should perhaps take a positive attitude towards the apparent lack of clear progression in the readability indices. And we should remember that these results are based on only one sweep through one set of readers. We also note that in spite of their lack of sequential progression in terms of difficulty, the four upper levels (XABC) overall are considerably more difficult on the Gunning-Fog Index of readability than are the four lower levels (DEFG): 6.47: 4.32.

We have already concluded that the tests are closer approximations to the EPER level allocations than are the readability indices: (0.89: 0.63). The two upper and two lower tests are appropriately located but the four middle tests are problematic. As Table 3 shows there are two problems: the first is that Test B is badly misplaced, and is much too easy. (Note that the sequence is disturbed only by the incorrect location of Test B which should be in third not sixth place.) The second problem relates to the lack of separation among these four tests. Even when test B is removed, tests C and D are too close (mean difficulties: 10.55: 10.44), and since the protocol observed for test administration requires that a candidate take two sequential tests, B and C are almost complete replications of D and E. There is an easy solution: it is to remove from use the pair B and C. Then we have an ordered declining sequence of mean test difficulties viz: X(12.25) A(11.65) D(10.44) E(9.89) F(9.47) G(8.33).

Given the redundancy across levels in the readers and the built-in overlap of the tests, removing tests B and C from the test battery would not affect assessment of progress and subsequent allocation to a reading level. Any worries about the adequacy of the distinction between tests D and A could be overcome by the use of the single Vocabulary test which provides statements about progress between these two levels.

It is time both to recall the purpose of these extensive reading tests and to remind ourselves of the 0.88 correlation between the mean test item difficulties and the EPER ordering. And here there is a dilemma because there are in fact two distinct purposes for the reading tests, not one. The first purpose is to provide a measure of progress up an ideal set of levels, each of which is discrete: that may be called the proficiency purpose. The other purpose is to provide feedback on progress on the actual materials in use, and as we have seen these are certainly not discrete in terms of levels. This might be regarded as the achievement purpose. As they stand, in spite of the redundancy and misplacement in the middle levels, the tests do a reasonable job on the first purpose; on the second I suggest they do exactly what is wanted in that they emphasise and capture the lack of discreteness and the interlocking of variables which is the nature of difficulty at those middle stages of graded reading where it is most critical for the habit of extensive reading to be given time to establish itself and thereby to grow. At the same time, a slow progression of test difficulty over those mid-levels is surely desirable. That can be readily achieved by revising Test B so as to raise its mean difficulty to a position between Tests C and A.

At the beginning of this paper we queried whether the assertion that the content dependence of achievement tests puts upper limits on the validity of which they are capable might always be justified. Our conclusion is both no and yes. No, because it does appear that tests can be more/less difficult than the materials on which they are based. Yes, because that correction (towards more/less difficult) can only be towards the syllabus on which in turn the materials are based. Doing further 'correction' would simply turn what are supposed to be achievement tests into proficiency tests.

Notes

1 A version of this paper was read at the annual meeting of the Language Testing Research Colloquium in Arnhem, August 1993.
  Address for correspondence: Aileen Irvine, University of Edinburgh, Dept of Applied Linguistics, 14 Buccleuch Place, Edinburgh EH8 9LN, Scotland, U.K.
2 In Hong Kong the EPER materials are known as the English Reading Scheme (ERS) materials.
3 Alan Davies was investigator and Aileen Irvine project officer. The project team consisted in addition of Sheena Davies, Gibson Ferguson, Eric Glendinning, David Hill, Brian Parkinson, Helen Reid-Thomas, Dan Robertson.

Appendix 1

Table 6

Scores Guide

E.P.E.R. EDINBURGH PROJECT ON EXTENSIVE READING

Assessment of extensive reading comprehension
Scores Guide for VERSION ONE tests

	Comprehension Scores Version 1	ADVICE ON ERS READING LEVEL	Vocabulary Scores Version 1
A & X	51 and over	level X mastered	65 and over
	40 – 50	reading at level X	60 – 64
	23 – 39	reading at level A	49 – 59
	22 and less	not yet at level A	48 and less
C & B	32 and over	level B mastered	49 and over
	21 – 31	reading at level B	43 – 48
	14 – 20	reading at level C	38 – 42
	13 and less	not yet at level C	37 and less
E & D	28 and over	level D mastered	38 and over
	19 – 27	reading at level D	34 – 37
	12 – 18	reading at level E	28 – 33
	11 and less	not yet at level E	27 and less
G & F	32 and over	level F mastered	28 and over
	21 – 31	reading at level F	20 – 27
	10 – 20	reading at level G	12 – 19
	9 and less	not yet at level G	11 and less

Appendix 1

Table 7

Ability Map for all Reading Comprehension Test Items (n = 188)

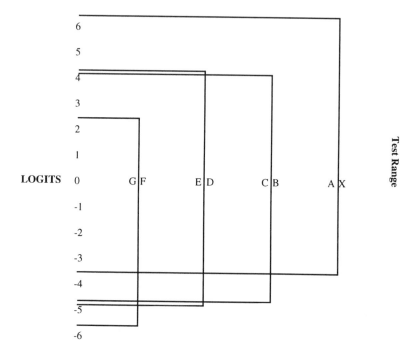

Appendix 2

Sample Reading Comprehension Test (Level F)

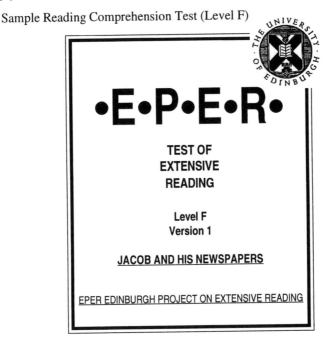

•E•P•E•R•

**TEST OF
EXTENSIVE
READING**

**Level F
Version 1**

JACOB AND HIS NEWSPAPERS

EPER EDINBURGH PROJECT ON EXTENSIVE READING

Jacob lived with his mother and father near a large city. His father was old and didn't have a job. His mother did cleaning work. She didn't make very much money. Jacob helped to earn some extra

Jacob and his Newspapers

money for the family. Every Saturday morning, he went into the city to sell newspapers.

One cold Saturday morning in winter, Jacob didn't want to get up early. He had worked hard all week at school. It was dark outside and he was feeling cold and tired.

'Get up Jacob,' said his mother. 'You'll be late for your bus.'

Jacob got dressed and ran to the bus stop.

He arrived there as the bus was leaving.

'You missed the bus!' said a man who was washing his car.

'When does the next bus come?' asked Jacob.

'Not for another half hour.'

Jacob sat at the bus stop. It was cold and the wind blew round his bare legs. He buttoned up his jacket and pulled his blue woollen hat down over his ears.

He felt very unhappy. He didn't know what to do. Other boys were always waiting to sell newspapers. He had to get to the depot before the manager gave his papers away.

Suddenly a car stopped. It was his neighbour.

'Where are you going, Jacob?' she asked.

'To the newspaper depot,' he replied, 'to collect my newspapers to sell. I'm very late.'

'Jump in, Jacob. I'll get you there in time.'

The manager was waiting at the depot.

'What happened to you, Jacob?' he asked. 'You're always on time.'

'I missed my bus!'

Jacob took his bag full of newspapers and hurried to his favourite position at some traffic lights on a busy road.

The newspapers were heavy. Jacob took some out of the bag and put them down beside the traffic lights. He had a stone in his pocket which he used to weight his papers down. But today he was in a hurry.

'Morning News! Morning News!' he shouted, jumping up and down to keep warm.

> Now answer questions 1 to 6 on your question sheet.

On the other side of the road there was a cafe. It was very busy. Jacob could smell chips cooking. He hadn't eaten any breakfast. He ran across the street to sell his papers outside the shop.

'Morning News!' he shouted. 'Morning News!'

'Quick, a newspaper!' shouted a driver.

Jacob ran to the car, holding out the Morning News.

Suddenly Jacob saw newspapers blowing everywhere.

He looked at the traffic lights where he'd left his papers.

'Oh no, I've forgotten the stone. They're my newspapers. They're blowing away! Help! Help me!' shouted Jacob. 'Help!'

The wind blew his newspapers everywhere.

Front-page news blew against car windscreens.

Business pages blew round the legs of people walking past. Sports pages blew into shop windows.

Jacob's newspapers were everywhere.

'What am I going to do now?' thought Jacob sadly. He slowly picked up the pages of his newspapers.

Some of the pages had blown away and got lost. Others were crumpled and torn. He pushed them all into his bag.

'I never want to see another newspaper again,' he said.

> *Now answer questions 7 to 12 on your question sheet.*

Jacob started walking slowly back towards the depot.

'What am I going to tell the manager? Nothing is going right today!'

He wanted to cry. It was cold and the wind blew dust into his eyes.

He walked across a square. An old woman was feeding bread to some pigeons there. He felt hungry and wanted some of the bread for himself.

Jacob came to a warehouse. There was a huge furniture van parked outside. He looked in through the front door and saw some men packing things into boxes.

It looked warm inside. Jacob stood near the door to get out of the wind.

One of the men who was packing saw Jacob at the door.

'Hello!' he said. 'Come inside. You'll be warmer in here.'

'Thank you,' said Jacob.

He was happy to hear a friendly voice.

'Perhaps the boy can help us,' said another man. 'We need some help.'

'Yes, I'll help you,' said Jacob. 'Tell me what to do'

'Take these plates,' said the man. 'Take them one at a time. Wrap each plate in a page of newspaper, then put it carefully in this box.'

When the boxes were full, the men loaded them onto the van.

> *Now answer questions 13 to 16 on your question sheet.*

'Oh no, we've run out of newspaper,' said one of the packers.

'Here!' said Jacob, 'I've got lots of newspapers.'

He took his crumpled papers out of his bag and gave them to the men.

In ten minutes they had finished packing.

The men were very pleased. They gave Jacob a carton of milk and some money.

'Thanks for your help, and your newspapers,' they said.

Jacob was very happy. The money was enough to pay for the lost papers.

Jacob ran back to the depot. He told the manager what had happened to him.

'You're a hard worker,' said the manager. 'Today isn't your day, is it?'

'You can pay me for newspapers you sold. We'll forget the others. I know it was an accident.'

'Great. Thanks,' said Jacob.

179

Jacob was very pleased. Now he had enough money for his family. And he had enough money to buy some lunch. He was really hungry now.

He walked back to the cafe and bought some chips.

They were hot and smelt good. The man wrapped them in newspaper. Jacob smiled.

'I never wanted to see another newspaper in my life,' he said. 'But I don't mind looking at a newspaper when it's wrapped around my hot chips!'

> *Now answer questions 17 to 22 on your question sheet.*

The Paper Chase: Diane Stewart. Heinemann 1991. Reproduced by permission of Heinemann International.

•E•P•E•R•

EPER EDINBURGH PROJECT ON EXTENSIVE READING

TEST OF EXTENSIVE READING

Level F
Version 1

JACOB AND HIS NEWSPAPERS

Name:_____

Class:_____

School:_____

Date:_____

Present Reading Level: _____

Read the story first and answer the questions when it tells you to.

You will have **30 minutes**.

Start when your teacher tells you.

Read the story first. When it says 'Now answer questions 1 to 6', do this.
*Answer **ONLY** questions 1 to 6.*

Put ONE word in each space.
Example: Jacob's job was to sell *newspapers*

1. Jacob's sold newspapers to help his_____.

2. One morning Jacob_____his bus.

3. His neighbour drove him in her_____.

Now give a short answer to questions 4 to 6.

Example: How did Jacob usually go to work? <u>by bus</u>

4.   Where did Jacob collect his papers?_____.

5.   Where did he usually sell the papers?_____.

6.   Did he put a stone on the papers that morning?_____.

> *Now continue to read the story. When it tells you to, answer*
> *questions 7 to 12. Answer **ONLY** questions 7 to 12.*
> *Put **ONE** word in each space.*

Jacob went and stood beside a (7)_____. A car stopped and the driver asked for a
(8)_____. Jacob left his newspapers and went over to the car. But there wasn't a
(9)_____ on the newspapers and they began to blow everywhere. They blew onto cars
and into the windows of (10)_____. Jacob started to pick up the (11)_____
and put them in his (12)_____.

> *Now continue to read the story. When it tells you to, answer*
> *questions 13 to 16. Answer **ONLY** questions 13 to 16.*
> *Put **ONE** word in each space.*

13. Jacob felt cold and _____.

14. He saw a big _____ outside a warehouse.

15. The men were packing things in _____.

16. Jacob began to _____ the men.

> *Now continue to read the story. When it tells you to, answer*
> *questions 17 to 22. Give a short answer.*

17. What did Jacob give the men? _____.

18. What did the men give Jacob? _____.

19. Was the manager kind or unkind to Jacob? _____.

20. Did Jacob pay the manager for all the newspapers? _____.

21. What did he buy with his money? _____.

22. What did the man put the chips in? _____.

References

Adams, R.J. and S.T. Khoo 1992. *Quest, the Interactive Test Analysis System.* Hawthorn, Victoria: A.C.E.R.

Davies, A. 1989. Testing reading speed through text retrieval. In C.N. Candlin and T.F. McNamara (eds.), *Language, Learning and Community.* New South Wales: NCELTR, pp.115–24.

Davies, A. and A. Irvine. 1992. *The EPER Hong Kong Test Project Final Report.* Unpublished report. University of Edinburgh.

Duran, R. P. 1988. Validity and language skills assessment: Non-English background students. In H. Wainer and H.I. Braun (eds.), *Test Validity.* Hillsdale, NJ: Lawrence Erlbaum, pp.105–27.

Hill, D.R. 1992. *The EPER Guide to Organising Programmes of Extensive Reading.* The Institute for Applied Language Studies. University of Edinburgh.

Hill, D. R. and H. Reid-Thomas. 1988. Survey review: Graded readers (Part 1). *English Language Teaching Journal* 42 (1).

Hill, D. R. and H. Reid-Thomas. 1989. Survey review: Seven series of graded readers. *English Language Teaching Journal* 43 (3).

Jones, N.1993. *Item banking.* Unpublished PhD thesis. University of Edinburgh.

Manning, W. H. 1987. Development of cloze-elide tests of English as a second language. *TOEFL Research Report* 23. Princeton, NJ: Educational Testing Services.

Messick, S. 1988. The once and future uses of validity: assessing the meaning and consequences of measurement. In H. Wainer and H. Braun (eds.), *Test Validity.* Hillsdale, N.J. Lawrence Erlbaum, pp.33–45.

Reid-Thomas, H. and D. R. Hill. 1993. Seventeen series of graded readers. *English Language Testing Journal* 48 (3).

10 Equating national examinations of foreign language reading comprehension

Rob van Krieken
CITO, Dutch National Institute for Educational Measurement

Background and rationale

National examinations in Holland consist of two parts, a school internal part which is constructed, set and marked by the individual schoolteacher, and a central part which is constructed by CITO, but set and marked according to procedures laid down by the committee for central examinations in secondary education (CEVO).

For foreign languages the central examination tests only reading comprehension and consists of 50 multiple choice items. The mother tongue, on the other hand, is centrally examined in two papers, one on reading comprehension, by means of a mixture of multiple choice and open-ended questions, and the other on writing by means of either an essay or a number of functional assignments. Characteristic of the procedures concerning central examinations is that every year for each examination the construction cycle starts all over again, that every year the cut-off score is set anew, within a narrow range, and that in general the CEVO prefers screening to pretesting.

Against this background it is not surprising that CITO has investigated the possibilities of relating the examinations to each other, providing information on their relative difficulty, in order to ascertain consistency of cut-off scores. To this end a first study consisting of a series of equatings has been carried out, resulting in the advice to introduce section post equating as a standard part of the procedure. This first study offered CITO the possibility of applying IRT based equating programs (Glas 1989) in real practice and of comparing the outcomes with classical equating using multiple matrix sampling (Shoemaker 1973).

In Parliament there has been some doubt as to whether the increasing numbers of pupils opting for higher forms of education has not been accompanied by declining standards. This has led to a major research project from the Inspectorate, conducted by CITO, into the level of cut-off scores and into the ability of candidates over the period 1981–1991. In this second study it was possible to use

Rasch homogeneous subscales to express the difficulties of all examinations on one common scale (Glas 1989).

First study

Design and methods

In the first study reading comprehension examinations were equated for several years up to 1990, starting with a pilot project in 1984 (Sanders and Goldebeld 1985) which led to an official experiment in 1988 and 1989. Here only the results for German, French, English and Dutch (L1) reading comprehension for 1987–90 are reported. In all cases the equating consisted of comparing the same previous examination (called the reference examination) with the current one. In most cases both examinations were split up into sections, and booklets were formed consisting of one section of each (see figure 1). Only the Dutch reading comprehension examinations could not be divided into sections as they contained questions comparing two or more texts, so these examinations were set as a whole, assuming that pupils who took one examination were equivalent to those who took the other. In all cases all the different versions were distributed within each class.

The examinations were meant for pupils completing the fourth and last year of the lowest type of general and vocational secondary education. For reasons of confidentiality, equating could not take place before the actual examination. Therefore the booklets were presented to pupils in the third year of a higher type of education in the week immediately following the actual examination. These pupils performed slightly differently from the actual examination population. As the purpose of the equation was a comparison within these non-equivalent groups this difference was of no statistical importance.

Figure 1

Distribution of sections from two examinations over booklets

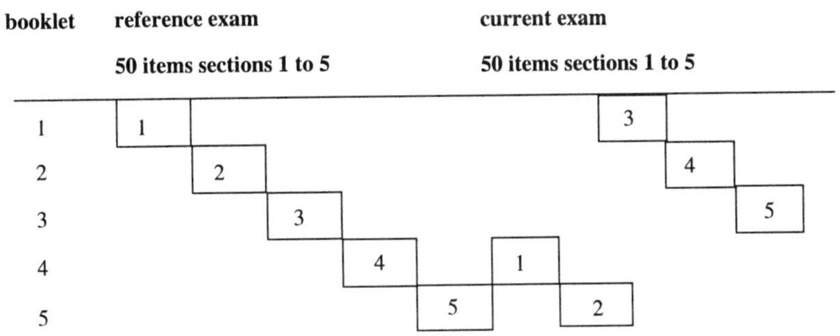

Mean scores for both examinations were estimated using MULTIMAX (Shoemaker 1973) for multiple choice examinations and VARCOM/GSS (Tormäkängas 1986) for the Dutch examination containing polytomous questions. The equivalent cut-off score for the current examination was estimated in the simplest possible way, by using only the difference between the means. So, if the mean score for the current examination proved to be two points lower than that for the reference examination, the advice would be to set the cut-off score two points lower than that for the reference examination. This seemed to be most transparent for subject specialists. In fact, differences in variance between examinations were slight and hardly affected the choice of cut-off scores.

To gather more information about the robustness of this method of estimating equivalent cut-off scores, the equating was replicated in three different ways. Out of eight replications, only one gave a minimally different result. It can therefore be concluded that they are sufficiently robust. A first replication, for the German examination of 1988, made use of pupils from the educational type the examination was meant for, instead of a non-equivalent group, one month before the examination, and produced Rasch analyses. This yielded the same results. Secondly, Rasch analyses were used in reanalysing the 1989 data for the three foreign languages. This too led to the same estimates as resulted from the classic equating. In a third replication, also for each of the three foreign languages, 1000 pupils from the authentic examination population with a score above guessing level were added to the design. Then all the pupils were divided into three score groups in each of which both examinations were equated using the Rasch model. Here there was one case out of nine where the result was different from before, though by only one point (Glas 1989: 106-9).

Results

From Figure 2 it is clear that examinations do show marked differences from the reference examination and from one year to another.

In five out of fourteen examinations the CEVO committee did not apply the advised equivalent cut-off score: three times they set a lower, twice a higher cut-off score (see Appendix 1 for more details). It is important to note that this committee is fully authorized to do that. The reasons for following another course were diverse. In three cases there were formal reasons: the equivalent cut-off scores would have fallen outside the permitted band or the difference from the usual cut-off score was too slight to change it. In two other cases arguments other than equivalence prevailed: in 1988 the advised equivalent cut-off score for English was thought to be too low for the large influx of pupils from vocational education, in 1989 the committee decided that the French reference examination and its cut-off score had become too difficult for this level.

Figure 2

Differences between current examinations and a reference examination

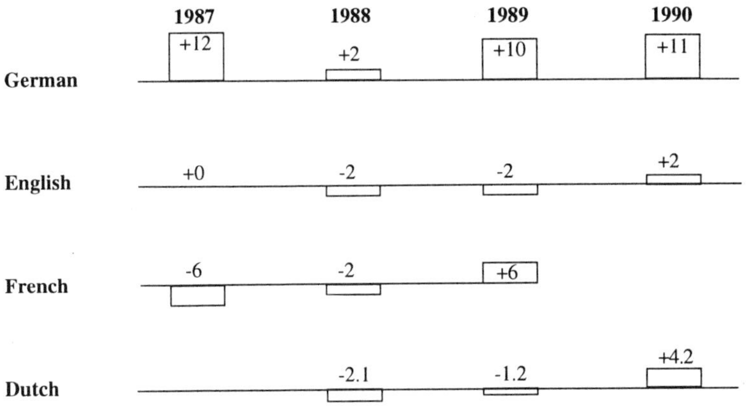

	1987	1988	1989	1990
German	+12	+2	+10	+11
English	+0	-2	-2	+2
French	-6	-2	+6	
Dutch		-2.1	-1.2	+4.2

+ : current examination is easier than reference examination (higher cut-off score)
- : current examination is more difficult (lower cut-off score)

From discussions with the committees responsible for the examinations it appeared that they found it difficult to understand how the equivalent cut-off scores were arrived at. Especially the use of within-group comparisons in non-equivalent groups was found hard to accept.

Second study

Design and methods

The second study consisted of two parts. In the first part examinations were distributed among teachers with experience in examination classes. They were asked to rate the difficulty of all questions from a number of examinations as well as the difficulty of the integral examinations. In the second part, sections of five central examinations were set for pupils preparing themselves for their examinations. By comparing the teachers' judgements with the pupils' results, their usefulness as predictors of difficulty could be evaluated. Figure 3 gives a survey of the examinations used in the second study.

Figure 3

Selection of examination years in the design

Language and Level*	81	82	83	84	85	86	87	88	89	90	91
German D		X		X		X		X			X
English C	X		X		X			X			X
English D	X		X		X			X			X
English HAVO	X		X			X			X	X	
English VWO					X	X	X		X		X
French VWO		X			X		X			X	X
Dutch C						X	X	X		X	X

* After four years of general secondary (MAVO) or preparatory vocational education (VBO, formerly called LBO) pupils may choose C or the higher D-level; HAVO-level is attained after five years of general secondary education preparing for higher vocational training and VWO-level is attained after six years of general secondary education preparing for academic study.

Teachers' estimations

In this part of the study groups of 13 to 21 teachers participated who had extensive experience in examination classes, and sometimes experience in examination construction as well. They all had been using previous examinations in the classroom, but were advised not to look up any information about their difficulty. They were asked to rate the difficulty of each item from the examinations in the design on a scale. The instruction they were provided with contained a scale with eight categories, each of them illustrated with one or more items. These examples were chosen from another examination and had difficulty indices at about the middle of each class as in Table 1.

The teachers' classifications were transformed to mean difficulty indices for total examinations by taking the middle of the category as the difficulty level and computing the mean over all items in the same examination. (In the Dutch examinations, reading comprehension questions were first weighted according to their maximum score.) Then interrater reliabilities were computed as well as correlations between the mean over all teachers' estimations and the mean pupils' scores (as estimated in the second part of study 2), and the differences between the two means (see Appendix 2).

Table 1

Difficulty categories with their corresponding difficulty level

category	difficulty level(% of maximum score)
1	approximately 30
2	approximately 45
3	approximately 55
4	approximately 65
5	approximately 70
6	approximately 75
7	approximately 85
8	approximately 95

Results of teachers' estimations

Table 2 offers a survey of the interrater reliabilities (ICC) and also of the correlation between the teachers' estimations of the difficulty and the difficulty as computed in the second part. The reliabilities are intra-class correlations for the whole group. They reflect agreement in order, not counting systematic differences in means. All groups were found to be highly or very highly reliable. This means that other estimations by the same or comparable groups would come to almost precisely the same estimations. The correlations between the teachers' estimations and the pupils' means clearly vary. For two groups they are very low, for two others moderate, and only for three of the seven groups are they really high.

Table 2

Teachers' estimates and equating data

	Teachers #	ICC	Correlation Teachers X Equating
German D	18	.97	.96
English C	21	.96	.29
English D	17	.99	.75
English HAVO	16	.92	.86
English VWO	13	.98	.75
French VWO	13	.80	.15
Dutch C	20	.99	.86

The usefulness of the estimations is illustrated by Table 3, which shows the difference between the mean teachers' estimates and the pupils' mean scores in percentages of the maximum score. Teachers are clearly optimistic, but not constantly to the same degree. Differences of 2% amount to one score point in the foreign language examinations. Teachers' estimates that are exactly right one year but two points wrong the following year are not sufficiently precise to be useful.

Table 3

Differences in means between teachers' and equating data

EXAMINATION	1	2	3	4	5
GERMAN	−4.1	−2.0	−0.7	−3.6	+0.6
ENGLISH C	−11.7	−6.3	−3.1	+1.8	−3.9
ENGLISH D	−12.2	−8.0	+2.9	−3.5	+3.9
ENGLISH HAVO	−0.9	−4.1	−1.8	−4.8	−3.3
ENGLISH VWO	−0.8	−4.9	−0.4	−4.4	−1.4
FRENCH VWO	−4.8	+3.5	+1.2	+3.8	−0.8
DUTCH C	−9.1	−12.9	−16.1	−8.5	−2.0

− = less difficult; + = more difficult than reference examination according to teachers

Conclusions

Teachers estimated the difficulty of examinations with a high enough degree of agreement to be called precise. Compared with data from equating, however, they underestimated the difficulty and they did this inconsistently. Their precise estimations were not correct. It is to be remembered that the study used old examinations which were known to the teachers and which they used to read with their classes. If teachers were to participate in a procedure to equate examinations that are quite new to them this would be unlikely to produce better results. The result made it abundantly clear that teachers' estimations cannot generally replace equating using data collected among pupils.

Data collected among pupils

Design and method

The same examinations that were judged by the teachers were also set to pupils reading for their finals. The administration took place two months before the actual examinations. At the beginning of the year the teachers had been instructed not to discuss the five examinations under study.

The total amount of texts and items was distributed among a large number of booklets in such a way that each booklet could be answered within two consecutive school periods and that there was some overlap among all the booklets (see the example in Appendix 3).

On the basis of the results the difficulties of all examinations were first estimated on one common scale. This was done by creating as many subscales as were necessary to fit the Rasch model and then combining them to form a common scale (Glas 1989). In a second step these difficulties were used together with the known score distributions of about 1000 authentic candidates on the most recent examination to estimate which scores these recent candidates would have got on each previous examination. This meant that two comparisons could be made: first of all the percentage failures that the most recent population would have shown had they taken a previous examination could be compared with percentage failures in the previous years' populations. This would answer the question whether there had been a decline in ability among the candidates. Secondly, equivalent cut-off scores could be estimated and compared with the actual cut-off scores. Estimating equivalent cut-off scores was performed by the equipercentile method: taking the percentage failures in the most recent population as a point of reference and looking up the score in every previous examination at which this same population would have produced almost the same percentage of fails. This would answer the question whether there had been a decline in standards.

Results

Detailed results of the equation are shown in Appendix 4. Here we present only differences between the actual and the equivalent cut-off scores and between populations. The differences between the most recent population (1991, except for English HAVO where the 1990 population was the most recent) and candidates from previous years is shown in Table 4.

Table 4

Differences between previous populations and the most recent one (% of maximum score)

EXAMINATION	1	2	3	4	5
GERMAN	0	+3	+2	+8	+3
ENGLISH C	0	−8	0	+2	+3
ENGLISH D	0	+3	+5	+5	−4
ENGLISH HAVO	0	+4	+1	+2	0
ENGLISH VWO	0	+1	−2	+3	+5
DUTCH C	0	+5	+7	+11	+7
FRENCH C	0	+1	+1	+5	+6

+ : earlier population scores higher than most recent population

Although most previous populations appear to have done better than the most recent population would have done, there is no clearly discernible decline in the sense that each new population scores lower than the previous one.

Table 5 shows the differences between the actual cut-off scores and those that have been estimated to be equivalent. Not all differences are meaningful, of course. Some might be due to statistical error. As the usual standard error of an examination is about 6% of its total score, it seems reasonable to take only differences of at least 7% into consideration. There are only five of these major differences in 28 examinations, randomly distributed over subjects and years. It is interesting to note, though, that in the only case where the actual cut-off score was much lower than that of 1991, the population had much lower scores than the 1991 population would have had. In the other cases higher, i.e. more severe actual cut-off scores correspond with higher performances by the actual previous populations. In fact, there is a correlation of .49 between differences in population and those in cut-off scores. This clearly suggests a tendency of the CEVO committee to use the score distribution and set the cut-off score at an acceptable failure percentage without taking into consideration that the whole population might perform better or worse than before.

Table 5

Differences between equivalent and actual cut-off (% of maximum score)

EXAMINATION	1	2	3	4	5
GERMAN	0	–2	0	0	–2
ENGLISH C	0	+10	2	–2	–2
ENGLISH D	0	–6	+2	–8	–2
ENGLISH HAVO	0	0	+2	0	+2
ENGLISH VWO	0	–4	0	–2	+2
DUTCH C	0	–5	–6	–10	–9
FRENCH C	0	–2	0	–2	–8

+ : earlier cut-off score lower (more lenient) than most recent one

Implications from both studies

The first study showed that examinations are clearly not at the same level of difficulty. When confronted by the difference between the current examination and an exemplary previous one the committees concerned have in most cases acted upon this information and set the advised equivalent cut-off score. The use of non-equivalent groups, however, and the statistical methods used have not been understood or accepted.

The second study confirmed the intuition of the teachers most directly involved in test construction, that they cannot be expected – as they are – to predict the difficulty of a new examination with sufficient precision. This would be a minor problem if we could assume that the ability level of the candidates remained constant over the years. Then, fluctuations in the mean scores between the current examination and previous ones that show up after the examinations have been analysed could be seen as pure indications of the difficulty of the examinations. This assumption turned out to be false too. Populations do vary (but, contrary to expectations, no decline could be demonstrated).

The second study also showed that one out of every six cut-off scores is clearly not equivalent to that of 1991 (not counting differences among the previous examinations themselves). In the case of Dutch reading comprehension this is the result of a well-considered decision to lower the norm. In other cases the non-equivalent cut-off scores could have been caused by the absence of an equating procedure. The first (exploratory) study providing this only covered part of the period 1981–1991, and did not cover 1991 at all, being discontinued immediately after the examinations of 1990. The future looks brighter, however. Acting upon the results of the second study, the State Secretary for Education and Sciences has funded the introduction of equating as a standard procedure for central examinations.

Note

I would like to thank Kees Glas and Maarten Groot for the way they have taken care of the psychometric part of the research, Michel Zwarts for his advice concerning the second study, Noud van Zuijlen for his many quick reactions to several drafts and the other people from the examinations department for the trouble they have taken to understand what we have been doing and to explain the use of it to their committees.

Appendix 1: Equating data first study

Language	Year	Pupils	Mean Score		Cut-Off Point		
			Reference (max. 50)	Current (max. 50)	Reference	Equivalent	Actual
GERMAN D	1987	539	30.4	36.4	27.5	33.5	31.5
	1988	890	30.1	31.4	27.5	28.5	28.5
	1989	579	31.1	35.9	27.5	32.5	32.5
	1990	1878	30.0	35.2	27.5	32.5	32.5
ENGLISH D	1987	775	34.8	34.9	29.5	29.5	29.5
	1988	522	33.7	33.1	29.5	28.5	29.5
	1989	874	37.5	36.5	29.5	28.5	28.5
	1990	1045	37.2	37.9	29.5	30.5	30.5
FRENCH C	1987	584	37.2	34.5	25.5	22.5	24.5
	1988	1111	37.3	36.3	25.5	24.5	24.5
	1989	644	36.1	38.9	25.5	28.5	26.5
DUTCH D	1988	257	30.6	28.5	27.5	25.5	24.5
	1989	445	30.6	29.4	27.5	26.5	26.5
	1990	1103	63.9%[1]	68%	55%	50%	50%

[1] From 1990 on the maximum score has been increased from 50 to 90 points.

Appendix 2: Second study, part one, teachers' estimations

A Language	B Yr	C X̄ %	D Teachers #	E Sd	F Pupils' mean %	G diff F–C
GERD	82	65.14	18	5.64	61	−4.14
GERD	84	69.01	18	7.00	67	−2.01
GERD	86	67.73	18	5.29	67	−0.73
GERD	88	66.60	18	6.25	63	−3.60
GERD	91	69.39	18	6.87	70	0.61
ENGC	81	69.74	21	4.51	58	−11.74
ENGC	83	72.26	20	5.92	66	−6.26
ENGC	85	70.90	21	5.08	74	3.10
ENGC	88	68.76	21	5.15	67	−1.76
ENGC	91	71.89	20	5.23	68	−3.89
ENGD	81	66.19	17	5.71	54	−12.19
ENGD	83	72.04	16	5.26	64	−8.04
ENGD	85	72.06	17	4.58	75	2.94
ENGD	88	70.47	17	4.17	67	−3.47
ENGD	91	70.12	16	5.82	74	3.88
ENGH	81	68.94	16	4.74	68	−0.94
ENGH	83	69.13	16	4.90	65	−4.13
ENGH	86	67.84	16	6.42	66	−1.84
ENGH	89	65.84	16	5.11	61	−4.84
ENGH	90	66.34	16	4.78	63	−3.34
ENGV	84	75.85	13	5.77	75	−0.85
ENGV	85	72.88	13	6.94	68	−4.88
ENGV	86	70.44	12	6.24	70	−0.44
ENGV	88	73.35	13	5.19	69	−4.35
ENGV	91	75.38	13	6.90	74	−1.38
FREV	81	67.76	10	6.15	63	−4.76
FREV	84	68.48	13	5.59	72	3.52
FREV	86	66.85	13	3.69	68	1.15
FREV	89	67.22	13	6.31	71	3.78
FREV	91	69.82	13	6.44	69	−0.82
DUTC	86	62.13	20	4.32	53	−9.13
DUTC	87	65.93	20	4.92	53	−12.93
DUTC	88	61.10	20	5.82	45	−16.10
DUTC	90	70.53	20	6.89	62	−8.53
DUTC	91	68.01	20	6.22	66	−2.01

Appendix 3: Distribution of exams over booklets, German-D

Booklets	Items from exam year				
	1981	1983	1985	1988	1991
1	1–8, 20–30	11–30			
2		11–30	1–10, 33–41		
3			1–10, 33–41	30–50	
4				30–50	11–31
5	9–19, 31–40				11–31
6	9–19, 31–40	31–50			
7		31–50	22–32	11–19	
8			22–32	11–19	32–50
9	41-50	1-10			32–38, 42–50
10	41–50	1–10	11–21, 42–50		
11			11–21	1–10, 20–29	
12	1–8 20–30			1–10, 20–29	
13		11–30	42–50		1–10
14	20–30		33–41		1–10

Appendix 4 : Equating data second study, part two

A LANG	B EXYR	C %Right EXPOP	D %Right REFPOP	E D – C Mean REFPOP – EXPOP	F Mean Ex – Mean REFEX	G Cut-Off ExYear	H Cut-Off Equiv to REFEX	I H – G
GERD	1982	64	61	–3	–9	55	53	–2
GERD	1984	75	67	–8	–9	55	53	0
GERD	1986	69	67	–2	–3	59	59	0
GERD	1988	66	63	–3	–7	57	55	–2
GERD	1991	70	70	0	0	63	63	0
ENGC	1981	61	58	–3	–10	49	47	–2
ENGC	1983	68	66	–2	–2	59	57	–2
ENGC	1985	74	74	0	6	63	65	2
ENGC	1988	59	67	8	–1	49	59	10
ENGC	1991	68	68	0	0	59	59	0
ENGD	1981	50	54	4	–20	41	39	–2
ENGD	1983	69	64	–5	–10	59	51	–8
ENGD	1985	80	75	–5	1	63	65	2
ENGD	1988	70	67	–3	–7	59	53	–6
ENGD	1991	74	74	0	0	61	61	0
ENGH	1981	68	68	0	5	59	61	2
ENGH	1983	67	65	–2	2	57	57	0
ENGH	1986	67	66	–1	3	57	59	2
ENGH	1989	65	61	–4	–2	53	53	0
ENGH	1990	64	63	–1	0	55	55	0
ENGV	1984	80	75	–5	1	63	65	2
ENGV	1985	71	68	–3	–6	57	55	–2
ENGV	1986	68	70	2	–4	57	57	0
ENGV	1988	70	69	–1	–5	59	55	–4
ENGV	1991	74	74	0	0	63	63	0
FREV	1981	69	63	–6	–6	59	51	–8
FREV	1984	77	72	–5	3	63	61	–2
FREV	1986	69	68	–1	–1	57	57	0
FREV	1989	72	71	–1	2	61	59	–2
FREV	1991	69	69	0	0	57	57	0
DUTC	1986	60	53	–7	–13	50	41	–9
DUTC	1987	64	53	–11	–13	51	41	–10
DUTC	1988	52	45	–7	–21	39	33	–6
DUTC	1990	67	62	–5	–4	49	44	–5
DUTC	1991	67	66	–1	0	49	49	0

Rob van Krieken

References

Glas, C.A.W. 1989. *Contributions to Estimating and Testing Rasch Models.* Proefschrift, Universiteit Twente.

Masters, G.N. 1982. A Rasch model for partial credit scoring. *Psychometrika* 47.

Sanders, P. and P. Goldebeld. 1985. *Het pre-equivaleren van examens.* ORD paper.

Shoemaker, D.M. 1973. *Principles and Procedures of Multiple Matrix Sampling.* Cambridge MA: Bollinger.

Tormäkängas, K. 1986. *The estimation of the variance components and their errors by utilizing generalized symetric sums.* Helsinki: The University of Jyväskyäl. Dept. of Statistics and Economies (unpublished).

11 A comparative study of four ESL placement instruments

Marjorie Wesche, T. Sima Paribakht, Doreen Ready
University of Ottawa

Theoretical background and rationale

The use of tests for placement of students in language programs, like testing for certification or achievement, raises the theoretical issue of method validity for given score interpretations and uses. Second language testing instruments are realizations of different methods through which the attempt is made to measure language ability. Tests vary in many ways (see Bachman 1990, for an analysis of method facets), and although there is little evidence of the effects of specific facets of tests, research has shown that fairly large differences in testing method can lead to systematic variance in test performance apart from ability (Shohamy 1990). One major cleavage in test methods is between tests which present language processing tasks and those in which testees report on their own knowledge or ability to do things in the second language. The former type of test may, among other things, vary according to the channel, mode and textual characteristics of the language input, the nature of the processing tasks that are set, characteristics of the required response scoring criteria, as well as features of the testing environment, test format, organization and presentation, scoring procedures and the interpretation of scores. In placement, the recommended practice is to use a test which reflects the nature and emphasis of instruction in its method. None the less, there is a tendency for large instructional programs to depend upon more easily tested receptive skills and constructed responses whatever the instructional emphasis.

Self-report procedures usually require candidates to rate their ability to 'do' certain things using their L2, or their 'knowledge' of particular elements or patterns of the L2. Sometimes, however, the criteria are less precisely defined, e.g., 'beginner' to 'advanced', or 'non-native' to 'nativelike'. Self-assessments are subject to poor reliabilities when candidates are either unable or unwilling to give an honest appraisal, the first case arising from unclear or unfamiliar criteria or the candidate's inability to analyze his or her own performance; the second case arises when there is a perceived advantage to a high or low rating. (See discussion in Ready 1991.) However, the successful use of such instruments for placement in some settings (LeBlanc and Painchaud 1985; Meara 1990) and their ease and limited expense of administration make them worth a second look by L2 instructional programs.

The practical questions for administrators are: how fine are the ability distinctions required for a given program, and, within the resource constraints under which all programs operate, what is the best feasible solution, be it a standardized or a carefully developed in-house or *ad hoc* language test, or a self-report procedure. The point is usually made that unlike the outcomes of certification tests, changes to poor initial placements are usually possible, and therefore a rough initial sorting is adequate for the purpose. However, poor placements and subsequent changes result in lost instructional time and frustrate students and teachers alike. The method issue thus remains important, even when it has become 'Which of the possible tests (methods) is best for this program?' rather than 'What is the best possible test (method) for this program?'

Purposes of the research

The present study, carried out in 1992, sought to compare the accuracy of three alternative placement instruments using different methods with the accuracy of the instrument currently in use in a multi-skill, intensive ESL summer program for Canadian high school graduates. Students came from varied L1 backgrounds, and included a large group of French L1 speakers. The study investigated placement accuracy at seven proficiency levels and overall, relative efficacy for students of the same versus different L1 backgrounds (French versus non-native French speakers) and relationships between the different measures.

Research questions

The following questions guided the research:
1 How well do the various instruments compare to the existing English Placement Test and to each other in terms of overall placement accuracy?
2 Which instruments work best at low, middle and high proficiency levels (as defined by criterion groups 1–2, 3–4, and 5–7)?
3 Are the instruments differentially effective in placing homogeneous L1 (i.e., francophone) vs. heterogeneous L1 (L2 French-speaking) students?
4 What are the implications regarding appropriate placement instruments for this (and other) program(s) and to what extent does testing method appear to play a role?

Research design and methods

Setting

The six-week summer ESL program is part of a national bursary program to provide intensive L2 exposure and practice to Canadian high school graduates and university students who wish to improve their English or French second language use skills. Official objectives of the program include the strengthening of oral skills and development of knowledge and appreciation of the L2 culture. Since students in the ESL program tend to have strong oral skills already, given the omnipresence of English throughout most of Canada as a language of the wider community and its prominence in the media, a four-skill approach is used at all levels. The program offers a variety of language activities in and out of the classroom, including daily morning classes organized around themes, featuring authentic materials of various kinds and a series of one-week afternoon workshops (e.g., film interpretation; preparation of a student newspaper).

Subjects

The subjects in the present study were high school graduates and university students from 18–25 years old. The group consisted of 56 francophone students and 37 L2 French-speaking students from a variety of other linguistic backgrounds, e.g., Arabic, Chinese, Spanish, Polish, Turkish.

Instruments

The main placement instrument was the English Placement Test (EPT) developed initially for the academic year comprehension-based program for beginners and intermediates at the Second Language Institute (SLI) of the University of Ottawa. This test had been carefully validated over the course of several regular academic semesters to provide accurate cut-off scores for these courses. The validation process consisted of comparisons of the scores obtained on the Placement Test with teacher assessments and rankings obtained at the beginning of the semester, with student mid-term marks and with student final marks. At the end of the semester, adjustments were made to the cut-off scores where it was thought to be necessary and then the process was repeated the following semester to verify any changes that were made. This process continued until the cut-off points were satisfactory. Since the summer bursary program includes students from a wide ability range, validation for this program at higher proficiency levels was carried out over three summers using the same criteria.

A Listening Dictation Test was developed in 1991 to provide supplementary information at lower proficiency levels in the summer bursary and other Institute programs. The other two instruments in the present study were more widely used self-report tests which offered considerable logistical appeal, as one was self-administered and scored and the other administered and scored by personal computer. All instruments demonstrated acceptable to very high reliabilities.

English Placement Test (EPT), SLI, University of Ottawa

The EPT is a text-based listening and reading test presenting varied tasks and short-answer formats. This test assesses the testees' reading and listening comprehension ability. Version II of the test which was used in this study has three listening comprehension sub-tests on different themes (i.e., two students discussing their exam schedules, a radio text on Mother's Day and a biographical sketch on Chopin). Students are given time to read the comprehension questions before listening to the text. After they have listened to the text, they are given time to answer the questions. The text is then played a second time and at the end students are given time to check their answers. The listening test takes about 20 minutes and students answer a total of 32 questions in a variety of formats (multiple choice, fill-in-the-blank, chart).

The reading comprehension part consists of three sub-tests on a variety of themes (i.e., a letter to a magazine editor, an announcement of a contest honouring the founding of a city and fitness levels in Canada). A variety of task formats (e.g., multiple choice, true or false, summary cloze) are used. There are a total of 32 questions in this part of the test, and students are given one hour to complete it. Both the listening and reading questions cover a range of comprehension tasks, ranging from identification of main ideas to finding specific information. The results have always been quite consistent and very few changes are generally made to initial placement levels. The main weakness that has been observed is that for some students the listening part of the test underestimates student ability at lower ranges of proficiency. This appears largely due to students' unfamiliarity with some of the tasks. For this reason, the Listening Dictation was developed in order to provide an additional measure of listening ability.

Listening Dictation, SLI, University of Ottawa

This test presents a listening text, based on a short biography of a youthful Canadian hero, which must be understood and written down by the student. Presented on cassette, it requires reconstruction of varied-length chunks of the original text which tax short-term memory. Testees are given one point for every identifiable word in the correct order (total of 147 words). They are not penalized for spelling errors, verbs with the wrong endings, singular instead of plural, etc., unless the word is unrecognizable and far from the original meaning. Extra words are ignored. Sentence or word inversions are scored as correct if the sentence and/or word still makes sense. The Listening Dictation is best described as a test of precision in listening comprehension.

Self-Assessment questionnaire, SLI, University of Ottawa

This instrument uses Likert scale ability estimates for descriptions of everyday language uses in an academic environment. The self-assessment instrument, which is administered in the student's L1 (either English or French), has been used for initial placement purposes in academic credit courses at the SLI, University of Ottawa, since 1985. It consists of a series of 60 statements which briefly outline situations in which students might find themselves having to use their second language receptively. They are asked to respond using a five-point scale ranging from 'I cannot do the task at all' to 'I can do it all the time.' The tasks are related either to listening or reading and are sequenced according to increasing difficulty. An example of a low level task is:

> *I can understand a notice announcing a class cancellation when it is only written in French.*

An example of a more difficult task is:

> *I can read a French newspaper and understand the gist of the stories on the front page.*

Experience has shown that there is a sufficient variety of tasks included in the self-assessment questionnaire to allow differentiation among the seven levels.

Eurocentres' Vocabulary size test (EVST) (Eurocentres, 1990)
The EVST, developed by Meara and his colleagues (cf. Meara and Jones 1990), belongs to a family of self-report checklist tests. Using words sampled from a word frequency list plus a set of imaginary words which would be possible in the given language, these tests ask students whether they 'know' sample words, and provide an overall estimate of learners' vocabulary size in the target language. The English language version is used by the Eurocentres for purposes of placement, on the authors' rationale that 'vocabulary knowledge is heavily implicated in all practical language skills' (Meara and Jones 1988: 80). An example from a French pencil and paper version is given below (Meara and Jones 1988: 81):

> *Look through the French words listed below. Cross out words that you do not know well enough to say what they mean. Keep a record of how long it takes you to do the test.*

VIVANT	MELANGE	MOUP	SOUTENIR
REPOS	GOUTER	ETOULAGE	DEMENAGER
AJURER	LEUSSE	LAVIRE	ORNIR
GOTER	TROUVER	LIVRER	VION
SIECLE	GANAL	FOULARD	ECARTER
POIGNEE	BARRON	CRUYER	SID
CERISE	PONTE	MAGIR	IVRE
LAGUE	TORVEAU	HARTON	EXIGER
MIGNETTE	EQUIPE	CLAGE	HESITER
ROMAN	PAPIMENT	ROMPANT	FOMBE
INONDATION	PRETRE	TOULE	AVARE
JAMBONNANT	MISSONNEUR	TOUTEFOIS	SURPRENDRE
CHIC	CONFITURE		

Meara and Jones (1990) have produced computer-administered versions of the earlier pencil and paper vocabulary tests in a number of languages which make the test even more practical for some settings. The computerized EVST has a 'Yes/No' format and consists of a bank of vocabulary items drawn from different frequency bands (up to a ceiling of 10,000 words in version E1.1/K10, MS DOS), as well as nonexistent words which conform to English word formation rules as a correction for guessing. The test begins with the easiest words, gets progressively more difficult, stops once it finds a sufficiently low level of performance and then does a detailed analysis at that level. Target words appear on the screen one at a time and the testee is asked to indicate if s/he knows the word well enough to be able to give its meaning. The imaginary words act as a built-in mechanism for adjusting scores for false claims and overestimates, and a correction factor based on the percentage of these is calculated into the final score (Meara and Buxton 1987). Meara and Jones (1988) noted the possibility that the test overestimates true vocabulary knowledge but Meara (1990) has subsequently revised this position based on experience with the test, to the effect that most people probably underestimate their knowledge, due possibly to inherent conservatism or to the inability to access little-known words presented in this way. In any case, we do not know what individuals do, and other studies of self-assessment of L1 proficiency suggest considerable inter-subject variability (Ready 1991). The EVST shows good test-retest reliability (Meara personal communication). Part of its attractiveness is that it is very easily administered, requiring approximately ten minutes on a personal computer, and is automated and self-scoring.

Procedures

All measures except the vocabulary test were administered to over 100 candidates at program entry. The vocabulary test was subsequently administered to those in levels 2–7 (N=93). Final placement level (based on information from the first three tests, in-class measures and teacher observation) was the criterion. The placement procedure was the following. Students were ranked in ascending order of their scores on the EPT and were then divided into seven approximately equal groups. The teachers administered both an oral exercise (each student interviewed and presented a classmate to the rest of the class) and a composition task to their initial groups during the first and second day of classes, and then received the scored Listening Dictation papers.

Based on this information and their own observations, the teachers reconsidered the appropriateness of the initial placement, particularly of the most and the least proficient students in each class. The teachers met together on the third day to compare information and decide upon placement changes, maintaining approximately equal groups. Approximately 2% of the students were changed from their initial group, mainly in cases where their oral proficiency was markedly different from the rest of their group. This percentage was particularly low compared to recent years. (Teachers reported that, due to the relatively large classes, they were reluctant to add students to their groups or to ask others to do so.)

Analyses

The following analyses were carried out. Descriptive statistics were calculated for all four instruments overall and at each final placement level (Table 1). Correlations were calculated among the four instruments plus the reading and listening sub-tests of the EPT and with final placement level for the overall population, for low, middle and high proficiency segments of the population and for all francophone and non-francophone subjects (Tables 2, 3 and 4).

Results

The results are reported in terms of the four research questions noted above.

1 How well do the various instruments compare to the EPT and to each other in terms of overall placement accuracy?

Table 1 shows the descriptive statistics for each instrument at each final placement level. While there is little overlap of scores between levels for the EPT, all four comparison instruments show a wide range of scores at each level with considerable overlap. The Listening Dictation shows a steady increase in the mean at each level, although the only difference between contiguous pairs that is statistically significant is that between levels 1 and 2. The Self-assessment test and the Vocabulary test do not consistently show increases in the mean from level to level and none of the differences between contiguous pairs of means is statistically significant.

Table 2 shows the relationship of each test with the final placement level for all subjects. As might have been expected, the EPT total score correlates most highly with the final placement level, followed closely by the EPT reading and listening sub-test scores. Of the other three instruments, the Listening Dictation correlation is highest (.82) while the Self-assessment and Vocabulary self-report correlations are both moderate (.58 and .52 respectively).

2 Which instrument or combination works best at low, intermediate and high proficiency levels?

Table 3 shows the correlations of the scores on various instruments and part scores with final placement grouped as low, intermediate and advanced proficiency levels. Only the total EPT score and the EPT reading sub-score correlate with final placement across all three proficiency levels. In both cases, the correlation is highest at the advanced proficiency level. At low levels of proficiency, Listening Dictation shows a somewhat tighter correlation with final placement level than the EPT listening sub-score but in both cases, the correlations are in the moderate range.

Table 1

Descriptive statistics for the four placement instruments (N=93)

	EPT Total				Listening Dictation		
Level	Range	$\overline{X}$	Std dev	Level	Range	$\overline{X}$	Std dev
1	15–30	22.2	4.3	1	34–114	73	21
2	26–33	31.5	3.0	2	77–122	97	15
3	36–46	42.1	3.3	3	67–142	111	20
4	46–53	48.6	2.6	4	85–142	120	15
5	53–62	55.6	2.3	5	89–140	127	13
6	58–63	50.9	1.8	6	117–145	138	7
7	63–69	65.9	1.9	7	135–147	141	3.5

	Self-assessment				Vocabulary		
Level	Range	$\overline{X}$	Std dev	Level	Range	$\overline{X}$	Std dev
1	60–283	161	59	1	—	—	—
2	148–250	193	31	2	2393–6398	4107	1165
3	115–262	196	35	3	2633–6504	3980	1115
4	158–251	210	30	4	1720–6518	5142	1409
5	171–269	227	27	5	3578–7600	5430	1289
6	202–292	241	26	6	3458–7714	5628	1420
7	169–295	236	34	7	3470–8616	6122	1247

Table 2

Correlation of placement instruments with final placement level (All Subjects)

	Placement Level
EPT Total	.96
EPT Reading	.91
EPT Listening	.90
Listening Dictation	.82
Self-Assessment	.58
Vocabulary	.52

The Self-assessment score is not significant at any of the three proficiency levels. (The Vocabulary test was not administered at the low proficiency level.) At intermediate levels of proficiency, the only other score besides EPT Total and EPT Reading that correlates with final placement level is that of the Vocabulary test. At advanced levels of proficiency both the Listening Dictation and the EPT Listening scores also correlate with final placement level but Self-assessment and the Vocabulary test do not.

Table 3

Correlations of placements test with final placement level for low, intermediate and advanced Groups

Group	EPT Total	EPT Listening	EPT Reading	Listening Dictation	Self-assessment	Vocabulary
Low	.80	.45	.66	.56	n.s.	—
Intermediate	.74	n.s.	.69	n.s.	n.s.	.43
Advanced	.91	.64	.74	.54	n.s.	n.s.

The correlation between the EPT and final level placement is almost certainly an overestimate of the relationship at lower levels but not at higher levels (Table 3). If initial student placement had been consistently changed on the basis of their Listening Dictation scores, approximately 8% of them at lower levels (1–3) would have been moved. This was not done, however, for the reasons previously indicated. At higher levels (high intermediate to advanced) the correlation is .91, at low intermediate levels .74, and at high beginner levels .80. It appears that this test works particularly well at higher proficiency levels and the listening part of the test works best with advanced students.

Table 4

Correlations among test scores and with final placement level for francophone and non-native French speaking students

(correlations for francophone students are given first followed by correlations for non-francophone students (bold)

	ETP–T	EPT–L	EPT–R	L-Dict	Self-a	Vocab
English Placement Test Total	—					
	—					
English Placement Test Listening	.91	—				
	.90	—				
English Placement Test Reading	.88	.60	—			
	.91	**.62**	—			
Listening Dictation	.82	.73	.75	—		
	.77	**.75**	**.64**	—		
Self-assessment	.67	.65	.54	.72	—	
	(.22)°	**(.21)°**	**(.19)°**	**.31**	—	
Vocabulary	.52	.43	.51	.49	.48	—
	.52	**.39**	**.55**	**.56**	**(.25)°**	—
Final Placement	.98	.88	.87	.79	.66	.51
	.96	**.85**	**.88**	**.77**	**(.27)°**	**.56**

° not significant

This may be partially due to a method effect, in that the novelty of listening item formats – including a variety of fill-in, matching, chart and multiple choice items – may create added difficulties for some lower level students. No such effect is seen in the reading part of the test, where students are not constrained by time.

3 **Are the instruments differentially effective in placing homogeneous L1 (francophone) and heterogeneous L1 (non-native French-speaking) students?**

Table 4 shows the correlations of the various instruments and sub-scores with each other and with the final placement level for francophone students (N=56) and non-native French speaking students (N=37). The pattern of correlations of the various instruments and sub-scores with final placement level is quite similar for the two populations except in the case of Self-assessment. That correlation is moderate for francophones but not significant in the case of non-francophones. The final question was:

4 **What are the implications regarding appropriate instruments for this (and other) program(s) and to what extent does testing method appear to play a role?**

The relevant findings are discussed in the following section.

Discussion and conclusions

The results of this study lead to the not surprising conclusion that tests which have been shown to work well in one context cannot be assumed to be appropriate in a seemingly similar new context. Overall, the tests requiring a demonstration of proficiency on the part of students worked best (EPT reading and EPT listening and Listening Dictation). These were, furthermore, text-based tasks. EPT content and tasks conformed most closely to the communicative instructional objectives and content of the summer ESL program even though it did not test productive skills. The EPT uses authentic (non-contrived) texts of general interest to university-age students, and tasks require global understanding through listening and reading of the kinds of information voluntary listeners and readers would be expected to retain. The texts are varied in subject matter and genre, and tasks also vary, unlike the Listening Dictation or Vocabulary test. The Listening Dictation is also based on an interesting extended text, but tests only listening comprehension and a threshold level of writing. These findings suggest that content validity is important in placement testing.

Neither self-report measure worked well, although the Self-assessment based on functional descriptions of language uses worked better than the vocabulary measure overall, particularly for francophone L1 students. Although all students taking the test had French as their first language of study, many were allophones, and for them, placement via the Self-assessment was unreliable. There are two possible explanations for this, one being the language factor in the instrument itself. This seems unlikely, however, as these students have done their high school work in French. The other possibility is that of cultural differences in English learning experiences and/or in ability and readiness to self-report one's language knowledge. The Vocabulary test also did not work well. Since the summer bursary course does not specifically aim to teach vocabulary, a vocabulary test may be less appropriate here than in other situations. Still, it should be remembered that the rationale for using this test for placement is that it is viewed as an indicator of language proficiency. In spite of its general ineffectiveness in this context, this test was reasonably effective at intermediate proficiency levels. An interesting question would be whether the relationship between vocabulary and general proficiency is strongest at this level, but this study provides no further evidence on this issue. Unlike the Self-assessment, this test was presented in the target language, English. However, the language of presentation and task was very straightforward, and what was required more than instructional language knowledge was, probably, a threshold comfort level with computers.

Finally, it should be noted that method factors do appear to influence language test performance in this study as in others, and that, for adequate placement in courses, tests developed for local needs and normed on representative populations are required.

Acknowledgement

We are grateful to Sandra Burger, Michael Massey, Paul Meara and to the 1992 ESL Summer School teachers and their students for their help with this study, and to Trixi Magyar for graphics and word-processing.

References

Bachman, L. F. 1990. *Fundamental Considerations in Language Testing.* Oxford: Oxford University Press.

LeBlanc, R. and G. Painchaud. 1985. Self-assessment as a second language placement instrument. *TESOL Quarterly* 19 (4): 673–87.

Meara, P. 1990. Matrix models of vocabulary acquisition. *AILA Review*: 66–74.

Meara, P. and B. Buxton. 1987. An alternative to multiple choice vocabulary tests. *Language Testing* 4 (2): 142–54.

Meara, P. and G. Jones. 1988. Vocabulary size as a placement indicator. In P. Grimwell (ed.), *Applied Linguistics in Society.* London: CILT pp. 80–7.

Meara, P. and G. Jones. 1990. *Eurocentres Vocabulary Size Test* (version E1.1/ K10, MS DOS). Zurich: Eurocentres Learning Service.

Ready, D. 1991. The role and limitations of self-assessment in testing and research. *Paper presented at the Thirteenth Annual Language Testing Research Colloquium.* Princeton, NJ.

Second Language Institute. 1986. *Self-Assessment Questionnaire.* Ottawa: Second Language Institute, University of Ottawa.

Shohamy, E. 1990. *The effect of contextual variables on test takers' scores on language tests.* Internal document, University of Tel Aviv.

12 Content validity in tests for well-defined LSP domains: an approach to defining what is to be tested

Alex Teasdale
British Council and Thames Valley University

A key concern in performance testing relates to the problem of sampling behaviour which is representative. Bachman (1990) bases his 'interactional/ ability' (IA) approach to test design and validation on the measurement of underlying constructs, making a useful distinction between the means of assessment and the abilities to be assessed. However, well-developed validated models of language competence for distinctive LSP domains are often not available, making the overt referencing of scores to construct difficult to justify. Criterion-referenced testing, which, in general, does not take underlying abilities as known or given entities, offers an alternative approach, but has received some criticism in recent years.

Many commentators have been less than sanguine about the application of criterion-referenced approaches to testing situations. Doubts include scepticism about the feasibility of adequately sampling the domain of interest (Skehan 1984), concern from proponents of criterion-referenced testing that test objectives are frequently inadequately specified (Nitko 1980; Popham 1980, 1993) and reservations that, whether alone or in combination, content validity and face validity are unable to provide evidence of validity (Bachman 1990; Messick 1975; Stevenson 1985). A further concern is that the attention to specificity of context and language use in such tests serves to inhibit generalisations because it focuses on contextualised tasks and not necessarily the constructs which underly them (Messick 1975; Bachman 1990).

This paper reports on research conducted in the course of the development of an English language test for newly-qualifying Air Traffic Control trainees. It describes research into a highly distinctive language area in which little or no construct research has been conducted, and the subsequent domain specification process in which analysis of language use plays a direct part in test design. The outcome of the research is a test design and development methodology centred upon recordings of authentic language use. The analysis of this corpus yields functional categories in which tokens of language use are classified according to criteria of context of occurrence and speaker's purpose. These categories then translate directly into test objectives avoiding recourse to a competence-based model of ATC language use 'which would at best be tentative' as the basis of test development.

Domain specification and the language of Air Traffic Control

Domain specification procedures

Domain specification implies the allocation of resources to Needs Analysis in order, firstly, to define a 'domain of behaviour' (Nitko 1980) and secondly, to identify relevant performance to which scores can be referenced. The identification and investigation of an adequate criterion sample of behaviour with the purpose of defining the domain allows content which is representative to be distinguished from content which is not. This is important for both design and validation, as criterion-referenced tests should be able to demonstrate a theoretically acceptable approach to the derivation and subsequent monitoring of test content. If such precise definition of test content is problematic for language tests, then the referencing of scores to relevant performance is even more so. For criterion-referenced tests where scores are referenced in this way, success in tasks which operationalise the relevant categories of performance amounts to evidence of mastery in the domain which has been specified. In highly complex areas such as language behaviour, where the outcomes from which mastery can be inferred are not necessarily defined by the test objectives, attempts to reference scores directly to relevant performances are seldom feasible. It is, therefore, only in the general sense of developing a clear framework for delimiting and describing the behaviours to be tested that many EFL and ESP tests can lay claim to being criterion-referenced.

A domain is described by Nitko (1980:465) as well-defined when it

> *is clear to both the test developer and test user which categories*
> *of performance (or which kind of tasks) should and should not be*
> *considered as a potential test item.*

However, domain specification, in common with construct-oriented approaches to test design, may face immediate difficulties. Lennon (1968:178) notes in relation to criterion referencing that:

> ... particularly in fields other than achievement, the area of
> concern to the tester is vastly more complex, multidimensional,
> and resistant to precise definition. The test-maker's task is made
> no easier by the unhappy circumstance that the domain which he
> is attempting to define may be in many respects *terra incognita.*
> (original emphasis)

The language of Air Traffic Control (ATC) is one such domain. And while the precise weighting, role and contribution of underlying abilities to performance is, as yet, unexplored, the generally well-ordered nature of the domain allows for a content-oriented approach to test design.

The linguistic needs analysis

The Eurocontrol standard exit test

The Eurocontrol Standard Test in English for Trainee Air Traffic Controllers has, as one of its overall aims, to define the minimum level of competence required to practise as an Air Traffic Control Officer (ATCO) in Europe. It has been developed specifically for trainee Air Traffic Controllers who are near the completion of their training and comprises a Listening section, an Interactive section and an optional Reading section. Wherever possible authentic ATC materials, including authentic sound recordings, have been used. Where this has not been possible materials have been simulated.

The Language of Air Traffic Control

Air Traffic Control language is one of the best defined LSP domains. For all common ATCO-pilot interactions, there exists recommended phraseology in the form of a treated reduced code which defines the content, form and ordering of elements of utterances, as well as specifying the circumstances in which specific phrases are to be used. In practice, phraseology, like other areas of language use, is subject to systematic and unsystematic local variation, personal language processing preferences and a host of other performance and processing characteristics which disturb the generally orderly and predictable nature of the domain. The use of greetings, polite forms, Air Traffic Control vernacular and pilot challenges/queries are examples of this. In addition there are situations for which standard phraseology does not exist, necessitating the use of 'appropriate subsidiary phraseology' (ICAO 1985), the nature of which is not clearly defined, but is generally taken to mean the realisation of (unspecified) messages in phraseological style. Domain specification must, therefore, be sensitive to issues of register and to violations of prescribed code if it is to act as a criterion by which the validity of test content is to be assessed.

In order to map this area of language use and specify the domain, a Needs Analysis of the work-specific language use of Air Traffic Controllers was conducted. The aims of the Needs Analysis stage were:
- to identify consistencies in the language use of Air Traffic Controllers and pilots so that test content could later be selected on a principled basis (the linguistic Needs Analysis);
- to classify salient features of Needs Analysis language data and Test tasks (e.g.

information density, L1 of speakers, standard/non-standard phraseology) in order to ensure representativeness of tasks and recordings used in the test and to provide a descriptive framework for future test users which will identify the main parameters under which assessment and live interaction occurs (the 'Test Characteristics' document);
–to investigate the views of the Air Traffic Control profession in Europe by means of a questionnaire distributed by the Project Team.
The domain specification was carried out through transcription and analysis of recordings of authentic Air Traffic Control communications, through an investigation of the conditions of assessment and through the analysis of responses to a questionnaire. The first of these, the analysis of authentic Air Traffic Control recordings, is the major focus of this paper. The investigation of conditions of assessment (the Test Characteristics) and their role in the domain specification procedure is also briefly described.

The questionnaire results (McCann 1992a) will not be extensively discussed as they relate more closely to test design rather than to overall development and validitation issues. There were 76 responses in all, from 15 different countries. Information was solicited on issues such as: the suggested balance of standard and non-standard phraseology, the desirability of using authentic materials in the final test forms and the degree to which listening, oral interaction, reading and writing should be represented in the final test.

Figure 1, below, gives an outline of how the linguistic analysis, the investigation of Test Characteristics and the information from questionnaire responses fed into domain specification, and test/task design.

The linguistic analysis

The main source data for the linguistic analysis were recordings of over twelve hours of uninterrupted ATC transmissions from Madrid, Paris, Athens, Maastricht, Frankfurt, London and Birmingham. Although the corpus contains samples of nearly all common ATC work contexts, it is not an entirely balanced representation of ATC language use. The principal areas of ATC work are all represented, but not necessarily in equal measure. Nor are all the participating administrations represented in each ATC professional area which was analysed.

Recommended phraseologies from the International Civil Aviation Organisation (ICAO) document *Rules of the Air and Air Traffic Services* (1985) and those of the Spanish Civil Aviation Authority document *Rules of the Air* (undated) were also included in the corpus. The ICAO phraseology document was included to ensure standard phraseology was fully represented as part of the Needs Analysis corpus. The Spanish Civil Aviation document ensured that phraseology for telephone coordination between ATC centres, a language context missing from the corpus of authentic ATC transmissions, was represented.

The corpus was analysed twice at different levels of complexity. The first

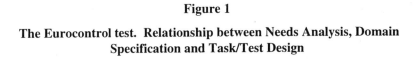

Figure 1

The Eurocontrol test. Relationship between Needs Analysis, Domain Specification and Task/Test Design

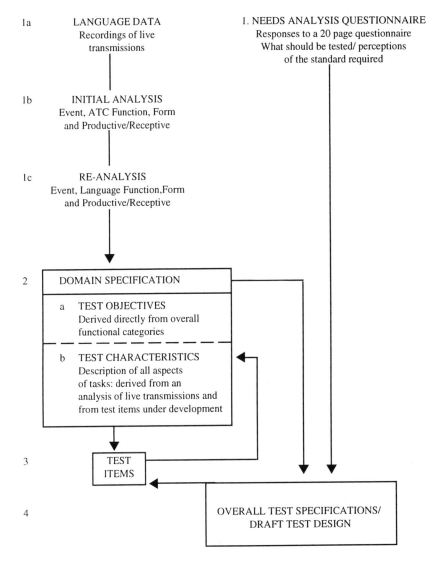

analysis was essentially work-procedure based, in that it grouped together utterances arising within the same phase of Air Traffic Control. The second analysis concentrated on the macro and micro language functions which occur in the corpus and allowed for the emergence of information about the language used in specific work procedures as well as for generalisations about language use across the entire corpus.

The initial analysis

The corpus was first analysed in terms of *Event, Function* and *Form* (McCann 1992b), in order to classify and group utterances into the Air Traffic Control contexts in which they occur:

EVENT	refers to the control service – in this case distinctions derived from ATC practice and procedures with categories reflecting the organisation of work in ATC. The categories are Tower (sub-divided into Clearance Delivery, Ground Movement Control and Local Control), Approach, En Route and Telephone Coordination. These sub-divisions are further divided into phases of a flight.
FUNCTIONS	refers to *ATC* functions (e.g. giving landing clearance).
FORMS	are listed under:

PRODUCTIVE skills:
Productive form: ATC: '[Callsign] cleared to land runway (number), wind (direction and speed)'
RECEPTIVE skills:
Receptive form: PILOT: 'Cleared to land runway (number), [callsign]'

The linguistic analysis took as its starting point utterances from the corpus of recorded material. Two examples of tokens of data from the corpus, in this case a clearance and the pilot's readback, are given below:

a. ATCO: [callsign] cleared for take-off runway (number) wind (direction and speed)
b. PILOT: [callsign] cleared for take-off on (runway number) copied the wind

(Note: 'copied the wind', indicates that the pilot has noted the current wind.)

These were coded into the following categories:

TOWER –   **LOCAL CONTROL** (*Event*)

         GIVING TAKE-OFF CLEARANCE (*ATC function*)

         PRODUCTIVE (*Form*)
         * [callsign] cleared for take-off runway (number) wind (direction and speed)

         RECEPTIVE (*Form*)
         * [callsign] cleared for take-off on (runway number) copied the wind

This initial categorisation of forms took as its fundamental unit of analysis the contexts of ATC work, grouping together utterances pertaining to the same set of Air Traffic Control procedures (labelled FUNCTION in this analysis). In the example above the two tokens of data, one productive, one receptive, are grouped as occurring within the function GIVING TAKE-OFF CLEARANCE. This ATC function occurs within TOWER – LOCAL CONTROL which is a distinct Air Traffic Control service.

In spite of the advantage of grouping utterances in this way, the approach provided only generalised information on the types of language arising within different phases of Air Traffic Control and, importantly, did not specifically identify the purposes for which language was used. A further exploratory analysis was, therefore, conducted (Teasdale forthcoming) to establish whether it was possible to account in a systematic and comprehensive way for the range of language functions which arise in ATC communications.

The subsequent analysis

The re-analysis of data began as an exploratory device to see if a framework of linguistic analysis would, as was anticipated, capture the systematic and repetitious nature of ATC language use. The analysis operated on a bottom-up principle, with the data determining the specific functional categories to be used in the analysis. These were then ordered into a set of general language functions which acted as an organising heuristic across the entire corpus and translated directly into Test Objectives (see Appendix A for an example of an elaborated Test Objective used in formal content validation).

For the subsequent analysis the original descriptive framework of *Event*, *Function* (renamed *ATC function*) and *Form* (*Productive/Receptive*), was retained, but the data were re-categorised within it to give information about the types of language function represented in the data. Figure 2 gives an overview of the levels and categories of description which arose from this re-analysis. *Event* was first divided into *Productive* and *Receptive*. Under each of these categories a series of *General Language Function* categories were established. These were developed while working with the data. A further classification into *ATC functions* was intended to reflect the Air Traffic Control procedures with which each of the utterances in the data is associated. Finally utterances were allocated to *Specific Language Functions*.

Figure 2

Re-analysis of corpus data – classification of forms into specific and general language functions

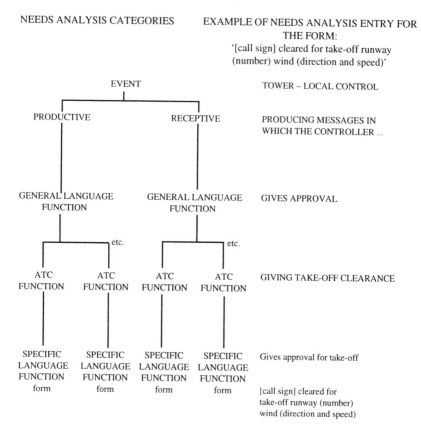

NEEDS ANALYSIS CATEGORIES

EXAMPLE OF NEEDS ANALYSIS ENTRY FOR THE FORM:
'[call sign] cleared for take-off runway (number) wind (direction and speed)'

EVENT — TOWER – LOCAL CONTROL

PRODUCTIVE / RECEPTIVE — PRODUCING MESSAGES IN WHICH THE CONTROLLER ...

GENERAL LANGUAGE FUNCTION / GENERAL LANGUAGE FUNCTION — GIVES APPROVAL

ATC FUNCTION / ATC FUNCTION / ATC FUNCTION / ATC FUNCTION — GIVING TAKE-OFF CLEARANCE

SPECIFIC LANGUAGE FUNCTION form / SPECIFIC LANGUAGE FUNCTION form / SPECIFIC LANGUAGE FUNCTION form / SPECIFIC LANGUAGE FUNCTION form —
Gives approval for take-off

[call sign] cleared for take-off runway (number) wind (direction and speed)

The revised framework differs from the initial analysis in that the primary classification of each utterance is in terms of language function rather than in terms of the phase of Air Traffic Control in which it occurs. This makes possible generalisations about the type of language use which arises in the whole, as well as in the sub-domains, of the corpus.

In the following example, the same language form used above to illustrate the coding procedure for the initial analysis is recoded using the revised analysis protocols. Three other language forms from the initial analysis are also included for illustrative purposes:

---

1. TOWER – LOCAL CONTROL *(Event)*

1.1. PRODUCING MESSAGES IN WHICH THE CONTROLLER:
(Productive/Receptive)

1.1.1. GIVES APPROVAL: *(General language function)*

> **[WHILE] GIVING TAKE-OFF CLEARANCE** *(ATC function)*
>
> > **1.1.1.1. Gives approval for take-off:** *(Specific language function)*
> >
> > *   [callsign] cleared for take-off runway (number) wind (direction and speed) *(Form)*
> >
> > **[WHILE] GIVING LANDING CLEARANCE** *(ATC function)*
> > **1.1.1.2. Gives approval to land:** *(Specific language function)*
> >
> > *   [callsign] cleared to land runway (number) wind (direction and speed) *(Form)*
> >
> > *   [callsign] cleared land runway (number) wind (direction and speed) *(Form)*

1.1.2. REQUESTS INFORMATION ABOUT: *(General language function)*

> **[WHILE] GIVING TAKE-OFF CLEARANCE** *(ATC function)*
> **1.1.2.1. Requests information about readiness for departure:**
> *(Specific language function)*
>
> *   are you ready for immediate departure ? *(Form)*

In this example:

TOWER – LOCAL CONTROL refers to the Air Traffic Control service. In this case the control of aircraft on short final approach or waiting for take-off clearance.

GIVES APPROVAL refers to the general language function (from which the test objectives are derived).

GIVING TAKE-OFF CLEARANCE refers to the Air Traffic Control operation which the utterance is related to.

GIVES APPROVAL FOR TAKE-OFF refers to the specific language function. '[callsign] cleared for take-off runway (number) wind (direction and speed)' is the actual language form as it appears in the corpus.

Utterances 1.1.1.2 and 1.1.2.1 are coded in the same manner.

Double-coding was necessary for some items which contained two separate and clearly distinguishable language functions. In the example below (as well as in the first three forms in the previous example) the utterance contains two distinct elements of information. In this case the utterance is a pilot readback. The coding classifies both elements of information as readbacks but separates the pilot readback of the take-off clearance given by the ATCO ('[callsign] cleared for take-off on (runway number)') from the stylised readback of the wind ('copied the wind'):

---

1. TOWER – LOCAL CONTROL

1.1 UNDERSTANDING MESSAGES BETWEEN PILOTS AND CONTROLLERS IN WHICH THE PILOT:

1.1.1 READS BACK:

    [WHILE THE CONTROLLER IS] GIVING TAKE-OFF CLEARANCE
    1.1.1.1a take-off clearance

    *   [callsign] <u>cleared for take-off on (runway number)</u> copied the wind

    1.1.1.1b reads back: wind
    *   [callsign] cleared for take-off on (runway number) <u>copied the wind</u> *(Form)*

After all the data had been coded the GENERAL LANGUAGE FUNC-TIONS generated by the analysis were extracted and translated into TEST OBJECTIVES (see below).

Test characteristics

Because the linguistic analysis is so heavily dependent on description in terms of language function, the Project Team felt that the domain was insufficiently characterised. A further level of analysis was therefore proposed to enhance the description of the domain. The 'Test Characteristics' are the result of this and serve two purposes: as information for test users on test content and testing methods, and as information which contributes to the specification of the domain.

A fixed category questionnaire with open-ended slots for comments was designed to investigate the test characteristics. The Listening test questionnaire investigates 19 parameters in some detail. Responses are required for each item group and focus on features such as: characteristics of task input, the length of recorded text, the number and type of speakers, the acoustic quality of recording, the amount of inference required to respond, the response characteristics and the ordering of information in the text. The purpose is to build up a detailed account, part quantitative (e.g. number of speakers in each audio recording), part qualitative (e.g. speakers' speed of delivery) and part descriptive (e.g. length of audio recording) of each item in the test. Although indigestible as a series of discrete descriptions, the information will, in summary form, provide an account of the conditions of assessment and will be made available as part of final test-user documentation. A fuller list of the features investigated and an edited section of the questionnaire used to elicit the test characteristics is included in Appendix B.

The approach adopted has been strongly influenced by Bachman's discussion of facets affecting measurement (1990) and by Weir's discussion of conditions of assessment (1993). The level and type of detail contained in the questionnaire also invites comparison with features of Popham's (1980) IOX test objectives and is intended to serve a rather similar purpose both in specifying the domain for the purposes of test development and as an aid to test interpretation.

Results

Overall the Needs Analysis generated 27 functional categories. These categories are used to define the Listening and the Interactive (Oral) Objectives. Figure 3 below illustrates the summarised Objectives for Listening:

Figure 3

The listening test objectives

```
4.   LISTENING OBJECTIVES
THE CONTROLLER:
4... SHOULD BE ABLE TO UNDERSTAND MESSAGES IN WHICH THE PILOT:
4.1 READS BACK/ACKNOWLEDGES ATCO'S MESSAGE
4.2 REQUESTS APPROVAL OR CLEARANCE
4.3 GIVES INFORMATION
4.4 REQUESTS INFORMATION
4.5 GIVES/REQUESTS REASONS
4.6 EXPRESSES READINESS TO DO SOMETHING
4.7 REQUESTS THE ATCO TO DO SOMETHING
4.8 CHECKS, CONFIRMS AND CLARIFIES WHERE NECESSARY
4.9 GIVES/DENIES APPROVAL AND CLEARANCE (ATCO'S ONLY)

5... SHOULD BE ABLE TO RECOGNISE THE COMMUNICATIVE FUNCTION
OF MESSAGES WITH AND WITHOUT EXPLICIT INDICATORS
```

All except Number 5, 'Recognition of Communicative Function', were derived directly from the General Language Functions identified in the Needs Analysis. As an objective 'Recognition of Communicative Function' arose from the occasional token of data in which implicature seemed to play a part. Such instances are rare, probably because of the legal restrictions on what constitutes allowable content in transmitted messages, the prescriptive nature of the recommended phraseology and the predictable relationship between communicative purpose and verbal realisation. Sarcasm and 'conversational implicature' (Brown and Yule 1983:31) are the most usual manifestations and are usually restricted to mild pilot sarcasm or reproach. One such example is the pilot utterance:

> '[Callsign] could you tell me please why we are so late, er... as my colleague has just informed you, when we taxied in, and we were in ahead of (name of company), why are we so late in leaving behind (name of company)'

This is coded as '... PILOT REQUESTS INFORMATION', but supports interpretation as either (or both) 'complaining' and 'giving reasons' (as to why they should be allowed to go earlier). Neither of these categories is represented in the analysis as Controllers are trained not to respond to challenges of this type. However, it must be recognised that implicature could arise during communications in an emergency situation and for this reason recognition of communicative function was included as an objective.

Linguistic analysis – discussion

The linguistic analysis began as an experimental tool in the search to define what was to be tested. A strong appeal was the potential for a direct link between source data and test objectives. For good reasons most Needs Analysis data used in the development of tests are subjected to a great many judgemental decisions before being translated into objectives. Two major considerations in investigating language behaviour are the wide range of possible utterances in any language use situation and the tremendous variety of contexts which arise. However, not all areas of language use are so open-ended and, for those which are more constrained, a data-driven approach may be suitable.

The approach described has led to a strong link between the findings of Needs Analysis and the test content specifications. The fact that communications take place in contexts in which the interactants share large amounts of information (about, for instance, the type, destination, routing and proposed altitude of particular aircraft, about current meteorological conditions and about the configuration of the airspace and position of traffic within it), which is not available to the eavesdropping researcher, means that some knowledge of ATC procedures is essential for the interpretation and analysis of the language data.

In the case of the ATC corpus the analysis revealed patterns of language use which might otherwise be hard to detect. Because utterances were listed together in subdomains (EVENTS) and into further sub-categorisations within them (ATC function) it was possible to confirm that interactions are more varied and open-ended while aircraft are still on the ground. Additionally, the grouping of similar functions provided evidence of a politeness register among native speaker pilots who often use indirect forms such as 'I wonder if ...', 'Would it be possible ...' in preference to the more precise and phraseologically correct form of Request .... While it is often possible to arrive at this type of information without systematically coding an entire data set, analysis does assist in revealing more accurately the frequency with which particular features occur.

Although the corpus was considered adequate and representative of European ATC communications there are some reservations, principally centred around sampling. Because of the sensitive nature of recordings of emergency and unusual ATC situations, they are poorly represented in the corpus. Indeed, it would be most unusual to capture any such transmission in 12 hours of random Air Traffic Control recordings, as unusual and emergency situations represent a tiny proportion of ATC language behaviour. Their importance in respect of ATC training and language use is, however, understandably out of all proportion to their frequency of occurrence. Analysis of language data of this type we did have access to suggests strongly that the range of general language functions were not, in fact different from those used in routine communications. This finding was reflected in the simulated emergency situations used in the Listening Test. The Interactive Test addressed the problem of emergency situations in a different way, with one component of this part of the test focusing on a mix of usual and unusual ATC language. In this way a range of less constrained language was introduced in order to compensate for the potentially serious possibility that the Needs Analysis sample is insufficient, and that emergency situations may, in some cases, manifest language use which is neither predictable nor conventional in the way suggested above.

A constant concern in all such studies, where there is a close and determining link between Needs Analysis data and Test Objectives, must be the size of the sample analysed. In this case over 12 hours of recording divides into numerous differentiated ATC sub-domains each with notably different patterns of language use. Some of these sub-domains are extremely constrained (for example, in Tower – Local Control, where the ATCO is responsible for arriving and departing traffic), others subject to wider variation (for example, in Tower – Clearance Delivery where there are often transactions concerning mislaid flight plans or delays which give rise to misunderstandings and opportunities for negotiation). Branching into sub-domains of use is a problem which is common to nearly all analysis of LSP use. What is important if Needs Analysis is to be amenable to a data-driven approach to test content, is that the sub-domains be clearly enough delineated, and that the language use is systematic enough to be open to meaningful analysis. The less this is the case, the larger the increase in sample size must be in order to establish the proportion of common and divergent elements within each sub-domain. Only then can a decision be taken as to whether the domain is sufficiently well-defined to allow for the test objectives to be directly derived from the data.

The approach also has other weaknesses, particularly in the restriction of its focus to single utterances and in the strong inferences it requires to conceptualise and specify the domain in terms of skills and processes. One implication of the restriction in focus to single utterances is that discoursal characteristics may not be properly accounted for. The 'principle of local interpretation', which 'instructs the hearer not to construct a context any larger than he needs to arrive at an interpretation' (Brown and Yule 1983:59), may on occasions demand that speakers and listeners look to a wider network of discoursal features than is reflected in the utterance-focused analysis of language data reported here.

In criterion-referenced testing, ways round the skill specification problem include concentration on the stimulus and response characteristics of the domain, implying the use of behavioural objectives (Nitko 1980), and the specification of the domain in terms of task (see for instance the RSA/UCLES Certificates in Communicative Skills in English which specify performance in terms of tasks, text types and degree of skill). To specify the domain in terms of stimulus and response characteristics would demand an acceptable theoretical framework through which language (as distinct from Air Traffic Control) task processes and outcomes could be defined and then related to concepts of mastery. As ATC language use is inseparably related to the movement of aircraft, an integrated set of task specifications would imply entirely faithful simulations of Air Traffic Control contexts of equal familiarity to candidates from all participating states. Varantola (1989) comments in relation to the language of Air Traffic Control that,

> .... *when the text is maximally economical the role of the context in its interpretation is extremely important. When the text is maximally explicit the role of the context or situation in which it is uttered is minimal ... Contextually dependent utterances are naturally short-lived or have limited interpretability.* (p.178).

The creation of fully contextualised tasks that would be equally familiar to all candidates is unfortunately impossible given the international nature of the test. As a consequence, 'limited interpretability' was accepted as a sufficient condition in the selection of items and tasks for the final test forms.

Evaluation and discussion

As final remarks, I would like to consider how such a data-driven approach might be further developed and incorporated into test design. It seems to me that a promising direction for Needs Analysis lies in corpus-based approaches, even if the domain is not restricted in the same way as Air Traffic Control communications.

In the language of Air Traffic Control the constraining influence inherent in the notion of permissible contributions, and the use of language as instrument in procedures which are unremittingly recurrent, permit an analysis of language use which will be more comprehensive than in most other domains. However, powerful insights are possible whatever the domain. With sufficiently large criterion samples, and a theory of how criterion and test performance might be related, the analysis of criterion and test performance might provide additional contributory evidence in the process of test validation. The relationship between language use in 'real-life' settings and that produced by candidates in test situations is an important area of enquiry for Performance Testing. The principal constraints are the feasibility of establishing theory-based predictions of how test and non-test behaviour might differ, the size of the criterion sample required and, related to this, the resources available to be allocated to Needs Analysis. While agreeing with Weir (1990:21) that, 'Perhaps the biggest danger is that there is a tendency for needs analysis to claim a disproportionate amount of the time and resources available for research, often at the expense of test development', we might wish to add that the legacy of inadequate research cannot be shed easily and may fatally weaken the claims to validity of the testing procedures which are developed.

The methodology adopted for the Eurocontrol Test, in which the analysis of the domain feeds into design/development decisions as well as test-user documentation, is intended to help ensure the validity of decisions made on the basis of test scores. The approach owes much to the influence of Popham and is also considerably influenced by Bachman's (1990) rigour in attempting to identify the nature, sources and magnitude of method effect. While Ebel's (1967) support for the primary role of content validity in test validation is perhaps difficult to endorse, the emphasis he gives to testers' judgements in the process of identifying constructs derived from measures, and in then relating test behaviours to them, is important in relation to construct validation:

> *The degree of **construct validity** of a test is the extent to which a system of hypothetical relationships can be verified on the basis of measures of the construct derived from the test. But this system of relationships always involves measures of observed behaviour **which must be defended on the basis of their content validity**. In every case quantitative validation builds on subjective validation. Statistical validation is not an alternative to subjective validation, but an extension of it. All statistical procedures for validating tests are based ultimately upon common sense agreement concerning what is being measured by a particular measurement process.*
> (p. 89: original emphasis)

In practice, test constructors are frequently faced with the same problem – that nomological validity (Campbell 1960) and a nomological network (Stevenson 1981), which might elucidate the relationships between observations and the construct, have not been established. With insufficient evidence to justify the use of given or derived models comprising traits as the basis of measurement, there may be little option but to pursue development paths which are not dependent on assumptions about the contributions of specific abilities to performance.

The approach I have described in relation to the design and development of the Eurocontrol test is closely related to Glaser and Nitko's (1971:653) definition of criterion-referencing:

> *A criterion-referenced test is one that is deliberately constructed to yield measurements that are directly interpretable in terms of specified performance standards. Performance standards are generally specified by defining a class or domain of tasks that should be performed by the individual. Measurements are taken on representative samples of tasks drawn from this domain, and such measures are referenced directly to this domain for each individual measured.*
> (original emphasis)

However, in common with many attempts at criterion-referencing for language tests, the approach described in this paper has difficulty with the notion of direct interpretability. Skehan (1984:217), 'in discussing the difficulties of applying criterion referencing to language tests', implies a more rigorous definition than Glaser and Nitko's, suggesting that true criterion referencing should be 'linked to ... specific performance which would allow a definite 'yes/no' judgement on whether a particular task can be accomplished'. While it would be highly desirable to conform to this second description of criterion referenced testing, it is difficult to imagine any test of a foreign language being able to meet such a demanding specification.

It is certainly true that domain specification procedures for language tests encounter difficulties in meeting the more rigorous requirements of strong-form criterion referenced approaches to testing. This does not, however, imply a total mismatch between language testing and criterion-referencing. Criterion-referencing, as Nitko (1980) shows, is not a unitary concept, but a robust and steadily diversifying set of approaches. For foreign language testing, criterion-referencing does not offer pre-packaged solutions. What it can offer, however, is a variety of ways, some complementary to other testing approaches and some not, of conceptualising the measurement process. This, and the test development paths which are implied in adopting a criterion-referenced approach, contribute to the usefulness of criterion referencing for performance tests, and, in particular, those addressing language areas in which the abilities underlying performance remain relatively unexplored.

Appendix A

4.8 CHECKS, CONFIRMS AND CLARIFIES WHERE NECESSARY

Includes:

– checking that information the pilot comprehends or has received is correct
  (e.g. 'Confirm turning right heading (heading)')
– requesting repetition
– confirming/disconfirming information being checked by ATCO
– clarifying information
– self-correcting (e.g. 'squawk 4382, disregard, 4328')

Does not include:
– acknowledgements that message has been received (e.g. 'roger')

Examples (in messages containing two functions see underlined sections only):

– <u>negative, negative</u>, we have retaxied,
  retaxied to change our position
– yes, <u>I understand now it's reverted
  to (x) minutes per departure</u> and what
  number are we please ?
– OK, <u>did you confirm, did you say that
  runway (number) would be available for
  us ?</u> That is our preference

– we have one hour delay, right?
– OK, <u>that means we start up now</u>
– I did not hear your reply
– OK, <u>you call us back for push-back?</u>
– I'm sorry, say again for callsign
– roger, <u>hold where ?</u>
– I do not understand
– cross runway (number) ?

Appendix B

(i) Overall categories covered in Test Characteristics document:

– Characteristics of task input
– Length of text
– Control service
– Number, type and characteristics of speakers
– Types of turn (short/long)
– Acoustic quality of recording
– Use of phraseology
– Realisation of messages in text – pragmatic encoding
– Topic
– Distribution of new information in text
– Types(s) of lexis
– Potential bias due to background knowledge
– Speed of processing required of candidate
– Characteristics of expected response to items
– Ordering of info in text compared with item ordering
– Item independence
– Identifiable strategies to respond to items
– Number of listenings

(ii) Sample extract from Item Characteristics document:

METHOD FACTORS		
Stimulus/Text		
10. Characteristics of task input	**Type**	
	a. Aural – recording	YES/NO
	b. Graphic	YES/NO
	c. Written Processing of input	YES/NO
	d. Time to process before tape played	YES/NO
	e. Example in which candidates perform Yes/No sample task using same type of input, task, and recording as actual items	YES/NO
	f. Written example only	YES/NO
	g. Other presentation of example (Please specify below)	YES/NO
	h. Quantity of input to be held in memory during task	NONE/LITTLE/A LOT
	i. Complexity of input to be held in memory during task	NONE/LITTLE/A LOT
	Comments – refer to items above if relevant:	

References

Bachman, L. F. 1990. *Fundamental Considerations in Language Testing.* Oxford: Oxford University Press.

Brown, G. and G. Yule. 1983. *Discourse Analysis.* Cambridge: Cambridge University Press.

Campbell, D.T. 1960. Recommendations for APA test standards regarding construct, trait, or discriminant validity. *American Psychologist* 15: 546–53.

Ebel, R. 1967. Evaluating Content Validity. In D. Payne and R. McMorris (eds.), *Educational and Psychological Measurement.* Waltham, MA: Blaisdell Publishing Company.

Glaser, R. and A. J. Nitko. 1971. Measurement in learning and instruction. In R. L. Thorndike (ed.), *Educational Measurement* (2nd edition). Washington D.C.: American Council on Education.

International Civil Aviation Organisation (ICAO) 1985. *Rules of the Air and Air Traffic Services, Doc 4444-RAC/501/12.* Montreal: ICAO.

Lennon, R. T. 1968. Assumptions underlying the use of content validity. In N. E. Gronlund (ed.), *Readings in Measurement and Psychology.* New York, NY: The Macmillan Company.

McCann, P. 1992a. *Eurocontrol Testing Project: Needs Analysis Phase. English for Air Traffic Control. Analysis of Questionnaire Results.* Luxembourg: Eurocontrol.

McCann, P. 1992b. *Eurocontrol Testing Project: Needs Analysis Phase. English for Air Traffic Control. Linguistic Analysis.* Luxembourg: Eurocontrol.

Messick, S. 1975. The standard problem: Meaning and values in educational measurement. *American Psychologist* 30: 955–66.

Nitko, A. J. 1980. Distinguishing the varieties of criterion-referenced tests. *Review of Educational Research* 50 (3): 461–85.

Popham, W. J. 1980. Domain specification strategies. In R. A. Berk, (ed.), *Criterion-referenced Measurement: The State of the Art.* Baltimore: The Johns Hopkins University Press.

Popham W. J. 1993. Educational testing in America: What's right and what's wrong? A criterion-referenced perspective. *Educational Measurement: Issues and Practice* 12,1.

Royal Society of Arts/University of Cambridge Local Examinations Syndicate: *Certificates in the Communicative Skills in English.* London/Cambridge: RSA/UCLES.

Skehan, P. 1984. Issues in the testing of English for specific purposes. *Language Testing* 1 (2): 202–20.

Spanish Civil Aviation Authority (undated). *Rules of the Air.* Madrid: SCAA.

Stevenson, D.K. 1981. 'All of the above': On problems in the testing of FL reading. *System* 9 (3): 267–273.

Stevenson, D.K. 1985. Authenticity, validity and a tea party. *Language Testing* 2 (1): 41–7.

Teasdale, A. (forthcoming). *Eurocontrol Testing Project. Needs Analysis Phase. English for Air Traffic Control. A Functional Analysis of Air Traffic Control Communications*. Luxembourg: Eurocontrol

Varantola, K. 1989. Natural languages vs. purpose-built languages. *Neuphilologische Mitteilungen* 2/XC.

Weir, C. J. 1990. *Communicative Language Testing*. New York, NY: Prentice Hall.

Weir, C. J. 1993. *Understanding and Developing Language Tests*. Hemel Hempstead: Prentice Hall International.

13 Decision dependability of subtests, tests and the overall TOEFL test battery

James Dean Brown
University of Hawaii at Manoa
Jacqueline A. Ross
Educational Testing Service

Introduction

Scores obtained on the *Test of English as a Foreign Language* (TOEFL) are frequently used to inform decisions regarding the readiness of non-native speakers to pursue academic studies in English at colleges and universities in the United States and Canada. As in all measurement, the reliability of the test instrument and the dependability of decisions made on the basis of test performance are of major concern to test developers and test score users. The internal consistency reliability of the TOEFL total and individual test scores has been shown to be high (based on either a classical theory approach or an item response theory approach), and the associated standard error of measurement is published as a means for decision makers to estimate the probable extent of error inherent in the test scores (ETS 1992: 30–1).

One useful extension of the classical theory approach to estimating the reliability of measurement was provided by with the introduction of generalizability theory by Cronbach, Rajaratnam and Gleser (1963). In their model, reliability 'resolves into a question of the accuracy of generalization, or generalizability' (Cronbach *et al.* 1972: 15), i.e., how well one can generalize from one observation to a universe of observations. Generalizability (G) theory views the observed score as if it were the universe score, generalizing from the sample to the universe of interest by means of specified estimation procedures (Shavelson and Webb 1981: 133–7).

As Suen (1990: 41–2) puts it, generalizability theory provides a conceptual framework to assess multiple sources and magnitudes of variation, or measurement error, within the context of a testing situation. In essence, analysis of variance (ANOVA) techniques are used to estimate components of variance associated with the various facets of measurement in a generalizability study (G-study). The ability to examine the sources of error in a multifaceted way provides a more comprehensive and differentiated explanation of variance than is possible in classical reliability theory (Shavelson and Webb 1981: 133). This information can be utilized in a decision study (D-study) wherein the results of various measurement designs can be manipulated. Test-design and score-use decisions can then be made that are based on a more accurate estimation of the error inherent in such choices. In turn, the dependability (analogous to reliability in classical theory) of such decisions can also be examined. All of these G-study and D-study techniques are amply demonstrated and exemplified for various statistical designs in Brennan (1983).

Application of G theory to language testing situations is discussed in Bolus, Hinofotis and Bailey (1982), who further iterate the usefulness of this systematic approach to the study of measurement error. Brown (1984) applied G theory to the study of numbers of items and passages used in measuring engineering English reading ability in EFL situations. Then Brown and Bailey (1984) studied the effect of numbers of raters and scoring categories on the dependability of writing scores. More recently, Stansfield and Kenyon (1992) applied G theory to the study of the effect of numbers of tests and raters on oral proficiency interview scores. Brown (1990, 1993) also applied G theory to the problems of estimating score dependability in criterion-referenced language tests.

Purpose

The purpose of this project is to explore two dimensions of the TOEFL that have hitherto received little attention. First, a test development policy issue will be addressed. This issue centers on deciding how many items and subtests to include on the TOEFL for maximum effectiveness. Formulas like the Spearman-Brown prophecy formula can be used to predict the effects on test reliability of different numbers of items. But, such formulas cannot help in determining the optimal combination of numbers of subtests and items that ought to be included on the TOEFL. Fortunately, generalizability theory, discussed above, is particularly well suited to addressing this issue. While this project was primarily designed to investigate the TOEFL test as it exists, it is possible within the generalizability theory framework to also include analyses that allow the results to be generalized to future versions of the TOEFL (e.g., TOEFL 2000) and to other test development projects around the world.

Second, while Educational Testing Service (ETS) has long reported the standard error of measurement (SEM) for the TOEFL to help score users make responsible decisions, there is one issue that continues to be potentially trouble-some: in general, tests are not equally reliable for making decisions at different cut-points (for an overview see Feldt and Brennan 1989: 123–4). Conditional SEM data provided by the in-house TOEFL reports indicates that the SEM is not currently the highest at the mean of the TOEFL test. Since the dependability of the scores has been found to be lowest at the mean elsewhere (Brennan 1984:

312–17), and since the dependability of the TOEFL along the entire range of possible decision points has not been demonstrated, cut-point dependability seems like an important, yet unresolved, issue. The second general goal of this project, then, is to determine whether differences in dependability exist at different cut-points for the total TOEFL scores (or the individual Listening Comprehension, Structure and Written Expression, and Reading Comprehension and Vocabulary test scores that make up the battery) and to examine the degree to which any such differences may affect the dependability and therefore the validity of score users' decisions.

To achieve the above goals, four research questions were formulated. These research questions apply not only to the overall TOEFL battery, but also to the various tests and sections that it includes:

1 What are the classical theory reliability estimates?
2 What are the relative contributions to error variance of persons, items, subtests, and their interactions?
3 What is the dependability for varying numbers of items and subtests?
4 What is the effect on score dependability of various cut-points?

Methods

Subjects

The subjects in this study all come from the May 1991 administration of the TOEFL. That administration included a total of 93,960 examinees with 26,371 in the United States and Canada and 67,589 at other test centers around the world. In fall 1992, the International Testing and Training Programs Area at ETS made available a data set (known as the 'Generic Data Set'), which was made up of 24,500 item response records from the May 1991 administration of the worldwide TOEFL. For the project reported here, a total of 20,000 students were randomly selected (from the 24,500 records in the generic data set) for convenience in analyzing the results.

Of the 20,000 subjects in this study 59.6 per cent were male and 40.4 were female. They were involved in both domestic (26.2%) and foreign (73.8%) administrations of the TOEFL. They reported themselves to be from a total of 144 different countries including Brazil (3.1%), Cyprus (2.8%), France (6.0%), Germany (4.7%), Greece (3.7%), India (4.3%), Indonesia (8.2%), Japan (8.2%), Jordan (1.6%), Republic of Korea (8.1%), Lebanon (1.2%), Malaysia (4.2%), Mexico (1.3%), Pakistan (3.7%), People's Republic of China (5.1%), Saudi Arabia (1.2%), Spain (1.9%), Switzerland (1.1%), Taiwan (2.3%), Thailand (8.3%), Turkey (5.7%), and 123 other countries with one per cent or less each (13.3%).

In terms of language background, the subjects reported themselves as being speakers of Arabic (8.3%), Chinese (8.0%), French (8.0%), German (6.2%), Greek (6.2%), Indonesian (8.2%), Japanese (8.2%), Korean (8.2%), Malay (4.1%), Portuguese (4.1%), Spanish (8.1%), Telugu (4.0%), Thai (8.3%), Turkish (6.1%), and Urdu (4.1%).

Their reasons for taking the TOEFL varied too, as follows: for undergraduate studies (37.0%), for graduate studies (46.2%), for another type of school (2.0%), for a license (1.8%), for a company (8.5%), other (3.5%), and no reason given (1.0%).

Materials

As pointed out in ETS publications (e.g., ETS 1992, 1993), the TOEFL test battery consists of three separately timed tests in multiple-choice format with four answer options for each test question printed in a test book. All responses are gridded on answer sheets that are later computer scored.

The first test, Listening Comprehension (LC Test), is designed to measure the ability to understand spoken English. The first part (LC1) requires the examinees to listen to a short sentence and to choose the option that is closest to it in meaning. The second part (LC2) consists of short conversations between two people, followed by a spoken question. The examinee decides which option best answers the question. Part 3 (LC3) presents several short talks and extended conversations about a variety of subjects, and requires the examinees to respond to oral questions about what they heard.

The second test, Structure and Written Expression (SWE Test), is designed to measure the ability to recognize selected points of English structure. In the first part of this test (SWE1), the examinee reads an incomplete sentence and must choose the word or phrase that best completes it. In the second part (SWE2), several words or phrases are underlined in a sentence, and the examinees must choose the underlined segment that is not an acceptable English usage.

The third test, Vocabulary and Reading Comprehension (VRC Test), was designed to test the ability to understand the meaning and use of words as well as the ability to comprehend a variety of reading materials. The first part (VRC1) of this test contains vocabulary items wherein a word or phrase is underlined in a sentence and the examinee must select a word or phrase that could be substituted and still preserve the original meaning of the sentence. In the second part (VRC2), the examinee reads a number of short passages on a variety of academic subjects and must answer questions based on what is stated or implied in the passage.

Procedures

The TOEFL being used here was administered under standard conditions in May 1991. Strict admission procedures were followed, and, during the test, examinees were not allowed to have anything other than the testing materials on their desks.

They were not permitted to take notes or make marks of any kind in their test books. Nor were they permitted to work on any section of the test before or after time was called.

After the administration, answer sheets were returned to Educational Testing Service (ETS) for scoring. The raw scores for each test are the number of questions answered correctly. There is no penalty for guessing. Raw scores are then converted to standardized scales based on the three-parameter item response theory model (T scores for the individual tests and CEEB scores for the battery as a whole). These scaled scores are reported to the examinees and to institutions that the examinees have selected to receive scores.

Analyses

The analyses in this project began with descriptive statistics and classical theory reliability estimates (split-half adjusted, Guttman, and Cronbach alpha) to provide background and a context for interpreting the generalizability studies (G-studies) and decision studies (D-studies). Five G-studies were conducted based on the overall structure of the TOEFL shown in Figure 1. The first G-study investigated the effects on the total TOEFL battery scores dependability of

Figure 1

TOEFL structure

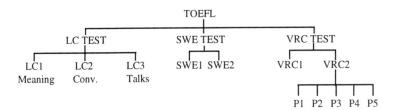

numbers of items (items facet) and numbers of test types (subtests facet based on the Listening Comprehension, Structure and Written Expression, and Reading Comprehension and Vocabulary tests) as shown in Figure 2A. The second, third, and fourth G-studies considered the effects on total test scores for the LC Test, the SWE Test, and the VRC Test of numbers of items and subtests (made up of different item types) on those tests as shown in Figures 2B through 2D. The fifth G-study focused on the Reading Comprehension section (VRC2) of the VRC Test. In this case, the effects of numbers of items and subtests (passages P1–P5) were investigated as shown in Figure 2E.

All of these G-studies were very similar in structure. In all cases, analysis of variance (ANOVA) procedures were run using all 20,000 subjects for a persons by items nested within subtests design, or p x (i:s). The result in all cases was a two-facet design with items and subtests as the facets. Random effects models were used in the ANOVAs so that the results would be generalizable to the development of the TOEFL 2000 project as well as to other test development projects around the world. However, in some places mixed model ANOVAs with fixed effects for the subtest facet were also used so that the results for the

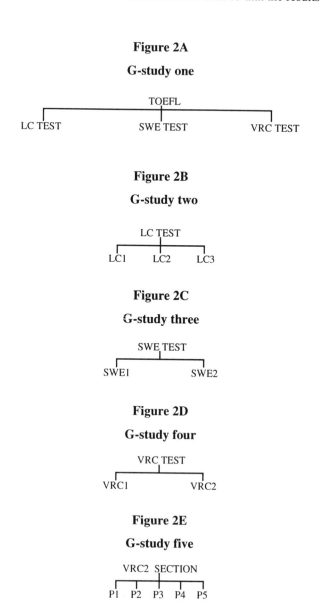

Figure 2A

G-study one

TOEFL

LC TEST   SWE TEST   VRC TEST

Figure 2B

G-study two

LC TEST

LC1   LC2   LC3

Figure 2C

G-study three

SWE TEST

SWE1   SWE2

Figure 2D

G-study four

VRC TEST

VRC1   VRC2

Figure 2E

G-study five

VRC2 SECTION

P1   P2   P3   P4   P5

current configuration of the TOEFL could be examined.

In the random effects model, it is assumed that persons, items, and subtests were randomly selected from the universes of all possible persons, items, and subtests. Shavelson and Webb (1981) argued that random effects models are reasonable if one can take an exchangeability perspective:

> *Viewed from the exchangeability perspective, the issue of fixed or random effects is not whether one can catalog (etc.) all possible members of a population but whether the members are exchangeable with other potential members. In terms of sampling, if one set of persons and items to which ρ^2 generalizability coefficient ... is generalizable is the set of such persons and items jointly exchangeable with the present sample, it is reasonable to consider the item facet random. The concept of exchangeability, at the minimum, provides reasonable grounds for considering whether a facet is random or fixed.*

Thus for those results in this paper that are based on a random effects model, random selection of items and subtests is assumed, while, for those results based on a mixed model (with fixed effects for subtests), no such assumption is made for the subtests facet.

Based on the mean squares obtained in the random effects model ANOVA procedures, variance components were estimated (as will be demonstrated in the *results* section). Interpreting these variance components helped in understanding the relative contribution of persons to the true score variance, as well as the contributions of items and subtests to the error variance. Five parallel D-studies followed the G-studies. In these D-studies, the variance components found in the G-studies were used to calculate statistics that can be directly interpreted in making decisions. Two types of error were considered:

a) lower-case delta error (δ) for relative decisions (i.e., norm-referenced decisions), and

b) upper-case delta error (Δ) for absolute decisions (i.e., criterion-referenced).

All relevant D-study statistics are reported in the *Results* section for the combination of items and tests under investigation in this project. In addition, G coefficients (based on lower case de'∙a) are reported for various numbers of items and subtests so that the reader can directly observe the effect on dependability of these two facets in various combinations of numbers of items and subtests.

The last step in each D-study was to calculate a squared-error loss agreement coefficient known as the phi(lambda), or $\phi(\lambda)$, at various cut-points from 10 per cent to 90 per cent. These analyses illustrate the effect of various cut-points on decision dependability. Phi(lambda) coefficients were calculated for both a random effects model (to provide generalizability of results to other tests) and a mixed model with fixed effects for subtests (to provide estimates for the TOEFL as it existed in this study).

Results

The results of this project will be discussed in the following stages with commensurate section headings: a) descriptive statistics for each of the five generalizability studies will be provided for background; b) classical theory reliability estimates will be presented for later comparison with the G-theory results; c) the variance components for the five G-studies will be presented and compared; d) the five parallel D-study results will be presented along with G coefficients for various numbers of items and subtests; and finally, e) squared-error loss agreement coefficients will be given for different cut-points within each of the D-studies.

Descriptive statistics

The descriptive statistics for the raw scores involved in each of the five generalizability studies are reported in Table 1. According to the labels across the top of the table, the mean, standard deviation (SD), and number of items (k) are given for the original test and for the G-study sampling. The original test includes the subtests and numbers of items just as they were administered. The G-study sampling results are based on the random samples that were taken from the original test to create balanced subtests (each containing the same number of items) for the generalizability studies.

The first G-study was on the effects of items and tests on the dependability of Total TOEFL battery scores. Thus descriptive statistics are given for the Total TOEFL and each of the tests which contribute to that Total score: Listening Comprehension (LC Test), Structure and Written Expression (SWE Test), and Vocabulary and Reading Comprehension (VRC Test). Notice that the original TOEFL had a total of 146 items and that the original LC, SWE, and VRC Tests had 50, 38, and 58 items, respectively. In order to create a balanced design, two of the tests had to be reduced in number of items to match the smallest of the tests. To achieve this, 38 items were randomly selected from the LC and VRC Tests to match the existing 38 items in the SWE Test. As a result, in the first G-study, all three tests were analyzed as 38 item tests with a TOEFL total of 114 items.

The second G-study was focused on the effects of items and subtests on the dependability of LC Test scores. Thus descriptive statistics are given in Table 1 for the whole LC Test and each of the subtests which contribute to the LC Test scores: LC1, LC2, and LC3. Notice that the original LC Test had a total of 50 items and that the original LC1, LC2, and LC3 sections had 20, 15, and 15 items, respectively. In order to create a balanced design, the longer section had to be reduced in number of items to match the other two sections. To achieve this, 15 items were randomly selected from the LC1 to match the existing 15 items in both the LC2 and LC3 sections. As a result, in the second G-study, all three sections were analyzed as 15 item subtests with an LC Test total of 45 items.

Table 1

Descriptive statistics

STUDY BATTERY TEST SUBTEST PASSAGE	ORIGINAL TEST			G-STUDY	SAMPLING	
	MEAN	STD	*k*	MEAN	STD	*k*
STUDY ONE						
TOTAL TOEFL	99.6788	27.2798	146	78.9712	21.3691	114
LC TEST	31.1660	10.5508	50	24.0095	8.1238	38
SWE TEST	27.5541	7.6467	38	27.5541	7.6467	38
VRC TEST	40.9588	11.6609	58	27.4077	7.7959	38
STUDY TWO						
LC TEST	31.1660	10.5508	50	27.7185	9.5038	45
LC1	12.6897	4.6491	20	9.2422	3.5805	15
LC2	9.5017	3.3634	15	9.5017	3.3634	15
LC3	8.9746	3.4902	15	8.9746	3.4902	15
STUDY THREE						
SWE TEST	27.5541	7.6467	38	20.4521	5.6912	28
SWE 1	10.5301	2.9676	14	10.5301	2.9676	14
SWE 2	17.0240	5.1066	24	9.9220	3.1298	14
STUDY FOUR						
VRC TEST	40.9588	11.6609	58	40.9588	11.6609	58
VRC 1	20.5785	6.4282	29	20.5785	6.2482	29
VRC 2	20.3804	6.0880	29	20.3804	6.0880	29
STUDY FIVE						
VRC 2	20.3804	6.0880	29	13.8102	4.3375	20
PASSAGE 1	5.5312	1.5248	7	3.1075	0.9972	4
PASSAGE 2	3.9047	1.2311	5	3.0894	1.0408	4
PASSAGE 3	4.4653	2.0514	7	2.5816	1.2644	4
PASSAGE 4	4.2770	1.7342	6	2.8295	1.2352	4
PASSAGE 5	2.2022	1.3318	4	2.2022	1.3318	4

The third G-study was on the effects of items and subtests on the dependability of SWE Test scores. Thus descriptive statistics are given for the whole SWE Test and each of the two sections which contributes to the SWE Test scores: SWE1 and SWE2. Notice that the original SWE Test had a total of 38 items and that the original SWE1 and SWE2 sections had 14 and 24 items, respectively. In order to create a balanced design, 14 items were randomly selected from the SWE2 section to match the existing 14 items in the SWE1 section. As a result, in the third G-study, the two sections were analyzed as 14 item subtests with a SWE Test total of 28 items.

The fourth G-study was on the effects of items and subtests on the dependability of VRC Test scores. Thus descriptive statistics are given for the whole VRC Test and each of the two sections which contributes to the VRC Test scores: Vocabulary and Reading Comprehension. Notice that the original VRC Test had a total of 58 items and, since each of the sections had 29 items, it was already balanced. Thus no modifications were necessary in preparing it for the fourth G-study.

The fifth G-study was on the effects of items and passages within the Reading Comprehension section (VRC2) on the dependability of VRC2 section scores. Thus descriptive statistics are given for the whole VRC2 section and the items associated with each of the passages which contributes to the VRC2 section scores: Passages 1 to 5. Notice that the original VRC2 section had a total of 29 items and that the original passages had 7, 5, 7, 6, and 4 items associated with them, respectively. In order to create a balanced design, the passages with larger numbers of items had to have the number of items reduced to match the shortest passage (i.e., Passage 5 with four items). To achieve this, four items were randomly selected from those associated with each of the larger passages. As a result, in the fifth G-study, all five passages were analyzed as four item sections with a VRC2 section total of 20 items.

Classical theory reliability

Classical theory reliability estimates are presented in Table 2. For ease of interpretation, Table 2 is organized in the same general manner as Table 1. The first classical theory reliability estimate given is the split-half correlation adjusted by the Spearman-Brown prophecy formula. Then the Guttman reliability is given followed by the Cronbach alpha coefficient. Notice that the first two estimates are consistently lower than the Cronbach alpha coefficients. Since theory indicates that the first two are more likely to be underestimates, the single best estimate is the Cronbach alpha. These estimates are given for the original tests and the G-study samplings (along with the numbers of items, or k) so that the effect of the reductions in test length on classical theory reliability can readily be seen.

Table 2

Classical theory reliahility statistics

STUDY BATTERY TEST SUBTEST PASSAGE	ORIGINAL TEST				G-STUDY SAMPLING			
	S–H	Guttman	Alpha	*k*	S–H	Guttman	Alpha	*k*
STUDY ONE								
TOTAL TOEFL	.8927	.8916	.9667	146	.8896	.8881	.9584	114
LC TEST	.8978	.8978	.9178	50	.8789	.8788	.8964	38
SWE TEST	.8752	.8652	.9016	38	.8752	.8652	.9016	38
VRC TEST	.8808	.8806	.9326	58	.8617	.8616	.9033	38
STUDY TWO								
LC TEST	.8978	.8978	.9178	50	.8941	.8930	.9077	45
LC1	.8209	.8209	.8349	20	.7706	.7669	.7845	15
LC2	.7541	.7512	.7618	15	.7541	.7512	.7618	15
LC3	.7457	.7437	.7677	15	.7457	.7437	.7677	15
STUDY THREE								
SWE TEST	.8752	.8652	.9016	38	.8520	.8513	.8686	28
SWE 1	.7565	.7478	.7726	14	.7565	.7478	.7726	14
SWE 2	.8263	.8113	.8574	24	.7466	.7370	.7723	14
STUDY FOUR								
VRC TEST	.8808	.8806	.9326	58	.8808	.8806	.9326	58
VRC 1	.8749	.8745	.8854	29	.8749	.8745	.8854	29
VRC 2	.8106	.8028	.8769	29	.8106	.8028	.8769	29
STUDY FIVE								
VRC 2	.8106	.8028	.8769	29	.7654	.7552	.8280	20
PASSAGE 1	.6232	.6101	.6124	7	.4735	.4684	.4542	4
PASSAGE 2	.5837	.5696	.5715	5	.5219	.5199	.5061	4
PASSAGE 3	.7205	.7100	.7323	7	.5903	.5903	.5910	4
PASSAGE 4	.7191	.7187	.7181	6	.6149	.6148	.6190	4
PASSAGE 5	.5823	.5822	.5964	4	.5823	.5822	.5964	4

Variance Components

Based on ANOVA procedures, G theory allowed for estimation of the relative contributions of persons, items, and subtests in terms of variance components. For example, for the first G-study of the Total TOEFL battery, which was a p x (i:s) design (like all of the others), the ANOVA results are shown in Table 3.

Table 3

G-study one – Total TOEFL battery

Source	SS	df	MS		EMS	Variance components
p	80306.73	199991	4.01553728	=	$\sigma^2\,(pi{:}s) + n_i\sigma^2\,(ps) + n_in_s\sigma^2\,(p)$	.03140424
s	4200.90	2	2100.45000000	=	$\sigma^2\,(pi{:}s) + n_i\sigma^2\,(ps) + n_p\sigma^2\,(i{:}s) + n_pn_i\sigma^2\,(s)$	.00247421
i:s	24395.20	111	219.77657658	=	$\sigma^2\,(pi{:}s) + n_p\sigma^2\,(i{:}s)$	.01098074
ps	17417.30	39998	0.43545427	=	$\sigma^2\,(pi{:}s) + n_i\sigma^2\,(ps)$	.00720131
pi:s	359188.37	2219889	0.16180465	=	$s^2\,(pi{:}s)$	.16180465

Based on the variance components that make up the estimated mean squares (*EMS*) as shown in Brennan (1983) or Kirk (1968), the variance components for persons as well as for the items and subtests facets were isolated from the observed mean squares (*MS*). The *EMS* shown in Table 3 were used systematically to derive the variance components in a step-by-step manner. First, because the estimated variance component for the interaction of persons and items nested within subtests, or $\sigma^2\,(pi{:}s)$, is equal to the *MS(pi:s)* for that interaction, .16180465 in this case, that variance component is easy to isolate. Formulaically, this process can be summarized as follows:

$$\sigma^2\,(pi{:}s) = MS(pi{:}s)$$

Second, because, as is shown in Table 3, it is known that the *EMS* for the *ps* interaction = $s^2\,(pi{:}s) + s^2\,(ps)$, the estimated variance component for this interaction, $s^2\,(ps)$, could be isolated by subtracting the *MS(pi:s)* from the *MS(ps)*, and dividing the result by the number of items, n_i, in each subtest (i.e., [.43545427 –.16180465]/38 in this case). Formulaically:

$$\sigma^2\,(ps) = [MS(ps) - MS(pi{:}s)]/n_i$$

Third, fourth, and fifth, using the known mathematical relationships shown in Table 3, the other three variance components in this design could then be calculated by using the following formulas:

$$\sigma^2\,(p) = [MS(p) - MS(ps)]/n_in_s$$
$$\sigma^2\,(i{:}s) = [MS(i{:}s) - MS(pi{:}s)]/n_p$$
$$\sigma^2\,(s) = [MS(s) - MS(i{:}s) - MS(ps) + MS\,(pi{:}s)]/n_pn_i$$

Note that the calculations in this example were based on MS values that have been rounded to eight places. Because the resulting variance components are often very small values, it was essential that nothing be rounded any more than was necessary until the final result was obtained.

Table 4

Variance components for five G-studies

	Variance components for				
	STUDY ONE:	STUDY: TWO:	STUDY THREE:	STUDY FOUR:	STUDY FIVE:
SOURCE	TOTAL TOEFL	LC TEST	SWE TEST	VRC TEST	VRC2 TEST
RAW COMPONENTS					
p	.03140424	.04055400	.03517126	.03614178	.03699441
s	.00237421	.00000000*	.00028243	.00060287	.00710587
i:s	.01098074	.01178236	.00924644	.01189282	.00762986
ps	.00720131	.00136198	.00148391	.00327638	.01234403
pi:s	.16180465	.18380686	.15119135	.15613306	.15143681
Total	.21386515	.23750520	.19737539	.20804691	.21551098

*This value was a negative variance component, which was rounded to zero after Brennan (1983: 47–8).

The variance components for each of the G-studies in this project (all calculated in similar manner) are shown in Table 4. Notice that the five G-studies are labeled across the top as columns and that the sources of variance (p, s, i:s, ps, and pi:s) are labeled at the left as rows. The totals in the last row represent the sums of the variance components isolated in each study.

D-Study results and generalizability coefficients

Summaries of the statistics found in the five D-studies are presented in Table 5. Notice that each D-study is presented in a separate column as labeled across the top of the table. The rows represent each of the statistics. First, the number of subtests (n_s) is given, then the number of items per subtest (n_i), then the total number of items (when the number of subtests is multiplied times the number of items per subtest). Then the estimated variance components (adjusted for the number of items and subtests in the particular D-study) are given for p, s, $i:s$, and their interactions. Notice that the variance components for p are the same as those reported in Table 4, while the variance components for s, $i:s$, and their interactions are different in the two tables because those in Table 5 have been adjusted for the numbers of items or subtests in the particular D-study design (after Brennan 1983). In the next row, the mean proportion scores $(\bar{x}_p)$ are given. These means are simply the average of each person's proportion score, which is calculated by dividing the number of correct responses by the number of items (but not moving the decimal two places to the right as would be done in calculating a per cent score).

Next, statistics are given for a random effects model. The random effects model estimates allow generalization of the results to other tests as discussed above. The statistics for this model include $\sigma^2(\tau)$, which is just another expression of $\sigma^2(p)$. The lower-case delta error term, $\sigma^2(\delta)$, (for relative decisions, i.e., norm-referenced interpretations) and the upper-case delta error term, $\sigma^2(\Delta)$ (for absolute decisions, i.e., criterion-referenced or domain referenced interpretations) are also given. Then the expected observed score variance, $E\sigma^2(X)$, and error variance associated with the grand mean, $\sigma^2(\bar{X})$, are presented. All of these statistics were used in calculating the generalizability coefficients for lower-case delta (norm-referenced) error, $E\rho^2(\delta)$, in the *S/N* ratios reported in this table, or in the phi(lambda) coefficients reported in the next section.

The G-coefficients, $E\rho^2(\delta)$, that are presented in Table 5 are analogous in interpretation to reliability coefficients. They are calculated by forming a ratio of the person's variance component for the particular number of subtests and items in the G-study over the same person's variance plus the appropriate error term. Thus G-coefficients for relative decisions would use δ error as follows:

$$E\rho^2(\delta) = \frac{\sigma^2(\tau)}{\sigma^2(\tau) + \sigma^2(\delta)} = \frac{\sigma^2(p)}{\sigma^2(p) + \sigma^2(\delta)}$$

Similarly, G-coefficients for absolute decisions would use D error as follows:

$$E\rho^2(\Delta) = \frac{\sigma^2(\tau)}{\sigma^2(\tau) + \sigma^2(\Delta)} = \frac{\sigma^2(p)}{\sigma^2(p) + \sigma^2(\Delta)}$$

The last statistic presented in the Random Effects part of Table 5 is the signal to noise ratio (S/N). This statistic can be interpreted as the ratio of systematic variance to random error (Brennan and Kane 1977), or, as Cronbach and Gleser (1964: 468) put it in an earlier discussion of communications systems, the 'signal to noise ratio compares the strength of the transmission to the strength of the interference.'

At the bottom of the table, the same statistics are presented for a mixed effects model (with subtests as a fixed effect). These results can only be generalized to the TOEFL battery as it was structured and studied here.

Notice that, as would be expected, the generalizability (or G) coefficients $E\rho^2$ (δ) for the mixed model are very similar to the Cronbach alpha values reported in Table 2 for the G-study sampling (.9584, .9077, .8686, .9326, and .8280,

Table 5

D-study results for

STUDY MODEL Statistic	STUDY ONE: TOTAL TOEFL	STUDY TWO: LC TEST	STUDY THREE: SWE TEST	STUDY FOUR: VRC TEST	STUDY FIVE: VRC2 SECTION
n_s	3	3	2	2	5
n_i	38	15	14	29	4
$n_i n_s$	114	45	28	58	20
$\sigma^2 (p)$	.0314	.0406	.0352	.0361	.0370
$\sigma^2 (s)$	.0008	.0000	.0001	.0003	.0014
$\sigma^2 (i{:}s)$	.0001	.0003	.0003	.0002	.0004
$\sigma^2 (ps)$	.0024	.0005	.0007	.0016	.0025
$\sigma^2 (pi{:}s)$	.0014	.0041	.0054	.0027	.0076
$(\bar{X}_p)$	.6927	.6160	.7304	.7062	.6905
RANDOM EFFECTS MODEL					
$\sigma^2 (\tau)$	.0314	.0406	.0352	.0361	.0370
$\sigma^2 (\delta)$	.0038	.0045	.0061	.0043	.0100
$\sigma^2 (\Delta)$	.0047	.0048	.0066	.0048	.0118
$E\sigma^2(X)$	.0352	.0451	.0413	.0405	.0470
$\sigma^2 (\bar{X}_p)$	.0009	.0003	.0005	.0005	.0018
$E\rho^2 (\delta)$	.8916	.8993	.8513	.8930	.7865
S/N	8.2251	8.9305	5.7249	8.3458	3.6838
MIXED EFFECTS MODEL					
$\sigma^2 (\tau)$	.0338	.0410	.0359	.0378	.0395
$\sigma^2 (\delta)$	.0014	.0041	.0054	.0027	.0076
$\sigma^2 (\Delta)$	.0015	.0043	.0057	.0029	.0080
$E\sigma^2(X)$	.0352	.0451	.0413	.0405	.0470
$\sigma^2(\bar{X}_p)$	.0001	.0003	.0003	.0002	.0004
$E\rho^2(\delta)$	.9597	.9094	.8693	.9335	.8390
S/N	23.8139	10.0375	6.6511	14.0376	5.2112

respectively). In addition, probably because of differences in numbers of items, these G-coefficients are slightly lower than the corresponding Cronbach alpha values reported in Table 2 for the original test (.9667, .9178, .9016, .9326, and .8769, respectively).

Naturally, the G-coefficients for the random effects model are more conservative than those for the mixed model because the random effects statistics can be generalized beyond the items and subtests of the current TOEFL to other batteries and tests. Tables 6 to 10 were created by expanding this random effects G-coefficient information. Each of these tables corresponds to one of the D-studies in this project and gives the coefficients that would arise from different numbers of items and subtests.

For instance, Table 6 is for the Total TOEFL battery and shows that the G-coefficient for three subtests with 38 items each (see the point where the 38th row and third column of coefficients intersect) is .892, which is equivalent (though rounded) to the random effects model G-coefficient of .8916 reported in Table 5. Notice in the bottom left corner of the table that the battery configured with the same 114 items but in one subtest instead of three is estimated to be dependable at .785, with two subtests of 57 (total 114), it is predicted to be .862 and, with three subtests of 38 (as shown at the top of this paragraph), it would be .892. Thus the effects of having the items divided up into smaller and smaller subtests are demonstrated.

Clearly, there is considerable dependability gained from having the TOEFL battery made up of three different subtests rather than of one long, homogeneous test. In other words, there is an increase in dependability due to increases in the number of subtests involved while holding the number of items constant. Moreover, these increases are above and beyond predictions that could be made by using formulas like the Spearman-Brown prophecy formula used in classical theory reliability studies.

Table 6 also allows for considering other potential combinations of numbers of items and subtests as part of the D-study to help in deciding what is the optimal number of items and subtests to include in future versions of this and other tests. For instance, by looking at the point where six subtests intersect with 19 items (also for a total of 114 items), the table reveals that a G-coefficient of .923 is predicted.

However, for actual policy decisions, factors other than dependability must come into play. For instance, 100 tests with seven items each are predicted to be dependable at .99, but such a 700 item test is not practical even though the dependability would be near perfect. Thus these dependability estimates for various numbers of items and subtests are meant to provide one piece of information among the many types of information that must be considered in making test development decisions.

Turning to Table 7 for the LC Test, notice that a single 45 item test would be

Table 6

Generalizability coefficients for the Total TOEFL

Items	1	2	3	4	5	6	7	8	9	10	11	12	13	14	15	16	17	18	19	20	30	40	50	60	70	80	90	100
1	.157	.271	.358	.426	.482	.527	.565	.598	.626	.650	.671	.690	.707	.722	.736	.748	.760	.770	.779	.788	.848	.881	.903	.918	.929	.937	.944	.949
2	.263	.416	.517	.588	.641	.681	.714	.740	.762	.781	.797	.811	.823	.833	.842	.851	.858	.865	.871	.877	.914	.934	.947	.955	.961	.966	.970	.973
3	.339	.507	.606	.673	.720	.755	.782	.804	.822	.837	.850	.860	.870	.878	.885	.892	.897	.902	.907	.911	.939	.954	.963	.969	.973	.976	.979	.981
4	.397	.569	.664	.725	.767	.798	.822	.841	.856	.868	.879	.888	.895	.902	.908	.913	.918	.922	.926	.929	.952	.963	.971	.975	.979	.981	.983	.985
5	.443	.614	.704	.760	.799	.826	.847	.864	.877	.888	.897	.905	.912	.917	.923	.927	.931	.935	.938	.941	.960	.969	.975	.979	.982	.984	.986	.988
6	.479	.648	.734	.786	.821	.846	.865	.880	.892	.902	.910	.917	.923	.928	.932	.936	.940	.943	.946	.948	.965	.974	.979	.982	.985	.987	.988	.989
7	.509	.674	.757	.806	.838	.861	.879	.892	.903	.912	.919	.926	.931	.935	.940	.943	.946	.949	.952	.954	.969	.976	.981	.984	.986	.988	.989	.990
8	.534	.696	.775	.821	.851	.873	.889	.902	.912	.920	.926	.932	.937	.941	.945	.948	.951	.954	.956	.958	.972	.979	.983	.986	.988	.989	.990	.991
9	.555	.714	.789	.833	.862	.882	.897	.909	.918	.926	.932	.937	.942	.946	.949	.952	.955	.957	.960	.961	.974	.980	.984	.987	.989	.990	.991	.992
10	.573	.729	.801	.843	.870	.890	.904	.915	.924	.931	.937	.942	.946	.950	.953	.956	.958	.960	.962	.964	.976	.982	.985	.988	.989	.991	.992	.993
11	.589	.741	.811	.851	.878	.896	.909	.920	.928	.935	.940	.945	.949	.953	.956	.958	.961	.963	.965	.966	.977	.983	.986	.989	.990	.991	.992	.993
12	.603	.752	.820	.859	.884	.901	.914	.924	.932	.938	.944	.948	.952	.955	.958	.960	.963	.965	.966	.968	.979	.984	.987	.989	.991	.992	.993	.993
13	.615	.762	.827	.865	.889	.906	.918	.927	.935	.941	.946	.950	.954	.957	.960	.962	.965	.966	.968	.970	.980	.985	.988	.990	.991	.992	.993	.994
14	.626	.770	.834	.870	.893	.909	.921	.931	.938	.944	.948	.953	.956	.959	.962	.964	.966	.968	.970	.971	.980	.985	.988	.990	.992	.993	.993	.994
15	.636	.777	.840	.875	.897	.913	.924	.933	.940	.946	.951	.954	.958	.961	.963	.965	.967	.969	.971	.972	.981	.986	.989	.991	.992	.993	.994	.994
16	.645	.784	.845	.879	.901	.916	.927	.936	.942	.948	.952	.956	.959	.962	.965	.967	.969	.970	.972	.973	.982	.986	.989	.991	.992	.993	.994	.995
17	.653	.790	.849	.883	.904	.919	.929	.938	.944	.949	.954	.958	.961	.963	.966	.968	.970	.971	.973	.974	.983	.987	.989	.991	.992	.993	.994	.995
18	.660	.795	.853	.886	.907	.921	.931	.939	.946	.951	.955	.959	.962	.964	.967	.969	.971	.972	.974	.975	.983	.987	.990	.991	.993	.994	.994	.995
19	.666	.800	.857	.889	.909	.923	.933	.941	.947	.952	.956	.960	.963	.965	.968	.970	.971	.973	.974	.976	.984	.988	.990	.992	.993	.994	.994	.995

Table 6 continued

20	.673	.804	.860	.891	.911	.925	.935	.943	.949	.954	.958	.961	.964	.966	.969	.970	.972	.974	.975	.976	.984	.988	.990	.992	.993	.994	.995	.995
21	.678	.808	.863	.894	.913	.927	.936	.944	.950	.955	.959	.962	.965	.967	.969	.971	.973	.974	.976	.977	.984	.988	.991	.992	.993	.994	.995	.995
22	.683	.812	.866	.896	.915	.928	.938	.945	.951	.956	.960	.963	.966	.968	.970	.972	.973	.975	.976	.977	.985	.989	.991	.992	.993	.994	.995	.995
23	.688	.815	.869	.898	.917	.930	.939	.946	.952	.957	.960	.964	.966	.969	.971	.972	.974	.975	.977	.978	.985	.989	.991	.993	.994	.994	.995	.995
24	.693	.818	.871	.900	.918	.931	.940	.947	.953	.957	.961	.964	.967	.969	.971	.973	.975	.976	.977	.978	.985	.989	.991	.993	.994	.994	.995	.996
25	.697	.821	.873	.902	.920	.932	.941	.948	.954	.958	.962	.965	.968	.970	.972	.974	.975	.976	.978	.979	.986	.989	.991	.993	.994	.995	.995	.996
26	.701	.824	.875	.903	.921	.933	.942	.949	.955	.959	.963	.966	.968	.970	.972	.974	.975	.977	.978	.979	.986	.989	.992	.993	.994	.995	.995	.996
27	.704	.826	.877	.905	.922	.935	.943	.950	.955	.960	.963	.966	.969	.971	.973	.974	.976	.977	.978	.979	.986	.990	.992	.993	.994	.995	.995	.996
28	.708	.829	.879	.906	.924	.936	.944	.951	.956	.960	.964	.967	.969	.971	.973	.975	.976	.978	.979	.980	.986	.990	.992	.993	.994	.995	.995	.996
29	.711	.831	.881	.908	.925	.936	.945	.952	.957	.961	.964	.967	.970	.972	.974	.975	.977	.978	.979	.980	.987	.990	.992	.993	.994	.995	.995	.996
30	.714	.833	.882	.909	.926	.937	.946	.952	.957	.961	.965	.968	.970	.972	.974	.976	.977	.978	.979	.980	.987	.990	.992	.993	.994	.995	.996	.996
38	.733	.846	.892	.916	.932	.943	.950	.956	.961	.965	.968	.970	.973	.975	.976	.978	.979	.980	.981	.982	.988	.991	.993	.994	.995	.995	.996	.996
40	.736	.848	.893	.918	.933	.944	.951	.957	.962	.965	.968	.971	.973	.975	.977	.978	.979	.980	.982	.982	.988	.991	.993	.994	.995	.996	.996	.996
50	.751	.858	.900	.923	.938	.948	.955	.960	.964	.968	.971	.973	.975	.977	.978	.980	.981	.982	.983	.984	.989	.992	.993	.994	.995	.996	.996	.996
57	.758	.862	.904	.926	.940	.949	.956	.962	.966	.969	.972	.974	.976	.978	.980	.980	.982	.983	.984	.984	.989	.992	.994	.995	.995	.996	.996	.997
60	.760	.864	.905	.927	.941	.950	.957	.962	.966	.969	.972	.974	.976	.978	.979	.981	.982	.983	.984	.984	.990	.992	.994	.995	.995	.996	.997	.997
70	.768	.868	.908	.930	.943	.952	.959	.964	.967	.971	.973	.975	.977	.979	.980	.981	.982	.983	.984	.985	.990	.992	.994	.995	.996	.996	.997	.997
80	.773	.872	.911	.932	.945	.953	.960	.965	.968	.971	.974	.976	.978	.979	.981	.982	.983	.984	.985	.986	.990	.993	.994	.995	.996	.996	.997	.997
90	.777	.875	.913	.933	.946	.954	.961	.965	.969	.972	.975	.977	.978	.980	.981	.982	.983	.984	.985	.986	.991	.993	.994	.995	.996	.996	.997	.997
100	.781	.877	.914	.934	.947	.955	.961	.966	.970	.973	.975	.977	.979	.980	.982	.983	.984	.985	.985	.986	.991	.993	.994	.995	.996	.996	.997	.997
114	.785	.879	.916	.936	.948	.956	.962	.967	.970	.973	.976	.978	.979	.981	.982	.983	.984	.985	.986	.986	.991	.993	.995	.995	.996	.996	.997	.997

Table 7

Generalizability coefficients for the LSC Test

Items	1	2	3	4	5	6	7	8	9	10	11	12	13	14	15	16	17	18	19	20	30	40	50	60	70	80	90	100
1	.180	.305	.397	.467	.523	.568	.605	.637	.663	.687	.707	.724	.740	.754	.767	.778	.788	.798	.806	.814	.868	.898	.916	.929	.939	.946	.952	.956
2	.303	.465	.566	.635	.685	.723	.753	.777	.796	.813	.827	.839	.850	.859	.867	.874	.881	.887	.892	.897	.929	.946	.956	.963	.968	.972	.975	.978
3	.393	.564	.660	.721	.764	.795	.819	.838	.854	.866	.877	.886	.894	.901	.907	.912	.917	.921	.925	.928	.951	.963	.970	.975	.978	.981	.983	.985
4	.462	.632	.720	.774	.811	.837	.857	.873	.885	.896	.904	.911	.918	.923	.928	.932	.936	.939	.942	.945	.963	.972	.977	.981	.984	.986	.987	.988
5	.515	.680	.761	.810	.842	.865	.882	.895	.905	.914	.921	.927	.933	.937	.941	.945	.948	.950	.953	.955	.970	.977	.982	.985	.987	.988	.990	.991
6	.559	.717	.792	.835	.864	.884	.899	.910	.919	.927	.933	.938	.943	.947	.950	.953	.956	.958	.960	.962	.974	.981	.984	.987	.989	.990	.991	.992
7	.595	.746	.815	.855	.880	.898	.911	.922	.930	.936	.942	.946	.950	.954	.957	.959	.961	.964	.965	.967	.978	.983	.987	.989	.990	.992	.992	.993
8	.625	.769	.833	.870	.893	.909	.921	.930	.937	.943	.948	.952	.956	.959	.962	.964	.966	.968	.969	.971	.980	.985	.988	.990	.991	.993	.993	.994
9	.651	.788	.848	.882	.903	.918	.929	.937	.944	.949	.953	.957	.960	.963	.965	.968	.969	.971	.973	.974	.982	.987	.989	.991	.992	.993	.994	.995
10	.673	.804	.860	.891	.911	.925	.935	.943	.949	.954	.958	.961	.964	.966	.969	.970	.972	.974	.975	.976	.984	.988	.990	.992	.993	.994	.995	.995
11	.692	.818	.871	.900	.918	.931	.940	.947	.953	.957	.961	.964	.967	.969	.971	.973	.974	.976	.977	.978	.985	.989	.991	.993	.994	.994	.995	.996
12	.709	.829	.879	.907	.924	.936	.945	.951	.956	.960	.964	.967	.969	.971	.973	.975	.976	.978	.979	.980	.986	.990	.992	.993	.994	.995	.995	.996
13	.723	.840	.887	.913	.929	.940	.948	.954	.959	.963	.966	.969	.971	.973	.975	.977	.978	.979	.980	.981	.987	.991	.992	.994	.995	.995	.996	.996
14	.737	.848	.894	.918	.933	.944	.951	.957	.962	.966	.969	.971	.973	.975	.977	.978	.979	.981	.982	.982	.988	.991	.993	.994	.995	.996	.996	.996
15	.749	.856	.899	.923	.937	.947	.954	.960	.964	.968	.970	.973	.975	.977	.978	.979	.981	.982	.983	.983	.989	.992	.993	.994	.995	.996	.996	.997
16	.759	.863	.904	.927	.940	.950	.957	.962	.966	.969	.972	.974	.976	.978	.979	.981	.982	.983	.984	.984	.990	.992	.994	.995	.995	.996	.996	.997
17	.769	.869	.909	.930	.943	.952	.959	.964	.968	.971	.973	.976	.977	.979	.980	.981	.983	.984	.984	.985	.990	.993	.994	.995	.996	.996	.997	.997
18	.778	.875	.913	.933	.946	.955	.961	.966	.969	.972	.975	.977	.979	.980	.981	.982	.983	.984	.985	.986	.991	.993	.994	.995	.996	.996	.997	.997
19	.786	.880	.917	.936	.948	.957	.963	.967	.971	.974	.976	.978	.979	.981	.982	.983	.984	.985	.986	.987	.991	.993	.995	.995	.996	.997	.997	.997
20	.794	.885	.920	.939	.951	.958	.964	.968	.972	.975	.977	.979	.980	.982	.983	.984	.985	.986	.986	.987	.991	.994	.995	.996	.996	.997	.997	.997

Table 7 continued

21	.800	.889	.923	.941	.952	.960	.966	.970	.973	.976	.978	.980	.981	.982	.984	.985	.986	.986	.987	.988	.992	.994	.995	.996	.996	.997	.997	.998
22	.807	.893	.926	.943	.954	.962	.967	.971	.974	.977	.979	.980	.982	.983	.984	.985	.986	.987	.988	.988	.992	.994	.995	.996	.996	.997	.997	.998
23	.813	.897	.929	.945	.956	.963	.968	.972	.975	.977	.979	.981	.983	.984	.985	.986	.987	.987	.988	.989	.992	.994	.995	.996	.996	.997	.997	.998
24	.818	.900	.931	.947	.957	.964	.969	.973	.976	.978	.980	.982	.983	.984	.985	.986	.986	.987	.988	.989	.992	.994	.996	.996	.997	.997	.997	.998
25	.823	.903	.933	.949	.959	.965	.970	.974	.977	.979	.981	.982	.984	.985	.986	.986	.987	.988	.988	.989	.993	.994	.996	.996	.997	.997	.998	.998
26	.828	.906	.935	.951	.960	.967	.971	.975	.978	.980	.982	.983	.985	.986	.986	.987	.988	.988	.989	.989	.993	.995	.996	.996	.997	.997	.998	.998
27	.832	.908	.937	.952	.961	.968	.972	.975	.978	.980	.982	.983	.985	.986	.987	.988	.988	.989	.989	.990	.993	.995	.996	.996	.997	.997	.998	.998
28	.837	.911	.939	.953	.962	.968	.973	.976	.979	.981	.983	.984	.985	.986	.987	.988	.988	.989	.990	.990	.993	.995	.996	.996	.997	.997	.998	.998
29	.840	.913	.940	.955	.963	.969	.974	.977	.979	.981	.983	.984	.986	.987	.987	.988	.989	.990	.990	.990	.994	.995	.996	.997	.997	.998	.998	.998
30	.844	.915	.942	.956	.964	.970	.974	.977	.980	.982	.983	.985	.986	.987	.988	.989	.989	.990	.990	.991	.994	.995	.996	.997	.997	.998	.998	.998
40	.872	.932	.953	.965	.971	.976	.979	.982	.984	.986	.987	.988	.989	.990	.990	.991	.992	.992	.993	.993	.995	.996	.997	.998	.998	.998	.998	.999
45	.882	.937	.957	.968	.974	.978	.981	.983	.985	.987	.988	.989	.990	.990	.991	.992	.992	.993	.993	.993	.996	.997	.997	.998	.998	.998	.999	.999
50	.889	.942	.960	.970	.976	.980	.983	.985	.986	.988	.989	.990	.991	.991	.992	.992	.993	.994	.994	.994	.997	.998	.998	.998	.998	.999	.999	.999
60	.902	.948	.965	.973	.979	.982	.985	.987	.988	.989	.990	.991	.992	.992	.993	.993	.994	.994	.995	.995	.997	.998	.998	.998	.999	.999	.999	.999
70	.910	.953	.968	.976	.981	.984	.986	.988	.989	.990	.991	.992	.993	.993	.994	.994	.995	.995	.995	.995	.998	.998	.998	.999	.999	.999	.999	.999
80	.917	.957	.971	.978	.982	.985	.988	.989	.990	.991	.992	.993	.994	.994	.994	.995	.995	.996	.997	.998	.998	.998	.998	.999	.999	.999	.999	.999
90	.923	.960	.973	.979	.983	.986	.988	.990	.991	.992	.993	.994	.994	.995	.995	.996	.996	.997	.998	.998	.999	.999	.999	.999	.999	.999	.999	.999
100	.927	.962	.974	.981	.984	.987	.989	.990	.991	.992	.993	.994	.995	.995	.996	.996	.996	.997	.997	.998	.998	.999	.999	.999	.999	.999	.999	.999

dependable at .882, while a similar 45 item test based on three subtests of 15 items each would only be slightly more dependable at .899, and a 45 item test based on five subtests of nine items each would only gain .004 points at .903. Thus the pay off in terms of gains in dependability due to increases in the number of subtests (while items are held constant) appears to be minimal for the LC Test.

Similarly, in Table 8 for the SWE Test, a 28 item test with only one subtest would be dependable at .836, while a similar 28 item test based on two subtests of 14 items each would only be slightly more dependable at .851, four subtests of seven items each would only be .859, seven subtests of four items each would only be .862, and fourteen subtests of two items each would be .865. In short, there is not nearly as much to gain by dividing the SWE Test into subtests – certainly not beyond two subtests – as there was in the Total TOEFL battery.

Table 9 for the VRC Test is somewhat different. The table seems to indicate that considerable dependability is gained by splitting the 58 items into two subtests, i.e., the one-subtest, 58 item dependability is .858, while the two subtests version (of 29 items each) dependability is considerably higher at .893. However, a three subtests version (of 20 items each) would only increase to .907 even though it is two items longer, and a four subtests version (of 15 items each) would only increase further to .914. Thus, like the SWE Test results, it appears that the present two subtest version of the VRC Test may include as many subtests as are necessary and practical.

Table 10 for the VRC2 section is more like the Total TOEFL in terms of the impact of subtests on dependability. For instance, the one subtest, 20 item dependability is .650, while the two subtest version (with 10 items each) is considerably higher at .729, and the four subtest version (with five items each) climbs to .776. Thus differences in the numbers of passages involved in VRC2 section appear to be relatively important to its overall dependability.

More D-study results: phi(lambda) dependability coefficients

Threshold loss agreement coefficients focus on the degree to which classifications in clear-cut categories have been consistent. Since it is known that such dependability may vary at different cut-points (Brennan 1980, 1984) and since TOEFL is widely used as an admissions tool for admit/no-admit decisions (though at different cut-points), one of the research questions in this study was the degree to which the dependability of TOEFL changes over the range of possible cut-points.

Table 11 gives the Phi(lambda), or $\phi(\lambda)$, coefficients for various cut-points (in percentage terms). In all cases, these coefficients are based on the p x i:s design and (Δ) error (as suggested by Brennan 1984) and are therefore more conservative than the (δ) error estimates would have been. Notice that such coefficients are reported for both random effects models and mixed models (with subtests as a fixed effects facet). In each set, the lowest value reported was that for a cut-point

Table 8

Generalizability coefficients for the SWE Test

Items	1	2	3	4	5	6	7	8	9	10	11	12	13	14	15	16	17	18	19	20	30	40	50	60	70	80	90	100
1	.187	.315	.409	.480	.535	.580	.617	.648	.675	.697	.717	.734	.750	.763	.776	.787	.797	.806	.814	.822	.874	.902	.920	.933	.942	.949	.954	.958
2	.313	.477	.578	.646	.695	.732	.762	.785	.804	.820	.834	.846	.856	.865	.873	.880	.886	.891	.897	.901	.932	.948	.958	.965	.970	.973	.976	.979
3	.404	.576	.670	.731	.772	.803	.826	.844	.859	.871	.882	.891	.898	.905	.910	.916	.920	.924	.928	.931	.953	.964	.971	.976	.979	.982	.984	.985
4	.472	.642	.729	.782	.817	.843	.862	.877	.890	.900	.908	.915	.921	.926	.931	.935	.938	.942	.944	.947	.964	.973	.978	.982	.984	.986	.988	.989
5	.526	.689	.769	.816	.847	.869	.886	.899	.909	.917	.924	.930	.935	.939	.943	.947	.950	.952	.955	.957	.971	.978	.982	.985	.987	.989	.990	.991
6	.569	.725	.798	.841	.868	.888	.902	.913	.922	.929	.935	.941	.945	.949	.952	.955	.957	.960	.962	.963	.975	.981	.985	.988	.989	.991	.992	.992
7	.604	.753	.821	.859	.884	.901	.914	.924	.932	.938	.944	.948	.952	.955	.958	.961	.963	.965	.967	.968	.979	.984	.987	.989	.991	.992	.993	.993
8	.633	.775	.838	.873	.896	.912	.924	.932	.939	.945	.950	.954	.957	.960	.963	.965	.967	.969	.970	.972	.981	.986	.989	.990	.992	.993	.994	.994
9	.658	.794	.852	.885	.906	.920	.931	.939	.945	.951	.955	.958	.962	.964	.967	.969	.970	.972	.973	.975	.983	.987	.990	.991	.993	.994	.994	.995
10	.679	.809	.864	.894	.914	.927	.937	.944	.950	.955	.959	.962	.965	.967	.969	.971	.973	.974	.976	.977	.985	.988	.991	.992	.993	.994	.995	.995
11	.698	.822	.874	.902	.920	.933	.942	.949	.954	.958	.962	.965	.968	.970	.972	.974	.975	.977	.978	.979	.986	.989	.991	.993	.994	.995	.995	.996
12	.714	.833	.882	.909	.926	.937	.946	.952	.957	.961	.965	.968	.970	.972	.974	.976	.977	.978	.979	.980	.987	.990	.992	.993	.994	.995	.996	.996
13	.728	.843	.889	.915	.931	.941	.949	.955	.960	.964	.967	.970	.972	.974	.976	.977	.979	.980	.981	.982	.988	.991	.993	.994	.995	.995	.996	.996
14	.741	.851	.896	.920	.935	.945	.952	.958	.963	.966	.969	.972	.974	.976	.977	.979	.980	.981	.982	.983	.988	.991	.993	.994	.995	.996	.996	.996
15	.753	.859	.901	.924	.938	.948	.955	.961	.965	.968	.971	.973	.975	.977	.979	.980	.981	.982	.983	.984	.989	.992	.993	.995	.995	.996	.996	.997
16	.763	.865	.906	.928	.941	.951	.957	.963	.967	.970	.973	.975	.977	.978	.980	.981	.982	.983	.984	.985	.990	.992	.994	.995	.995	.996	.996	.997
17	.772	.871	.910	.931	.944	.953	.960	.964	.968	.971	.974	.976	.978	.979	.981	.982	.983	.984	.985	.985	.990	.993	.994	.995	.996	.996	.997	.997
18	.781	.877	.914	.934	.947	.955	.961	.966	.970	.973	.975	.977	.979	.980	.982	.983	.984	.985	.985	.986	.991	.993	.994	.995	.996	.996	.997	.997
19	.788	.882	.918	.937	.949	.957	.963	.968	.971	.974	.976	.978	.980	.981	.982	.983	.984	.985	.986	.987	.991	.993	.995	.996	.996	.997	.997	.997
20	.795	.886	.921	.940	.951	.959	.965	.969	.972	.975	.977	.979	.980	.982	.983	.984	.985	.986	.987	.987	.992	.994	.995	.996	.996	.997	.997	.997

Table 8 continued

21	.802	.890	.924	.942	.953	.960	.966	.970	.973	.976	.978	.980	.981	.983	.984	.985	.986	.987	.988	.992	.994	.995	.996	.996	.997	.997	.998
22	.808	.894	.927	.944	.955	.962	.967	.971	.974	.977	.979	.981	.982	.983	.984	.985	.986	.988	.988	.992	.994	.995	.996	.996	.997	.997	.998
23	.814	.897	.929	.946	.956	.963	.968	.972	.975	.978	.980	.981	.983	.984	.985	.986	.987	.988	.989	.992	.994	.995	.996	.997	.997	.998	.998
24	.819	.900	.931	.948	.958	.964	.969	.973	.976	.978	.980	.982	.983	.984	.985	.986	.988	.988	.989	.993	.994	.996	.996	.997	.997	.998	.998
25	.824	.903	.933	.949	.959	.966	.970	.974	.977	.979	.981	.982	.984	.985	.986	.987	.988	.989	.989	.993	.995	.996	.996	.997	.997	.998	.998
26	.828	.906	.935	.951	.960	.967	.971	.975	.977	.980	.981	.983	.984	.985	.986	.988	.988	.989	.989	.993	.995	.996	.997	.997	.997	.998	.998
27	.832	.909	.937	.952	.961	.968	.972	.975	.978	.980	.982	.983	.985	.986	.987	.988	.988	.990	.990	.993	.995	.996	.997	.997	.997	.998	.998
28	.836	.911	.939	.953	.962	.968	.973	.976	.979	.981	.983	.984	.985	.987	.987	.988	.989	.990	.990	.994	.995	.996	.997	.997	.997	.998	.998
29	.840	.913	.940	.955	.963	.969	.974	.977	.979	.981	.983	.984	.986	.987	.987	.989	.990	.990	.991	.994	.995	.996	.997	.997	.998	.998	.998
30	.844	.915	.942	.956	.964	.970	.974	.977	.980	.982	.983	.985	.986	.987	.988	.989	.990	.990	.991	.994	.995	.996	.997	.997	.998	.998	.998
40	.870	.930	.952	.964	.971	.976	.979	.982	.984	.985	.987	.988	.989	.990	.990	.991	.992	.992	.993	.995	.996	.997	.998	.998	.998	.998	.999
50	.886	.940	.959	.969	.975	.979	.982	.984	.987	.988	.988	.989	.990	.991	.992	.992	.993	.993	.994	.996	.997	.997	.998	.998	.998	.999	.999
60	.898	.946	.963	.972	.978	.981	.984	.986	.988	.989	.990	.991	.991	.992	.992	.993	.994	.994	.994	.996	.997	.998	.998	.998	.999	.999	.999
70	.906	.951	.967	.975	.980	.983	.985	.987	.989	.990	.991	.991	.992	.992	.993	.994	.994	.995	.995	.997	.997	.998	.998	.999	.999	.999	.999
80	.912	.954	.969	.977	.981	.984	.986	.988	.990	.990	.991	.992	.993	.993	.994	.994	.995	.995	.995	.997	.998	.998	.999	.999	.999	.999	.999
90	.917	.957	.971	.978	.982	.985	.987	.989	.990	.991	.992	.993	.993	.994	.994	.995	.995	.995	.996	.997	.998	.998	.999	.999	.999	.999	.999
100	.922	.959	.972	.979	.983	.986	.988	.989	.991	.992	.992	.993	.994	.994	.994	.995	.995	.996	.996	.997	.998	.998	.999	.999	.999	.999	.999

Table 9

Generalizability coefficients for the RCV Test

Items	1	2	3	4	5	6	7	8	9	10	11	12	13	14	15	16	17	18	19	20	30	40	50	60	70	80	90	100
1	.185	.312	.405	.476	.531	.576	.613	.645	.671	.694	.714	.731	.747	.760	.773	.784	.794	.803	.812	.819	.872	.901	.919	.932	.941	.948	.953	.958
2	.308	.471	.571	.640	.690	.727	.757	.780	.800	.816	.830	.842	.852	.862	.870	.877	.883	.889	.894	.899	.930	.947	.957	.964	.969	.973	.976	.978
3	.395	.566	.662	.723	.766	.797	.821	.839	.855	.867	.878	.887	.895	.901	.907	.913	.917	.922	.925	.929	.951	.963	.970	.975	.979	.981	.983	.985
4	.461	.631	.719	.774	.810	.837	.857	.872	.885	.895	.904	.911	.917	.923	.928	.932	.936	.939	.942	.945	.962	.972	.977	.981	.984	.986	.987	.988
5	.512	.677	.759	.807	.840	.863	.880	.893	.904	.913	.920	.926	.932	.936	.940	.944	.947	.950	.952	.954	.969	.977	.981	.984	.987	.988	.990	.991
6	.552	.712	.787	.831	.860	.881	.896	.908	.917	.925	.931	.937	.941	.945	.949	.952	.954	.957	.959	.961	.974	.980	.984	.987	.989	.990	.991	.992
7	.586	.739	.809	.850	.876	.894	.908	.919	.927	.934	.940	.944	.948	.952	.955	.958	.960	.962	.964	.966	.977	.983	.986	.988	.990	.991	.992	.993
8	.613	.760	.826	.864	.888	.905	.917	.927	.935	.941	.946	.950	.954	.957	.960	.962	.964	.966	.968	.969	.979	.984	.988	.990	.991	.992	.993	.994
9	.637	.778	.840	.875	.898	.913	.925	.933	.940	.946	.951	.955	.958	.961	.963	.966	.968	.969	.971	.972	.981	.986	.989	.991	.992	.993	.994	.994
10	.657	.793	.852	.884	.905	.920	.931	.939	.945	.950	.955	.958	.961	.964	.966	.968	.970	.972	.973	.975	.983	.987	.990	.991	.993	.994	.994	.995
11	.674	.805	.861	.892	.912	.925	.935	.943	.949	.954	.958	.961	.964	.967	.969	.971	.972	.974	.975	.976	.984	.988	.990	.992	.993	.994	.995	.995
12	.689	.816	.869	.899	.917	.930	.940	.947	.952	.957	.961	.964	.966	.969	.971	.973	.974	.976	.977	.978	.985	.989	.991	.993	.994	.994	.995	.996
13	.703	.825	.876	.904	.922	.934	.943	.950	.955	.959	.963	.966	.968	.971	.973	.974	.976	.977	.978	.979	.986	.990	.992	.993	.994	.995	.995	.996
14	.715	.834	.883	.909	.926	.938	.946	.952	.958	.962	.965	.968	.970	.972	.974	.976	.977	.978	.979	.980	.987	.990	.992	.993	.994	.995	.995	.996
15	.725	.841	.888	.914	.930	.941	.949	.955	.960	.964	.967	.969	.972	.974	.975	.977	.978	.979	.980	.981	.988	.991	.992	.994	.995	.995	.996	.996
16	.735	.847	.893	.917	.933	.943	.951	.957	.961	.965	.968	.971	.973	.975	.977	.978	.979	.980	.981	.982	.988	.991	.993	.994	.995	.995	.996	.996
17	.744	.853	.897	.921	.935	.946	.953	.959	.963	.967	.970	.972	.974	.976	.978	.979	.980	.981	.982	.983	.989	.991	.993	.994	.995	.995	.996	.997
18	.752	.858	.901	.924	.938	.948	.955	.960	.965	.968	.971	.973	.975	.977	.978	.980	.981	.982	.983	.984	.989	.992	.993	.995	.995	.996	.996	.997
19	.759	.863	.904	.926	.940	.950	.957	.962	.966	.969	.972	.974	.976	.978	.979	.981	.982	.983	.984	.984	.990	.992	.994	.995	.995	.996	.996	.997
20	.765	.867	.907	.929	.942	.951	.958	.963	.967	.970	.973	.975	.977	.979	.980	.981	.982	.983	.984	.985	.990	.992	.994	.995	.996	.996	.997	.997

Table 9 continued

21	.771	.871	.910	.931	.944	.953	.959	.964	.968	.971	.974	.976	.978	.979	.981	.982	.983	.984	.985	.990	.993	.994	.995	.996	.997
22	.777	.875	.913	.933	.946	.954	.961	.965	.969	.972	.975	.977	.978	.980	.981	.982	.983	.984	.986	.991	.993	.994	.995	.996	.997
23	.782	.878	.915	.935	.947	.956	.962	.966	.969	.973	.975	.977	.979	.980	.982	.983	.984	.985	.986	.991	.993	.994	.996	.996	.997
24	.787	.881	.917	.937	.949	.957	.963	.967	.971	.974	.976	.978	.980	.980	.982	.983	.984	.985	.986	.991	.993	.995	.996	.997	.997
25	.791	.884	.919	.938	.950	.958	.964	.968	.972	.974	.977	.979	.980	.981	.983	.984	.985	.986	.987	.991	.993	.995	.996	.997	.997
26	.796	.886	.921	.940	.951	.959	.965	.968	.972	.975	.977	.979	.981	.981	.983	.984	.985	.986	.987	.991	.994	.995	.996	.997	.997
27	.800	.889	.923	.941	.952	.960	.965	.969	.973	.976	.978	.980	.981	.982	.984	.985	.985	.986	.987	.992	.994	.995	.996	.997	.997
28	.803	.891	.925	.942	.953	.961	.966	.970	.974	.976	.978	.980	.982	.982	.984	.985	.986	.987	.988	.992	.994	.995	.996	.997	.997
29	.807	.893	.926	.943	.954	.962	.967	.970	.974	.977	.979	.980	.982	.983	.984	.985	.986	.987	.988	.992	.994	.995	.996	.997	.998
30	.810	.895	.927	.945	.955	.962	.968	.971	.975	.977	.979	.981	.982	.983	.985	.985	.986	.987	.988	.992	.994	.995	.996	.997	.998
40	.834	.910	.938	.953	.962	.968	.972	.976	.978	.981	.982	.984	.985	.986	.988	.988	.989	.990	.990	.993	.995	.996	.997	.997	.998
50	.850	.919	.944	.958	.966	.971	.975	.978	.981	.983	.984	.985	.987	.988	.989	.989	.990	.990	.991	.994	.996	.996	.997	.998	.998
58	.858	.924	.948	.960	.968	.973	.977	.980	.982	.984	.985	.986	.988	.989	.989	.990	.990	.991	.992	.995	.996	.997	.998	.998	.998
60	.860	.925	.949	.961	.968	.974	.977	.980	.982	.984	.985	.987	.988	.989	.990	.990	.991	.991	.992	.995	.996	.997	.998	.998	.998
70	.868	.929	.952	.963	.970	.975	.979	.981	.983	.985	.986	.987	.989	.990	.990	.991	.992	.992	.992	.996	.997	.997	.998	.998	.998
80	.874	.933	.954	.965	.972	.976	.980	.982	.984	.986	.987	.988	.989	.991	.992	.992	.992	.992	.993	.996	.997	.998	.998	.998	.999
90	.878	.935	.956	.966	.973	.977	.981	.983	.985	.986	.988	.989	.990	.991	.992	.992	.992	.993	.993	.997	.997	.997	.998	.998	.999
100	.882	.937	.957	.968	.974	.978	.981	.984	.985	.987	.988	.989	.990	.991	.992	.992	.993	.993	.993	.997	.997	.998	.999	.999	.999

Table 10

Generalizability coefficients for the VRC2R subtest

Items	1	2	3	4	5	6	7	8	9	10	11	12	13	14	15	16	17	18	19	20	30	40	50	60	70	80	90	100
1	.184	.311	.404	.475	.530	.575	.613	.644	.670	.693	.713	.730	.746	.760	.772	.783	.793	.803	.811	.819	.871	.900	.919	.931	.941	.948	.953	.958
2	.296	.457	.558	.627	.677	.716	.746	.771	.791	.808	.822	.834	.845	.855	.863	.870	.877	.883	.889	.894	.926	.944	.955	.962	.967	.971	.974	.977
3	.371	.541	.639	.702	.746	.779	.805	.825	.841	.855	.866	.876	.884	.892	.898	.904	.909	.914	.918	.922	.946	.959	.967	.972	.976	.979	.981	.983
4	.424	.596	.689	.747	.787	.816	.838	.855	.869	.881	.890	.898	.905	.912	.917	.922	.926	.930	.933	.936	.957	.967	.974	.978	.981	.983	.985	.987
5	.465	.634	.722	.776	.813	.839	.859	.874	.886	.897	.905	.912	.919	.924	.929	.933	.937	.940	.943	.946	.963	.972	.977	.981	.984	.986	.987	.989
6	.496	.663	.747	.797	.831	.855	.873	.887	.899	.908	.915	.922	.928	.932	.937	.940	.944	.947	.949	.952	.967	.975	.980	.983	.986	.987	.989	.990
7	.521	.685	.766	.813	.845	.867	.884	.897	.907	.916	.923	.929	.934	.938	.942	.946	.949	.951	.954	.956	.970	.978	.982	.985	.987	.989	.990	.991
8	.542	.703	.780	.826	.855	.877	.892	.904	.914	.922	.929	.934	.939	.943	.947	.950	.953	.955	.957	.959	.973	.979	.983	.986	.988	.990	.991	.992
9	.559	.717	.792	.835	.864	.884	.899	.910	.919	.927	.933	.938	.943	.947	.950	.953	.956	.958	.960	.962	.974	.981	.984	.987	.989	.990	.991	.992
10	.574	.729	.801	.843	.871	.890	.904	.915	.924	.931	.937	.942	.946	.950	.953	.956	.958	.960	.962	.964	.976	.982	.985	.988	.989	.991	.992	.993
11	.586	.739	.810	.850	.876	.895	.908	.919	.927	.934	.940	.944	.949	.952	.955	.958	.960	.962	.964	.966	.977	.983	.986	.988	.990	.991	.992	.993
12	.597	.748	.816	.856	.881	.899	.912	.922	.930	.937	.942	.947	.951	.954	.957	.960	.962	.964	.966	.967	.978	.983	.987	.989	.990	.992	.993	.993
13	.607	.755	.822	.860	.885	.902	.915	.925	.933	.939	.944	.949	.952	.956	.959	.961	.963	.965	.967	.969	.979	.984	.987	.989	.991	.992	.993	.994
14	.615	.762	.827	.865	.889	.906	.918	.927	.935	.941	.946	.950	.954	.957	.960	.962	.964	.966	.968	.970	.980	.985	.988	.990	.991	.992	.993	.994
15	.622	.767	.832	.868	.892	.908	.920	.930	.937	.943	.948	.952	.955	.958	.961	.963	.966	.967	.969	.971	.980	.985	.988	.990	.991	.992	.993	.994
16	.629	.772	.836	.872	.895	.911	.922	.931	.939	.944	.949	.953	.957	.960	.962	.964	.966	.968	.970	.971	.981	.985	.988	.990	.992	.992	.993	.994
17	.635	.777	.839	.874	.897	.913	.924	.933	.940	.946	.950	.954	.958	.961	.963	.965	.966	.969	.971	.972	.981	.986	.989	.991	.992	.993	.993	.994
18	.641	.781	.842	.877	.899	.914	.926	.934	.941	.947	.951	.955	.959	.961	.964	.966	.968	.970	.971	.973	.982	.986	.989	.991	.992	.993	.994	.994
19	.646	.785	.845	.879	.901	.916	.927	.936	.942	.948	.952	.956	.959	.962	.965	.967	.969	.970	.972	.973	.982	.986	.989	.991	.992	.993	.994	.995
20	.650	.788	.848	.881	.903	.918	.929	.937	.944	.949	.953	.957	.960	.963	.965	.967	.969	.971	.972	.974	.982	.987	.989	.991	.992	.993	.994	.995

Table 10 continued

21	.654	.791	.850	.883	.904	.919	.930	.938	.945	.950	.954	.958	.961	.964	.966	.968	.970	.971	.973	.974	.983	.987	.990	.991	.993	.993	.994	.995
22	.658	.794	.852	.885	.906	.920	.931	.939	.945	.951	.955	.958	.962	.964	.967	.969	.970	.972	.973	.975	.983	.987	.990	.991	.993	.994	.994	.995
23	.662	.796	.854	.887	.907	.921	.932	.940	.946	.951	.956	.959	.962	.965	.967	.969	.971	.972	.974	.975	.983	.987	.990	.992	.993	.994	.994	.995
24	.665	.799	.856	.888	.908	.922	.933	.941	.947	.952	.956	.960	.963	.965	.967	.969	.971	.973	.974	.975	.983	.988	.990	.992	.993	.994	.994	.995
25	.668	.801	.858	.889	.910	.923	.934	.941	.948	.953	.957	.960	.963	.966	.968	.970	.972	.973	.974	.976	.984	.988	.990	.992	.993	.994	.995	.995
26	.671	.803	.859	.891	.911	.924	.934	.942	.948	.953	.957	.961	.964	.966	.968	.970	.972	.973	.975	.976	.984	.988	.990	.992	.993	.994	.995	.995
27	.673	.805	.861	.892	.912	.925	.935	.943	.949	.954	.958	.961	.964	.966	.969	.971	.972	.974	.975	.976	.984	.988	.990	.992	.993	.994	.995	.995
28	.676	.806	.862	.893	.912	.926	.936	.943	.949	.954	.958	.962	.964	.967	.969	.971	.973	.974	.975	.977	.984	.988	.990	.992	.993	.994	.995	.995
29	.678	.808	.863	.894	.913	.927	.936	.944	.950	.955	.959	.962	.965	.967	.969	.971	.973	.974	.976	.977	.984	.988	.991	.992	.993	.994	.995	.995
30	.680	.810	.865	.895	.914	.927	.937	.944	.950	.955	.959	.962	.965	.968	.970	.971	.973	.975	.976	.977	.985	.988	.991	.992	.993	.994	.995	.995
40	.696	.821	.873	.902	.920	.932	.941	.948	.954	.958	.962	.965	.968	.970	.972	.973	.975	.976	.978	.979	.986	.989	.991	.993	.994	.995	.995	.996
50	.706	.828	.878	.906	.923	.935	.944	.951	.956	.960	.964	.967	.969	.971	.973	.975	.976	.977	.979	.980	.986	.990	.992	.993	.994	.995	.995	.996
60	.713	.833	.882	.909	.926	.937	.946	.952	.957	.961	.965	.968	.970	.972	.974	.975	.977	.978	.979	.980	.987	.990	.992	.993	.994	.995	.996	.996
70	.718	.836	.884	.911	.927	.939	.947	.953	.958	.962	.966	.968	.971	.973	.975	.976	.977	.979	.980	.981	.987	.990	.992	.994	.994	.995	.996	.996
80	.722	.839	.886	.912	.929	.940	.948	.954	.959	.963	.966	.969	.971	.973	.975	.977	.978	.979	.980	.981	.987	.990	.992	.994	.995	.995	.996	.996
90	.725	.841	.888	.913	.930	.941	.949	.955	.960	.963	.967	.969	.972	.974	.975	.977	.978	.979	.980	.981	.988	.991	.992	.994	.995	.995	.996	.996
100	.727	.842	.889	.914	.930	.941	.949	.955	.960	.964	.967	.970	.972	.974	.976	.977	.978	.980	.981	.982	.988	.991	.993	.994	.995	.995	.996	.996

at the mean. Hence the $\phi(\lambda)$, values for the cut-point at the mean $\phi(X)$ are reported below all of the others in each type of model and the mean percentages (upon which the $\phi(\lambda)$ values are based) are given for reference.

To interpret this table, it is first necessary to decide whether it is results that are generalizable to other tests that are of interest (Random Effects Model), or results that pertain only to the present TOEFL items and subtests that are of interest (Mixed Effects Model). Consider the Mixed Effects Model for the present TOEFL battery which is presented in the bottom half of the first column. Notice that $\phi(\lambda)$ coefficients are presented for decisions made at 10%, 20%, etc. up to 90%. Notice further that the lowest of these is .957 at the 70% cut-point. It turns out here and in the other columns that the lowest value will be that closest to the mean. In fact, decisions made at the mean will generally turn out to be the least dependable. Hence, the $\phi(\lambda)$ at the mean is presented along with that mean in the last two rows of both the upper and lower portions of Table 11.

Discussion

In interpreting the above results, it is important to remember that most of the dependability estimates (i.e., all except those found in the VRC Test analyses in Study Four) are based on fewer items than actually used in the tests because it was necessary to design the various studies so that there would be equal numbers of items on each subtest. Since shorter tests tend to be less reliable, the effect of these reduced numbers of items (if there is any) would be to provide low estimates of dependability. As a result, it is reasonable to interpret the results as conservative underestimates of the true state of affairs. In other words, if the dependability estimates are in error, they will err on the low side and should *not* provide overestimates of the dependability of these measures.

The remainder of this discussion will directly address the original research questions posed at the outset of this project. To help organize the discussion, the research questions will be used as headings.

What are the classical theory reliability estimates?

As reported elsewhere in the literature, the Total TOEFL battery and its component tests – the LC Test, SWE Test, and VRC Test – proved to be very reliable from a classical theory perspective. The results in Table 2 indicate that these tests in their existing form (labeled Original Test in the table) were reliable at .97, .92, .90, and .93, respectively, using Cronbach alpha. Predictably, the VRC2 section, which was only a portion of the VRC Test, was less reliable at .88 than the tests and battery considered above because it is considerably shorter than they are. For the sake of comparison, Table 2 also presents the classical theory estimates for the items used in the G-study sampling (done to create balanced designs). These Cronbach alpha estimates later turned out to be comparable to the G-coefficients (for δ error) for the mixed models, as would be expected.

Table 11

Summary of the phi (lambda) results

STUDY MODEL Cut-point	STUDY ONE: TOTAL TOEFL	STUDY TWO: LC TEST	STUDY THREE: SWE TEST	STUDY FOUR: VRC TEST	STUDY FIVE: VRC2 SECTION
RANDOM EFFECTS MODEL					
90%	.939	.962	.906	.938	.870
80%	.899	.939	.857	.902	.799
70%	.866	.908	.843	.881	.749
60%	.892	.894	.887	.907	.786
50%	.934	.918	.930	.942	.858
40%	.961	.948	.956	.964	.910
30%	.975	.967	.971	.976	.941
20%	.983	.978	.980	.984	.959
10%	.988	.985	.985	.988	.970
$\phi(\bar{X})$	.865	.894	.840	.880	.748
$\bar{X} =$	69%	62%	73%	71%	69%
MIXED EFFECTS MODEL					
90%	.981	.965	.918	.963	.913
80%	.968	.945	.876	.941	.865
70%	.957	.917	.864	.928	.831
60%	.965	.904	.902	.944	.856
50%	.979	.926	.939	.965	.905
40%	.987	.953	.962	.978	.939
30%	.992	.970	.975	.986	.960
20%	.995	.980	.982	.990	.972
10%	.996	.986	.987	.993	.980
$\phi(\bar{X})$	.957	.904	.861	.928	.831
$\bar{X} =$	69%	62%	73%	71%	69%)

What are the relative contributions to error variance of persons, items, subtests, and their interactions?

Examining the variance components shown in Table 4 for the five G-studies in terms of their relative magnitude reveals the relative contributions of persons, subtests, and items nested within subtests, as well as their interactions. For instance, from inspection of the variance components themselves, it is clear that the lion's share of variance in all of these studies is taken up by persons and those interactions involving persons. This is as it should be because the purpose of a norm-referenced test is to differentiate among persons. However, it should be noted that the variance component for the persons by subtests interaction is far smaller than that for the persons by items nested within subtests interaction – though the persons by subtests interaction is fairly high in Study Five. It is also true in all cases that the variance component due to items nested within subtests is far larger than the component for subtests. Particularly in Study Two (LC Test) and Study Three (SWE Test), the subtests variance component is very small. The subtests component is somewhat larger in Study Four (VRC Test). However, in Study One (Total TOEFL), the variance component for subtests is much more important, amounting to about one-twelfth of the persons component and about one-quarter of the items nested within subtests component. In Study Five (VRC2), the subtests variance component is even more important since it is almost one-fifth as large as the persons component and almost equal in magnitude to the items nested within subtests component. These observations will be further illuminated in the next section.

What is the dependability for varying numbers of items and subtests?

Tables 6 to 10 provided a multitude of direct answers to this research question. In all cases, the subtests facet was shown to have some influence on the predicted dependability indices as indicated by the fact that in no D-study was the dependability the same for one subtest and more than one subtest with the number of items held constant. In other words, in all cases the dependability was enhanced by having an increased number of subtests even though the number of items was kept the same.

However, a pattern emerged in examining the results across tables which was consistent with the variance component findings in the previous section. The influence of subtests was greatest in Studies One (Total TOEFL) and Five (VRC2), and to a lesser degree in Study Four (VRC Test). In considering the Total TOEFL results, it might at first glance appear that the effect would be larger here than in the other studies because the length of the subtests themselves was longer at 38 items each than in any of the other studies. However, this reasoning is contradicted by the fact that an even larger effect for subtests was found in the

VRC2 results, which was based on four items in each subtest – the smallest number of items per subtest reported in any of the D-studies in this project.

It should be noted that Studies One and Five were quite different from each other in structure. The relatively large differences in dependability due to subtests in Study One were due to differences between tests (i.e., the LC Test, SWE Test, and VRC Test), while those observed for Study Five were due to differences between reading passages (i.e., Passages 1 to 5).

What is the effect on score dependability of various cut-points?

The results shown in Table 11 for D-studies One, Two, and Four indicate that, for the existing (i.e., using a Mixed Effects Model) Total TOEFL battery, LC Test, and VRC Test, the dependability of decisions is not greatly different at various cut-points, and in any case, at the lowest point they are acceptably dependable (at .957, .904, and .928, respectively). The third D-study indicates that the dependability at the mean is more markedly different at .861 from the dependabilities at other cut-points. Thus, though .861 is not problematic dependability, it would be most responsible to apply additional caution in interpreting decisions on the SWE Test that are at or near the mean (approximately 50 on the standardized scores). (It is also important to note that the .861 found here is probably an underestimate of the existing state of affairs because it is based on two subtests of 14 items while the original subtest was based on two subtests of 14 and 24 items). In short, decisions based on the current TOEFL battery and individual tests of the TOEFL can still be considered dependable even if those decisions are made right at the mean score (of approximately 500 for the battery or approximately 50 for the separate tests).

In the upper portion of Table 11, the Random Effects Model results turned out to be more conservative than the Mixed Effects results, showing both lower dependability in general and a more marked decline in the dependability at and near the mean. Recall that this difference was expected due to the fact that these results are generalizable to other test development projects.

Conclusion

Test dependability

The effects on dependability of different numbers of subtests and items (based on the random effects model) are shown in Table 4 as variance components and in Tables 6 through 10 as G coefficients. One pattern that emerged is that the effect of having multiple tests (i.e., the subtest facet) on the Total TOEFL battery seems to have a strong beneficial effect on the dependability of scores for the

Total TOEFL battery. In other words, including component tests like the LC Test, SWE Test, and VRC Test in the Total TOEFL battery has proven to be a sound policy decision from the dependability perspective. In addition, based on Table 6, further policy decisions can be made about the relative merits of adding further items and/or component tests or cutting down on their numbers.

Similarly, the effect of having multiple passages (the subtest facet) in the VRC2 section seems to have a positive advantageous effect on the dependability of scores for the VRC2 section. To some degree, the effect of having both the reading comprehension and vocabulary subtests on the VRC Test also appears to have a beneficial effect on the dependability of this test – though the strong increases in dependability do not appear to extend beyond two such subtests. In contrast, the individual subtests within the LC Test and SWE Test, while they do make some difference, appear to have less impact on the dependability of the scores on these tests.

It is possible that in G-studies One, Four and Five, where the subtests facet did have an important impact, the subtests involved were significantly different from each other and thus contributed to the overall variance on the test above and beyond the contribution made by items. In contrast, in G-studies Two and Three, the subtests involved may be testing very much the same things.

In terms of developing future versions of the TOEFL (including TOEFL 2000) and other test development projects around the world, recall that the results presented in Tables 4 and 6–10 were for random effects models and that they were therefore generalizable to other versions of the test and other testing projects. In short, the analyses in this project indicate that subtests can make substantial contributions to the variance of test scores and thus may affect dependability in important ways. However, these results also make it clear that, in some cases, subtests may have a negligible impact on dependability. Thus, while inclusion of subtests or the expansion of the number of subtests on a test may have a substantial beneficial effect on the dependability of the scores on that test, this relationship cannot be taken as a forgone conclusion.

Decision dependability and validity

The results of this study are also related to the notions of decision dependability and validity. At the beginning of this paper, concern was expressed about the possibility that test scores may not be equally reliable for making decisions at different cut-points in the score range. Since the dependability of a test is often lowest at the mean and since many decisions are made at or near the mean on TOEFL, this was a legitimate concern. Portions of this project were therefore designed to examine the degree to which these differences may affect the dependability and therefore the validity of score users' decisions. The lower portion of Table 11, which reports the $\phi(\lambda)$ coefficients when a mixed effects model is applied, indicates that on the present TOEFL the lowest dependabilities along the range are still very high. Thus, while it initially seemed like a potential problem for score users, there appears to be no need to worry about differential dependability at different cut-points on the existing test. In other words, regardless of the cut-point that current TOEFL score users may decide to be valid for their own reasons, the effect on dependability of various cut-points is apparently not an issue of great concern. In addition, ETS is currently implementing automated item selection procedures to assemble TOEFL tests which will help to insure that each section will provide high information (or low error variance) at the middle ability range. Naturally, any such validity decisions should be also studied in the actual context(s) in which the decisions are to be made.

In terms of future versions of the TOEFL and other testing projects around the world, the upper portion of Table 11, which reports the $\phi(\lambda)$ coefficients when a random effects model is applied, indicates that there may be more variation in dependability estimates across the range of possible decision points. Thus, while such differential dependability is apparently not a problem on the current TOEFL, it is an issue that should continue to concern developers of other tests and future versions of the TOEFL.

Future research

In the course of conducting this project, a number of questions have occurred to us. They are presented here in the hope that they will be investigated in the future:

1 Would similar results be obtained if these studies were replicated with other TOEFL data sets?
2 Would similar results be obtained if such studies were replicated using other tests as the basis?
3 What could generalizability theory tell us about the effects of raters on the scores of the *Test of Written English?*
4 What could generalizability theory tell us about the effects of items and raters on the scores of the *Test of Spoken English?*
5 What could be learned about the TOEFL battery and other tests by applying classical theory approaches to decision reliability/dependability at different cut points (for an overview of these approaches, see Feldt and Brennan 1989: 123–4)?

References

Bolus, R. E., F. B. Hinofotis and K.M. Bailey. 1982. An introduction to generalizability theory in second language research. *Language Learning,* 32: 245–58.

Brennan, R. L. 1980. Applications of generalizability theory. In R.A. Berk (ed.), *Criterion-referenced Measurement: The State of the Art.* Baltimore, MD: Johns Hopkins University Press.

Brennan, R. L. 1983. *Elements of Generalizability Theory.* Iowa City, IA: American College Testing Program.

Brennan, R. L. 1984. Estimating the dependability of the scores. In R.A. Berk (ed.), *A Guide to Criterion-referenced Test Construction.* Baltimore, MD: Johns Hopkins University Press.

Brennan, R. L. and M. T. Kane. 1977. Signal/noise ratios for domain-referenced tests. *Psychometrika* 42: 609–25.

Brown, J. D. 1984. A norm-referenced engineering reading test. In A.K. Pugh and J.M. Ulijn (eds.), *Reading for Professional Purposes: Studies and Practices in Native and Foreign Languages.* London: Heinemann Educational Books.

Brown, J. D. 1990. Short-cut estimators of criterion-referenced test consistency. *Language Testing* 7: 77–97.

Brown, J.D. 1993. A comprehensive criterion-referenced testing project. In D. Douglas and C. Chapelle (eds.), *A New Decade of Language Testing Research* pp. 163–84. Alexandria, VA: TESOL.

Brown, J. D. and K. M. Bailey. 1984. A categorical instrument for scoring second language writing skills. *Language Learning* 34 (4): 21–42.

Cronbach, L.J. and G.C. Gleser 1964. The signal/noise ratio in the comparison of reliability coefficients. *Educational and Psychological Measurement* 24: 467–80.

Cronbach, L. J., G. C. Gleser, H. Nanda and N. Rajaratnam. 1972. *The Dependability of Behavioral Measurements: Theory of Generalizability for Scores and Profiles.* New York, NY: John Wiley.

Cronbach, L. J., N. Rajaratnam and G. C. Gleser. 1963. Theory of generalizability: A liberalization of reliability theory. *British Journal of Statistical Psychology* 16: 137–63.

Educational Testing Service (ETS). 1992. *TOEFL Test and Score Manual.* Princeton, NJ: ETS.

Educational Testing Service (ETS). 1993. *Bulletin of Information for TOEFL, TWE, and TSE.* Princeton, NJ: ETS.

Feldt, L.S. and R.L. Brennan. 1989. Reliability. In R. L. Linn (ed.). *Educational Measurement* (3rd edn.). New York, NY: Macmillan.

Kirk, R.E. 1968. *Experimental Design: Procedures for the Behavioral Sciences.* Belmont, CA: Brooks/Cole.

Shavelson, R.J. and N.M. Webb. 1981. Generalizability theory: 1973–1980. *British Journal of Mathematical and Statistical Psychology* 34: 133–66.

Stansfield, C.W. and D.M. Kenyon. 1992. Research of the comparability of the oral proficiency interview and the simulated oral proficiency interview. *System* 20: 347–64.

Suen, H.K. 1990. *Principles of Test Theories*. Hillsdale, NJ: Lawrence Erlbaum.

14 Taking a multifaceted view of the unidimensional measurement from Rasch analysis in language tests

Tony Lee
Centre for Applied Linguistics and Languages
Griffith University

Introduction

The advent of Item Response Model (IRM) to the field of language testing (e.g. Henning 1984; Henning, Hudson and Turner 1985; Griffin 1985; Woods and Baker 1985; Pollitt and Hutchinson 1987; Choi and Bachman 1992) has been among the most important developments in the recent history of the discipline. IRM has given language testing a rigorous basis for the measurement dimension. The catch, though, is that IRM has been conceived as a measurement model with little or no immediate implications for language testing research. Specifically, the unidimensionality assumption in IRM has been an initial stumbling block for many language testers. It is argued that, if language is inherently complex, it would be straitjacketing language testing research by forcing the unidimensional condition onto all language data. (See Bachman 1990 for an interesting discussion.)

Theoretical discussions of IRM within language testing (e.g. Reckase 1979; Henning, Hudson and Turner 1985, Henning 1992; Choi and Bachman 1992) have helped to define the scope of the unidimensionalty assumption and to resolve the apparent dilemma. In addition, research designs encompassing an IRM component and development within IRM itself have made it a true research tool.

Rasch model as a research model

Wright and Masters (1982) maintain that the unidimensionality assumption is a 'universal characteristic of all measurement' (p.2). This, however, should not in theory preclude analyses over and above an IRM based analysis. Jensen (1978), for example, warns of '... a flagrant conceptual and scientific blunder ... to *apply* orthogonal rotation of principal components or factors without first extracting the general factor (i.e. the first principal component or first principal factor)'. (italics mine) Indeed, IRM can easily be conceptualized as a rigorous way to extract the general factor. The standardized residuals from an IRM analysis would provide data for further analysis as envisaged by Jensen. Lee (1993) analyses the residuals in a study on the construct validity of an ESL reading test.

Many-faceted Rasch analysis

Many-faceted Rasch analysis (Linacre 1989a) is the expansion of the one-parameter Rasch model to encompass analyses of facets in the data. This has enabled IRM to be employed in diverse research design and analysis configurations and data collection schedules.

Linacre (1989b) argues and demonstrates the possibility of extending the initial one-parameter (or two-facet) Rasch model to n-facet models. This is an interesting development. Constituents within a complex human behavioural context can now be accommodated within the same IRM model for analysis. Typically facets can include judges of human performance (e.g. in a writing test), or subgroupings of subjects/candidates, or item groups. With the flexibility introduced, research designs can now be developed which would do greater justice to unavoidable features in human behaviour (e.g. varying degrees of severity of judges, cultural and/or economic background of subjects). Within a many-faceted model, all facets entered into an analysis are combined to produce the calibrations and are themselves calibrated regarding consistency. In addition, FACETS (Linacre and Wright 1990), which is the software implementation of multifaceted Rasch analysis, can generate interaction analysis of the facets.

The study

The background

The study reported in this paper originated from a need to design a short EAP proficiency test for incoming mature undergraduate students. A policy decision of the Hong Kong Baptist College to admit former non-degree graduates into undergraduate programs resulted in a situation where the minimum entry requirement in the English language was not met by some of the entrants. It was rather difficult for those students to retake the official Use of English examinations and rather uneconomical to administer a facsimile version of Use of English. The Language Centre of the Hong Kong Baptist College was given the task of finding a means to establish the equivalence of the required minimum ESL level for entry into degree programs.

The approach to solving the problem was to focus on establishing consistent person comparison between the students in question and a reference group with a known ESL proficiency level that met the required minimum standard. The comparison was made on the basis of a short ESL proficiency test taken by both groups of candidates.

The EAP test

Practical and monetary constraints resulted in the choice of the modified cloze format based on a single reading passage. Two sets of questions were prepared. The first consisted of 52 proofreading items relating to grammatical features in the first part of the passage. The second set consisted of 44 gapfilling items relating to cohesion features in the latter part.

The test was first piloted on a group of undergraduate students covering the whole range of Use of English grade levels. The test was then given to 200 mature students. A reference group of students (n = 59) with the required minimum Use of English grade was also given the test.

The research design

The aim of this study was to obtain a comparison between the 'student' group and the 'reference' group based on the EAP test. As the reference group was a sample of those who had achieved the required minimum English language standard for entry into universities those in the 'student' group that would match the level of the 'reference' group in the EAP test were deemed as having an equivalent level of English language ability.

The analysis

To achieve the objectives described above it was necessary to have a stable and consistent ability scale and to make the required comparison of the two groups of candidates beyond the particular EAP test given. This is a typical sample free test calibration and test free person measurement in IRM. In addition, the analysis needed to calibrate the two subgroups of candidates (student and reference). Multifaceted Rasch analysis was thus necessary. It was also thought relevant to calibrate the two parts of the EAP test to see if mastery of grammar and cohesive features were distinguishable in the EAP test.

FACETS (Linacre and Wright 1990) was employed. Four facets were included in the analysis: the candidates, the two candidate subgroups: 'Student' and 'Reference', the two sub-sets of items and the test items.

Results

Unidimensionality

An informal test of unidimensionality was performed via maximum likelihood factor analysis. A first factor containing 21% of overall variance was obtained. This was considered sufficient to make a unidimensionality claim for Rasch analysis (Reckase 1979; Henning, Hudson and Turner 1985).

Item calibration

Table 1 contains detailed item calibrations of the EAP test. The leftmost column contains descriptive statistics: '*Score*' is the raw score of the item across all candidates; '*Count*' is the number of score points and '*Average*' the item facility value. The second column contains the item calibration statistics: the logit and its associated standard error. The third column contains the fit statistics. FACETS includes two types of fit statistics: the Infit and the Outfit. The former is an information-weighted mean-square fit statistic and the latter the conventional mean-square. The expected value is 1 in both. Values greater than 1 would indicate noise in the Infit statistic and an outlier in the Outfit statistic.

The range of item difficulties reported in Table 1 extend from logit –4.58 (Item 48) to 4.41 (Items 61 and 68). Most of the items are accepted by the model with the exception of Item 18 (Infit: 1.0, Outfit 1.3), Item 42 (Infit: 1.0, Outfit: 1.2), Item 70 (Infit: 1.0, Outfit: 1.5). Items 51 and 93 were answered correctly by none.

The test has thus 91 items accepted by the model with a fairly wide range of difficulty levels.

FACETS also reports a test of the overall calibration of a facet. These are found at the bottom of Table 1. *RMSE* is the root mean-square standard error; *Adj. S.D.* is the standard deviation of the estimates after removing measurement error; *Separation* is a measure of the relative spread of the estimates; *Reliability* is the Rasch equivalent to the KR-20 or Cronbach Alpha statistics. *Fixed chi square* is the goodness of fit test for the elements (i.e. items) sharing the same measure after allowing for measurement error. In the case of the item calibration, the differences (separations) among the items are found to be reliably distinct (reliability: 0.98). The measurement variable established is, thus, consistent.

Table 1

Item Calibration

Score	Count	Average	Measure Logit	Model Error	Infit MnSq	Std	Outfit MnSq	Std	Nu	Item	
211	259	0.8	-2.28	0.16	1.0	0	0.9	0	1	Q4	(V_A)
7	259	0.0	2.97	0.38	1.0	0	0.9	0	2	Q5	(Prep)
15	259	0.1	2.16	0.27	1.0	0	1.0	0	3	Q6	(PhV)
133	259	0.5	-0.78	0.13	1.0	0	1.0	0	4	Q7	(V_T)
138	259	0.5	-0.86	0.13	1.0	0	1.0	0	5	Q8	(V_T)
68	259	0.3	0.36	0.14	1.0	0	1.0	0	6	Q9	(Prep)
70	259	0.3	0.32	0.14	1.0	0	1.0	0	7	Q10	(N_A)
85	259	0.3	0.03	0.14	1.0	0	1.0	0	8	Q11	(N_N)
75	259	0.3	0.22	0.14	1.0	0	1.0	0	9	Q12	(V_F)
185	259	0.7	-1.69	0.14	0.9	0	0.9	0	10	Q13	(Adv)
61	259	0.2	0.51	0.51	1.0	0	1.0	0	11	Q14	(Prep)
226	259	0.9	-2.73	0.19	1.0	0	0.9	0	12	Q15	(V_A)
20	259	0.1	1.85	0.23	1.0	0	1.0	0	13	Q16	(Prep)
103	259	0.4	-0.28	0.13	1.0	0	1.0	0	14	Q17	(N_N)
140	259	0.5	-0.89	0.13	1.0	-1	1.0	-1	15	Q18	(V_F)
176	259	0.7	-1.51	0.14	0.9	-1	0.9	-1	16	Q19	(V_T)
127	259	0.5	-0.68	0.13	1.0	0	1.0	0	17	Q20	(V_A)
3	259	0.0	3.83	0.58	1.0	0	1.3	0	18	Q21	(Prep)
22	259	0.1	1.75	0.22	1.0	0	1.1	0	19	Q24	(PhV)
60	259	0.2	0.54	0.15	1.0	0	1.1	0	20	Q25	(Adv)
197	259	0.8	-1.94	0.15	0.9	0	0.9	-1	21	Q26	(Art)
191	259	0.7	-1.81	0.14	1.0	0	1.0	0	22	Q27	(Prep)
186	259	0.7	-1.71	0.14	1.0	0	1.0	0	23	Q28	(N_N)
42	259	0.2	0.99	0.17	1.0	0	1.0	0	24	Q29	(Prep)
16	259	0.1	2.09	0.26	1.0	0	0.9	0	25	Q30	(Art)
109	259	0.4	-0.39	0.13	1.0	0	1.0	0	26	Q31	(V_T)
118	259	0.5	-0.53	0.13	1.0	0	1.0	1	27	Q32	(N_N)
68	259	0.3	0.36	0.14	0.9	0	0.9	-1	28	Q33	(V_F)
17	259	0.1	-2.03	0.25	1.0	0	1.0	0	29	Q34	(Conj)
184	259	0.7	-1.67	0.14	1.0	0	1.0	0	30	Q35	(V_F)
163	259	0.6	-1.28	0.13	1.0	0	1.0	0	31	Q36	(N_N)
93	259	0.4	-0.11	0.13	1.1	1	1.1	2	32	Q37	(Art)
215	259	0.8	-2.39	0.17	1.0	0	0.9	0	33	Q38	(Spell)
10	259	0.0	2.59	0.32	1.0	0	1.0	0	34	Q39	(N_F)
23	259	0.1	1.70	0.22	1.0	0	1.1	0	35	Q40	(Prep)
40	259	0.2	1.05	0.17	1.0	0	1.1	0	36	Q41	(Pr_A)
156	259	0.6	-1.16	0.13	1.0	0	1.0	0	37	Q42	(V_F)
144	259	0.6	-0.96	0.13	1.1	2	1.1	2	38	Q43	(Art)
34	259	0.1	1.25	0.19	1.0	0	1.1	0	39	Q44	(N_N)
198	259	0.8	-1.96	0.15	1.0	0	1.0	0	40	Q45	(V_F)
84	259	0.3	0.05	0.14	1.0	0	1.0	0	41	Q47	(Pr)
240	259	0.9	-3.36	0.24	1.0	0	1.2	0	42	Q48	(Art)
15	259	0.1	2.16	0.27	1.0	0	1.0	0	43	Q49	(Prep)
151	259	0.6	-1.08	0.13	1.0	0	1.0	0	44	Q50	(N_N)
7	259	0.0	2.97	0.38	1.0	0	1.1	0	45	Q52	(Prep)
156	259	0.6	-1.16	0.13	1.0	0	1.0	0	46	Q53	(Art)

Score	Count	Average	Measure Logit	Model Error	Infit MnSq	Std	Outfit MnSq	Std	Nu	Item	
89	259	0.3	-0.57	0.13	1.0	0	1.1	1	47	Q54	(often)
249	259	1.0	-4.58	0.32	1.0	0	1.0	0	48	Q55	(that)
10	259	0.0	2.06	0.32	1.0	0	0.8	0	49	Q56	(those)
222	259	0.9	-3.13	0.18	1.0	0	1.1	0	50	Q57	(mainly)
0	259		Maximum						51	Q58	(whether)
98	259	0.4	-0.73	0.13	1.0	0	1.0	0	52	Q59	(without)
75	259	0.3	-0.31	0.14	1.0	0	1.0	0	53	Q60	(them)
206	259	0.8	-2.68	0.16	1.0	0	1.1	1	54	Q61	(their)
133	259	0.5	-1.31	0.13	1.0	0	1.0	0	55	Q62	(in)
45	259	0.2	0.38	0.17	1.0	0	0.9	0	56	Q63	(and)
35	259	0.1	0.68	0.18	1.0	0	0.9	0	57	Q64	(as)
54	259	0.2	0.14	0.16	1.0	0	0.9	0	58	Q65	(rather)
61	259	0.2	-0.02	0.15	1.0	0	1.0	0	59	Q66	(it)
16	259	0.1	1.56	0.26	1.0	0	1.0	0	60	Q67	(not)
1	259	0.0	4.41	1.00	1.0	0	0.7	0	61	Q68	(instead)
32	259	0.1	0.79	0.19	1.0	0	0.9	0	62	Q69	(when)
116	259	0.4	-1.03	0.13	1.1	2	1.1	1	63	Q70	(then)
4	259	0.0	3.01	0.50	1.0	0	1.0	0	64	Q71	(its)
96	259	0.4	-0.70	0.13	1.0	0	1.0	0	65	Q72	(this)
35	259	0.1	0.68	0.18	1.0	0	1.0	0	66	Q73	(where)
101	259	0.4	-0.78	0.13	1.0	0	1.0	0	67	Q74	(by)
1	259	0.0	4.41	1.00	1.0	0	0.5	0	68	Q75	(whose)
89	259	0.3	-0.57	0.13	1.0	0	1.0	0	69	Q76	(sometimes)
9	259	0.0	2.17	0.34	1.0	0	1.5	1	70	Q77	(they)
23	259	0.1	1.16	0.22	1.0	0	1.2	0	71	Q78	(then)
108	259	0.4	-0.90	0.13	0.9	-1	0.9	-2	72	Q79	(who)
21	259	0.1	1.27	0.23	1.0	0	1.1	0	73	Q80	(credits)
15	259	0.1	1.63	0.27	1.0	0	0.8	0	74	Q81	(that)
45	259	0.2	0.38	0.17	1.0	0	1.0	0	75	Q82	(by)
38	259	0.1	0.58	0.18	1.0	0	1.1	0	76	Q83	(that)
69	259	0.3	-0.19	0.14	1.0	0	1.1	0	77	Q84	(those)
59	259	0.2	0.3	0.15	0.9	0	0.9	-1	78	Q85	(those)
41	259	0.2	0.49	0.17	1.0	0	1.1	0	79	Q86	(but)
103	259	0.4	-0.82	0.13	1.0	0	1.0	0	80	Q87	(and)
214	259	0.8	-2.89	0.17	1.0	0	1.0	0	81	Q88	(than)
72	259	0.3	-0.25	0.14	1.0	0	1.0	0	82	Q89	(better)
180	259	0.7	-2.12	0.14	1.0	0	1.0	0	83	Q90	(like)
140	259	0.5	-1.43	0.13	1.0	1	1.0	1	84	Q91	(now)
192	259	0.7	-2.36	0.15	1.0	0	1.0	0	85	Q92	(and)
49	259	0.2	0.27	0.16	1.0	0	1.0	0	86	Q93	(though)
31	259	0.1	0.82	0.19	1.0	0	1.0	0	87	Q94	(they)
123	259	0.5	-1.15	0.13	0.9	-2	0.9	-2	88	Q95	(but)
23	259	0.1	1.16	0.22	1.0	0	1.0	0	89	Q96	(so)
25	259	0.1	1.07	0.21	1.0	0	0.9	0	90	Q97	(also)
30	259	0.1	0.86	0.20	1.0	0	1.0	0	91	Q98	(one)
187	259	0.7	-2.26	0.14	0.9	-1	0.9	-1	92	Q99	(as)
0	259		Maximum						93	Q100	(provided)
34	259	0.1	0.72	0.19	1.0	0	0.9	0	94	Q101	(those)
32	259	0.1	0.79	0.19	1.0	0	0.9	0	95	Q102	(only)
35	259	0.1	0.68	0.18	1.0	0	1.0	0	96	Q103	(it)

Score	Count	Average	Measure Logit	Model Error	Infit MnSq	Std	Outfit MnSq	Std	Nu	Item
88	259	0.3	-0.00	0.20	1.0	0.1	1.0	0.1		Mean of Count:
70	0	0.3	1.71	0.14	0.0	0.6	0.1	0.8		S.D. 96

RMSE: 0.25, Adj S.D.: 1.70, Separation: 6.86, Reliability: 0.98
Fixed (all same)   chi-square: 5237.64   d.f.: 93   significace: .00
Random (normal distribution) chi-square: 89.30   d.f.: 92   significance: .56

The Sub-test

Table 2 reports the calibration of the two sections of the test. Part 2 (cohesive features logit 0.14) is found to be more difficult than Part 1 (grammatical features logit –0.14). The fit statistics are all within the acceptability level.

Table 2

Sub-test calibration

Score	Count	Average	Measure Logit	Model Error	Infit MnSq	Std	Outfit MnSq	Std	N	Test
4782	11914	0.4	-0.27	0.02	1.0	0	1.0	0	1	Part 1
3666	12432	0.3	0.27	0.02	1.0	0	1.0	0	2	Part 2
4244.0	12173.0	0.3	0.00	0.02	1.0	0.1	1.0	-0.1		Mean of Count:
558.0	259.0	0.1	0.27	0.00	0.0	0.3	0.0	0.4		S.D. 2

RMSE: 0.02, Adj S.D.: 0.26, Separation: 11.23, Reliability: 0.99
Fixed (all same)   chi-square: 254.36   d.f.: 1   significance: .00
Random (normal distribution) chi-square: 1.00   d.f.: 0   significance: 1.00

The students

Owing to the large number of candidates it was not practicable to include a detailed person measurement report in this paper. The overall range of candidate ability is between logit –1.15 to 1.42. Table 3 reports the calibration report of the two candidate sub-groups: *Student* and *Reference*. The Reference group (logit: 0.93) is calibrated higher than the Student group (logit: 1.16).

Table 3

Candidate group calibration

Score	Count	Average	Calib Logit	Model Error	Infit MnSq	Std	Outfit MnSq	Std	N Group
7021	20774	0.3	-1.02	0.02	1.0	0	1.0	0	Student
1427	3572	0.4	-0.79	0.04	1.0	0	1.0	0	Reference
4244.0	12173.0	0.4	-0.91	0.03	1.0	0.2	1.0	-0.1	Mean of Count:
2797.0	8601.0	0.0	0.12	0.01	0.0	0.2	0.0	0.2	S.D. 2

RMSE: 0.03, Adj S.D.: 0.11, Separation: 3.47, Reliability: 0.92
Fixed (all same)   chi-square: 26.03 d.f.: 1   significance: .00
Random (normal distribution) chi-square: 1.00 d.f.: 0   significance: 1.00

Discussion

The principal research question in the study: the establishment of equivalence between the Reference and Student groups has been achieved through the use of FACETS. The logit level of the Reference group (-0.93) can be taken as equivalent to the minimal required ESL level for entry into the university. The concept of equivalence should be correctly understood. Equivalence here refers to the two groups of candidates on the basis of the test administered. It does not refer to the EAP test and the Use of English examinations. Thus, while the two groups of candidates have been compared regarding ESL ability, they have not been compared regarding possible equivalence in the results of the Use of English examinations.

The calibration of the two parts of the test is interesting in that it enables analysis of groupings of test items. The analysis reported is in fact a construct validation study as suggested by Wright and Masters (1982:93):

> *The pattern of item calibration provides a description of the reach and hierarchy of the variable. This pattern can be compared with the intentions of the item writers to see if it confirms their expectations concerning the variable they wanted to construct. To the extent that it does, it affirms the construct validity of the variable.*

The finding that cohesive features require a more advanced (difficult) ESL ability than grammar seems to confirm a common point of view in applied linguistics and TESL.

As an item oriented technique Rasch analysis can be used for item oriented construct validation (e.g. Lee 1993). As FACETS allows for facets of item subgroups to be included in the analysis, construct validation can also be carried out on item subgroups using Rasch analysis. In the study reported it may not be very instructive to estimate the construct validity directly from the items. Using the groupings of the items as it has been done would make more sense in terms of both computation and applied linguistic theory. The construct validation of item groups (or sub-tests) via many-faceted Rasch analysis provides an answer to a long-standing problem in construct validation: that of item oriented and test oriented construct validation. (See Bachman 1990, Lee 1994.)

Conclusions and implications

The study reported has demonstrated possible extensions of the Rasch model in terms of both item calibration and person measurement through the employment of FACETS. Indeed the package allows for a maximum of nine facets to be calibrated simultaneously. Such extensions are particularly attractive to those who, while appreciating the rigour in measurement offered by the Rasch model, would not be totally comfortable with the unidimensionality in Rasch. What has been demonstrated in the paper is that FACETS is able to maintain the rigour of the Rasch model and to provide the applied linguist with interesting research design possibilities. By so doing, FACETS enhanced the Rasch model from being a strictly measurement model to a general research tool and enables language testers to 'devote their creative powers to designing tests which involve deeper and more relevant evidence of competence ...' (Linacre 1989b:10).

References

Bachman, L.F. 1990. *Fundamental Considerations in Language Testing.* Oxford: Oxford University Press.

Choi, I.-C. and L. F. Bachman. 1992. An investigation into the adequacy of three IRT models for data from two EFL reading tests. *Language Testing* 9 (1): 51–78.

Griffin, P.E. 1985. The use of latent trait models in the calibration of tests of spoken language in large scale selection placement programs. In Lee *et al.* (eds.), *New Directions in Language Testing:* 149–61. Oxford: Pergamon.

Henning, G. 1984. Advantages of latent trait measurement in language testing. *Language Testing* 1 (2): 123–33.

Henning, G. 1992. Dimensionality and construct validity of language tests. *Language Testing* 9 (1): 1–11.

Henning, G., T. Hudson and J. Turner. 1985. Item response theory and the assumption of unidimentionality for language tests. *Language Testing* 2 (2): 141–54.

Jensen, A.R. 1978. g: Outmoded Theory or Unconquered Frontier? *Creative Science and Technology* 2 (3).

Lee, Y.P. 1993. Construct validation of language test via Rasch analysis. Occasional Papers in *Applied Language Studies.* Hong Kong: Hong Kong Baptist College, Language Centre.

Lee, Y.P. 1994. Problems and issues in communicative language testing. In J. Boyle and P. Falvey (eds.), *Language Testing in the 90s*: 173–90. Hong Kong: The Chinese University Press.

Linacre, J. M. 1989a. *Many-faceted Rasch Measurement.* Chicago, IL: MESA Press.

Linacre, J .M. 1989b. *Constructing Measurement from Judge-awarded Ratings with a Many-faceted Rasch Model.* Chicago, IL: MESA Press.

Linacre, J. M. and B. D. Wright. 1990. *FACETS.* Chicago, IL: MESA Press.

McKay, P., C. Hudson and M. Sapuppo. 1992. The NLLIA ESL Band scales. In *NLLIA E5L Development: Language and Literacy in Schools Project Report* Volume 1. Canberra: National Languages and Literacy Institute of Australia.

Pollitt, A. and C. Hutchinson. 1987. Calibrating graded assessments: Rasch partial credit analysis of performance in writing. *Language Testing* 4 (1): 72–92.

Reckase M. D. 1979. Unifactor latent trait models applied to multi factor tests: results and implications. *Journal of Educational Statistics* 4.

Woods, A. and R. Baker. 1985. Item response theory, IRT, *Language Testing* 2 (2).

Wright, B. D. and G. N. Masters. 1982. *Rating Scale Analysis.* Chicago, IL: MESA Press.

15 Early bilingualism, cognition and assessment

Ludo Verhoeven
Tilburg University

Introduction

It is a common pattern that ethnic minority groups live in a country where another language is dominant and where native speakers of this dominant language do not speak or understand most of these minority language varieties. Intergroup communication is most likely to take place in the majority language. However, the language norms for intragroup communication do not need to be adopted for intragroup communication. Given the fact that language can have a core value of cultural identity, the ethnic group language is often used for communication in the ethnic community (itself). Group membership turns out to be an important explanatory factor in the language behavior of ethnic minorities (cf. Extra and Verhoeven 1993a).

For many ethnic minority children first language (L1) starts from a favorable position (cf. Tosi 1984). Its development benefits from rich input from the family and the neighborhood, but later the conditions of exposure to L1 may become very poor. At school the mother tongue is often banned; at best it constitutes only a minimal portion of the curriculum. Depending on the channels of language input in the home environment, a large variation in first and second language acquisition patterns among ethnic groups can be expected. Sociolinguistic studies have shown that environmental factors, such as the child's social background, his language contacts, and the social and physical situation in which language behavior takes place may lead to differences in rate of first and second language development (cf. Verhoeven 1991). Day care and kindergarten play an important role in children's early language learning. The interaction with peers who speak L1 or L2 as a native language will enhance their language development. Institutional contexts also give minority children the opportunity to use language in a meaningful way and to receive feedback from professional caretakers. In many studies it has been found that the quality of interaction patterns is extremely relevant for minority children's progress in second language development (see McLaughlin 1985:145–63).

A fundamental problem of the study of language proficiency and language development concerns the unique nature of linguistic structures. Though the assumption that innate mechanisms underlie human language ability seems quite valid, the conception of a localized language organ is not consistent with modern biological theory. Edelman (1992) has claimed that the neural substrata underlying human linguistic ability do not appear to be separated from other aspects of human cognitive ability. Thus, it can be assumed that the process of language acquisition must represent an interaction between universal grammar and other cognitive functions. With respect to the processes associated with first and second language development in ethnic minority children, the notion of interdependency is highly important. While focusing on the acquisition of cognitive/ academic language skills, Cummins (1983) proposed the interdependency hypothesis which says that:

> *To the extent that instruction in a certain language is effective in promoting proficiency in that language, transfer of this proficiency to another language will occur, provided there is adequate exposure to that other language (either in the school or environment) and adequate motivation to learn that language.*

The hypothesis predicts transfer not only from L1 to L2, but also from L2 to L1, unless the exposure and motivation conditions are negative.

In a bilingual program, the interdependency hypothesis would predict that instruction in one language leads not only to cognitive skills in that language, but also to a deeper conceptual and linguistic proficiency which is strongly related to cognition and general academic skill in the other language. In other words: although surface aspects of linguistic proficiency, such as fluency, develop separately, an underlying proficiency is presupposed which is common across languages. This common underlying proficiency is said to facilitate the transfer of cognitive/academic skills across languages.

Cummins (1984) attempted to conceptualize language proficiency in such a way that the developmental interrelationships between academic achievement and language proficiency in both L1 and L2 can be more fully understood. He integrated his earlier distinction between basic interpersonal and cognitive/ academic language skills in a new theoretical framework by conceptualizing language proficiency along two continuums; a horizontal and a vertical continuum. The horizontal continuum relates to the range of contextual support for expressing or receiving meaning. The extremes of this continua are described as 'context-embedded' versus 'context-reduced'. In context-embedded communication, meaning is said to be actively negotiated by participants who give each other feedback and supply paralinguistic cues in case meaning is not fully understood. In context-reduced communication, learners are said to be entirely dependent on linguistic cues for meaning and to suspend knowledge-of-the-world in some cases in order to interpret the logic of the communication.

The vertical continuum in Cummins' framework is intended to address the developmental aspects of language proficiency in terms of the degree of active cognitive involvement for appropriate performance on a task. Cognitive involvement is conceptualized in terms of the amount of information which must be processed simultaneously or in close succession by the individual. As such, the upper part of the vertical continuum refers to tasks in which language processes become largely automatized, while at the lower end active cognitive involvement is required.

According to Cummins (1989,1991), the above framework permits the developmental interrelationships between proficiency in L1 and L2 to be conceptualized. First, he proposed that such interrelationships can predominantly take place in the case of performance on academic tasks. A task is defined as more academic as the context-reduction and the cognitive demands increase. From a review of studies on bilingual development, it can be concluded that research evidence shows support for the principle of linguistic interdependency in at least some linguistic domains (Verhoeven, 1994).

In the present study (see Verhoeven *et al.* 1993) an attempt is made to assess the bilingual proficiency of Turkish, Moroccan and Antillean children, living in the Netherlands. A bilingual proficiency test was constructed monitoring children's cognitive and language development at kindergarten level. A report will be given on its construction and validation. The goals of the present study were:

1 To assess the first and second language proficiency in Turkish, Moroccan and Antillean children in the Netherlands at kindergarten level.
2 To explore the dimensions underlying children's performance on first and second language tasks.
3 To test the hypothesis that children's level of bilingual proficiency is related to background characteristics, such as age, institutional care, socio-economic background, and language contact.
4 To determine to what extent there is empirical evidence for interdependency in the processes of first and second language development.

Design of the study

Informants

In the present study we examined the patterns of first and second language development of 77 Turkish, 70 Moroccan and 70 Antillean children, born and living in the Netherlands. For an overview of the sociolinguistic background of these ethnic groups, see Extra and Verhoeven (1993b). Turks form the largest minority group in the Netherlands. In 1990 they numbered 185,000, and there were 33,700 Turkish children in Dutch primary schools. Moroccans constitute 144,000, the second largest minority group. In 1990 there were 33,000 Moroccan children enrolled in Dutch primary schools. Turkish and Moroccan children are from the second generation, the children of immigrants who moved to the

Netherlands during the past decades. The language patterns of these children can be characterized as follows: they are living in primarily ethnic group language speaking homes with mothers who are almost always monolingual speakers of the ethnic group language. The early language input of the children is restricted to this language, and the Dutch language enters into their lives only gradually, through Dutch playmates and school.

The language situation of Antillean children in the Netherlands, on the other hand, is totally different (cf. Narain and Verhoeven 1993). The children originate from the islands of Aruba and Curaçao which are part of the Dutch Antilles, a former colony. Whereas in Aruba and Curaçao Papiamentu is used officially and unofficially in almost all domains, in the Netherlands the use of Papiamentu is reduced to intragroup communication. Dutch is becoming the language of intergroup communication and the exclusive language used in school. At this moment there are about 70,000 people from the Dutch Antilles living in the Netherlands. The profile of the Antillean immigrant in the Netherlands has changed drastically during the past decade. Until the 1960s, most of the immigrants were élite students eager to be admitted into Dutch society and willing and able to exchange their mother tongue for the Dutch language. Nowadays the greater part of the Antillean ethnic minority in Holland is made up of young Papiamentu speaking Antilleans – with hardly any education – who left their home country because of economic deterioration on the islands. The families consist mostly of single mothers with young children. Their low level of schooling in Curaçao generally brings about a low proficiency in Dutch.

The children were recruited from 43 kindergarten classrooms in 15 fairly big cities spread over the country. The interaction in these classrooms was in Dutch. Only the Turkish and Moroccan children had interaction in their native language also for two hours a week. The children's age varied from 4.0 to 6.2 years with a mean age of 5.1 years.

Instruments

In order to assess children's language proficiency equivalent tests were taken in L1 and L2, measuring phonological, lexical, morphosyntactic and textual abilities. On the lexical level, vocabulary measures were taken, not only for content words, but also for cognitive concepts (i.e. color names, quantifiers, temporal and spatial terms). Departing from a hierarchical structure of language proficiency distinct tasks were administered, measuring equivalent phonological, lexical, syntactic and textual abilities in L1 and L2.

Sound manipulation

Sound manipulation (SM): perception and production of minimal phonemic differences in monosyllabic words in the languages under consideration (25 items). In this task children were asked to repeat minimal word pairs (Dutch example: beer – peer). The score on this task is determined by calculating the number of correctly reproduced word pairs.

Cognitive categorization

Cognitive categorization (CC): comprehension of reference to the concepts of colour (15 items), shape (15 items), quantity (15 items), space (10 items) and cause-effect (10 items). These aspects can be labeled 'linguistic universals': language features which are common to all languages and related to some innate predisposition of perception and cognition (cf. Clark and Clark 1977). In the items of this task children were given three pictures, together with an aural production of a stimulus sentence whose meaning corresponded with one of the pictures. The total number of correct items determined the score on this task.

Receptive and productive vocabulary

Receptive vocabulary (RV): comprehension of content words (40 nouns and 20 verbs). In this task words were spoken as the child was shown four pictures, one of which corresponded to the correct meaning of the word. The total of 60 items were arranged in increasing difficulty; when the child failed to respond correctly to five consecutive items, the task was ended. The score was determined as the total number of items responded to correctly.

Productive vocabulary (PV): production of content words (30 nouns and 10 verbs). For this task, pictures of objects and actions were shown, and the child was asked to describe each picture. For this task too, items were arranged in increasing difficulty; the task was stopped when the child missed five consecutive items.

In order to arrive at more or less equivalent vocabulary measures for the four languages under consideration the following procedure was followed. A corpus of 7000 Dutch words, evaluated by 200 teachers on the criterion whether they thought that a particular word on the list, given in context, should be understood by six-year-old native Dutch children, was taken as a starting point. The words on the list were placed in the order of teacher agreement ratings. For the first words nearly every teacher agreed that a six-year-old should understand the word, whereas for the last words only 25 per cent of the teachers thought so. The next step was to randomly select one out of any 20 successive words on the list. From the resulting shorter list culture specific words were excluded, e.g., kerk ('church'), varken ('pork'). As a third step, Turkish, Papiamentu and Moroccan-Arabic equivalents were sought for all words. Words that could only be expressed by a compound, or three or more words, were eliminated. A list of 200 words was the result. The fourth step was to hand this list to groups of native language speaking teachers working in Dutch schools with the request to mark the words they thought six-year-old native Turkish, Antillean and Moroccan children in the Netherlands could understand, if presented in context. After the teachers had worked through the list, the words were ordered according to their agreement ratings. The final list of words was considered to be relatively culturally unbiased. Two samples of words were taken: 60 words for receptive vocabulary tasks and 40 words for productive vocabulary tasks in the four languages. As a validity check, the rankings of Turkish, Antillean, Moroccan and Dutch teachers for the words in these samples were correlated. The correlations were above .75. This result can be seen as support of the assumption that there was no strong cultural bias.

Sentence imitation

Sentence imitation (SI): reproduction of 40 critical morphosyntactic cues in current sentences. In this task 20 sentences that contained a rich variety of grammatical morphemes and syntactic structures were offered in each language. The mean length of stimulus sentences, as well as the mean number of nominal and verbal phrases, was held constant over the four languages. After presentation of each sentence the child was asked to reproduce each sentence as soon as it was spoken. If the child did not respond, the sentence was repeated once. The grammatical aspects under investigation in the task were function words and word order characteristics. The total number of correctly reproduced items determined the child's score on this task.

Text comprehension

Text comprehension (TC): comprehension of explicit information (10 items) and implicit information (10 items) in oral texts. The task consisted of four short texts which were read by the experimenter. After each text was read, five questions were asked referring to information that is explicitly given in the text and to implicit information in the text. The score on this task was the total number of questions correctly answered by the child.

In addition to these language proficiency measures, several measures were taken, referring to the background of the children: age, socio-economic stratum (SES), period of institutional care (including kindergarten), contact with minority language speaking peers and contact with Dutch language speaking peers at home as well as at school (as marked by the classroom teacher on five-point scales, running from no contact to intensive contact).

Procedure

Item-test score-correlations (Rit's) and Cronbach's alpha were measured in order to estimate the internal consistency of the language tasks under consideration. Moreover, One-Parameter-Maximum-Likelihood-analyses (OPML) (cf. Verhelst and Eggen 1989) were carried out on the same tasks to test the homogeneity of the measures taken.

By means of t-test analysis it was determined to what extent differences in patterns of bilingual proficiency for each ethnic group were significant. Factor analysis (PA-2) was used to determine whether the six proficiency measures in the children's first and second language could be reduced to unidimensional traits. In order to find out to what extent language skills in L1 and L2 are related to background characteristics correlations were computed between test scores and the measures of age, SES, period of institutional care, contact with minority language speaking peers and second language speaking peers. In order to test Cummins' interdependency hypothesis correlations were computed between L1 and L2 factor scores.

Results

Internal consistency of test measures

Table 1 presents for each measure in L1 and L2 the value of Cronbach's alpha, the mean Rit, and the Chi-square-test results for the OPML-testing. It can be seen that all test measures involved show reasonable results. In all cases the value of Crobach's alpha is above .80. Moreover, in no cases did the assumption of fit of the OPML-model need to be rejected.

Table 1

**Cronbach's alpha, mean Rit and test characteristics
one-parameter item response-model per group and per test**

	alpha	Rit	χ^2	df	p
Turkish					
Sound manipulation	.90	.56	25.7	24	.40
Cognitive categorization	.90	.38	44.94	64	.92
Receptive vocabulary	.90	.47	36.35	39	.63
Productive vocabulary	.85	.39	9.63	37	.99
Sentence imitation	.95	.58	22.88	39	.99
Text comprehension	.89	.57	15.37	19	.70
Papiamentu					
Sound manipulation	.92	.63	21.53	24	.61
Cognitive categorization	.92	.42	54.86	64	.62
Receptive vocabulary	.91	.48	33.04	38	.75
Productive vocabulary	.92	.57	27.73	26	.40
Sentence imitation	.96	.62	29.44	39	.90
Text comprehension	.93	.64	5.66	19	.99
Moroccan					
Sound manipulation	.87	.50	20.08	24	.69
Cognitive categorization	.83	.30	80.85	64	.06
Receptive vocabulary	.90	.47	37.25	39	.62
Productive vocabulary	.89	.53	23.18	22	.41
Sentence imitation	.94	.52	31.67	39	.82
Text comprehension	.87	.53	15.28	19	.70
Dutch					
Sound manipulation	.87	.50	24.84	24	.42
Cognitive categorization	.89	.36	75.43	64	.11
Receptive vocabulary	.95	.52	67.39	56	.07
Productive vocabulary	.90	.63	9.04	15	.89
Sentence imitation	.95	.59	23.44	39	.97
Text comprehension	.91	.60	19.16	19	.60

Patterns of bilingual proficiency

Turks

Table 2 presents the means, standard deviations and t-test statistics for the Turkish group. It can be seen that, except for color names, Turkish children are dominant in L1.

Table 2

**Means, standard deviations and t-test statistics
for the group of Turkish children**

	L1	L2	t	df	P
Sound manipulation	19.59	15.67	6.19	75	.001
Cognitive categorization					
– total	36.71	27.69	9.29	75	.001
– color names	9.57	9.44	.44	75	n. s.
– form names	7.24	5.84	4.53	75	.001
– quantifiers	9.36	5.45	11.90	75	.001
– spatial terms	5.33	3.89	5.25	75	.001
– cause-effect terms	5.22	3.30	6.58	75	.001
Receptive vocabulary	31.93	15.08	6.58	75	.001
Productive vocabulary	18.55	3.46	25.80	75	.001
Sentence imitation	20.09	7.33	12.64	74	.001
Text comprehension	11.07	2.54	14.30	74	.001

Figure 1

**Mean proportion correct scores for the
Turkish children per language and per task**

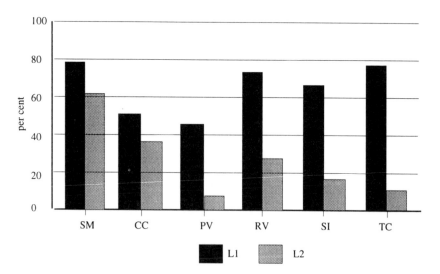

Figure 1 shows the mean per cent correct scores for the Turkish children on the L1 and L2 tests. It can be seen that the Turkish children are most dominant in L1 (especially at lexical, syntactic and textual tasks).

Antilleans

In Table 3 the means, standard deviations and t-test statistics for the Antillean group are presented. It can be seen that for the measures of sound manipulation, form names and text comprehension the children are dominant in Papiamentu. For the categorization of color names the children turn out to be dominant in Dutch, whereas on other measures no differences between L1 and L2 scores are found.

Table 3

Means, standard deviations and t-test statistics for the group of Antillean children

	L1	L2	t	df	P
Sound manipulation	19.59	15.93	4.25	69	.001
Cognitive categorization					
– total	34.67	33.86	.55	69	n.s
– color names	9.31	11.15	–4.08	69	.001
– form names	9.43	7.73	4.24	69	.001
– quantifiers	7.46	6.19	3.17	69	.01
– spatial terms	4.93	4.86	.21	69	n.s.
– cause-effect terms	3.54	3.93	–1.21	69	n.s.
Receptive vocabulary	30.78	28.21	1.50	69	n.s.
Productive vocabulary	10.23	9.50	.60	69	n.s.
Sentence imitation	18.17	15.37	1.69	69	n.s.
Text comprehension	9.46	7.74	2.11	69	.05

Figure 2

Mean proportion correct scores for the Antillean children per language and per task

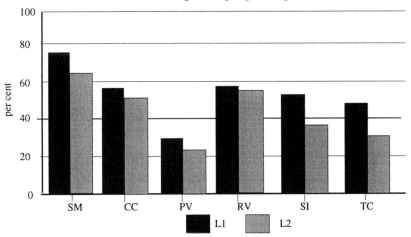

285

In Figure 2 the mean per cent correct scores for the Antillean children on the L1 and L2 tests are given. It can be seen that the language pattern for the Antillean children is more or less balanced.

Moroccans

Table 4 presents the means, standard deviations and t-test statistics for the Moroccan group. It can be seen that the children are dominant in the mother tongue for the measures of sound manipulation, categorization of quantifiers, receptive and productive vocabulary, sentence imitation and text comprehesnion. For the categorization of names, referring to form, space and cause-effect no differences between languages can be found. For color names the children turn out to be better in their second language.

Table 4

**Means, standard deviations and t-test statistics
for the group of Moroccan children**

	L1	L2	t	df	P
Sound manipulation	15.63	13.50	2.70	69	.01
Cognitive categorization					
– total	30.50	29.67	.65	69	n.s
– color names	7.31	8.51	–2.61	69	.01
– form names	7.30	6.80	1.54	69	n.s.
– quantifiers	7.17	6.37	2.36	69	.05
– spatial terms	4.63	4.20	1.48	69	n.s.
– cause-effect terms	4.09	3.79	1.33	69	n.s.
Receptive vocabulary	26.44	21.47	2.54	69	.05
Productive vocabulary	14.37	7.37	8.40	69	.01
Sentence imitation	15.84	12.16	2.80	69	.01
Text comprehension	8.27	6.16	2.94	69	.01

Figure 3 presents the mean per cent correct scores for the Moroccan children on the L1 and L2 tests. It can be seen that the Moroccan children are also dominant in L1, although the L1/L2 contrast is not as large as with the Turkish group.

Figure 3

**Mean proportion correct scores for the
Moroccan children per language and per task**

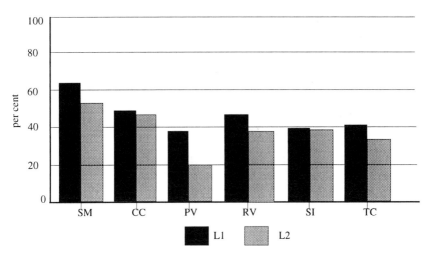

Relationship between tests

Common Factor Analysis for the L1 and L2 proficency measures yielded a one-factor solution in all cases. Table 5 presents the proportions explained variance for each of these solutions.

Table 5

**Proportions explained variance for
Common Factor Analyses per language, per group**

Group	L1	L2
Turks	62	66
Antilleans	63	66
Moroccans	58	66

Table 6 gives the factor loadings of the six proficiency measures for the two languages in each ethnic group. It can be seen that all tests, except for sound manipulation, show high loadings on the factors displayed. The factor loadings for sound manipulation can be called moderate.

Table 6

Factor loadings of the L1 and L2 proficiency measures in the three ethnic groups

Test	Turks		Antilleans		Moroccans	
	L1	L2	L1	L2	L1	L2
Sound manipulation	.58	.55	.53	.55	.75	.55
Cognitive categorization	.87	.85	.88	.85	.77	.85
Productive vocabulary	.78	.85	.77	.85	.79	.85
Receptive vocabulary	.80	.88	.83	.88	.67	.88
Sentence imitation	.81	.83	.88	.83	.84	.84
Text comprehension	.84	.86	.82	.86	.83	.86

Determinants of bilingual proficiency

Table 7 presents for the three ethnic groups the correlations between underlying factor scores in L1 and L2 and the background variables Age, Institutional Care, SES and Language Contact. The results make clear that in each group there is a substantial correlation between the children's first and second language proficiency and age and period of institutional care. Moderate significant correlations were obtained between language proficiency and language contact. The correlation between language proficiency and SES turned out to be weak. This may be due to the small variation in socio-economic background in the groups under consideration.

Table 7

Correlations between L1 and L2 factor scores and background variables in the three ethnic groups

	Turks		Antilleans		Moroccans	
	L1	L2	L1	L2	L1	L2
Age	.66***	.51***	.40***	.51***	.49***	.51***
Institutional care	.44***	.40***	.38***	.40***	.60***	.40***
SES	.22*	.14	.18	.14	.20*	.14
Language contact at home	.10	.20*	.24*	.26**	.13	.20**
Language contact at school	.22*	.15*	.35**	.15*	.26**	.15*

In order to test Cummins' claim on interdependency of linguistic skills in bilingual development the relations between L1 and L2 factor scores in the three ethnic groups were explored. The results are presented in Table 8. A significant positive correlation was indeed found between the children's linguistic proficiency scores in the two languages. However, clear intergroup differences are evidenced:

for the Turkish group the correlation is high, for the Moroccan group it is moderate, for the Antillean group it is low. The low correlation for the Antillean children can be explained by the fact that social factors, as exemplified by language contact, have the greatest impact on first and second language development in this group. It can be assumed that the higher the impact of social factors on bilingual development, the more the correlation between L1 and L2 will be suppressed.

Table 8

**Correlations between L1 and L2
factor scores in the three ethnic groups**

	Correlation between L1 and L2
Turks	.72***
Antilleans	.25**
Moroccans	.47***

Conclusions

From the present study several conclusions can be drawn. First of all, it is clear that the patterns of bilingual development can be very different for different ethnic groups. In our study the Turkish children tended to be quite dominant in their mother tongue. The language proficiency levels of the Antillean children, on the other hand, tended to be much more balanced. The Moroccan children seem to be in an intermediate position. Different socio-cultural factors may be responsible for these different patterns of development (see Verhoeven 1991). Besides intergroup differences in bilingual proficiency, intragroup differences could also be evidenced. For instance, their overall proficiency being stronger in L1, Antillean and Moroccan children did better on the categorization of color names in L2. This result can be explained from the fact that the naming of colors is highly focused on in kindergarten.

The present study also makes clear that one factor underlies the children's abilities in L1 and L2 proficiency. The scores on formal linguistic tasks, such as sound manipulation, sentence imitation and text comprehension, on the one hand, and cognitive tasks, such as vocabulary and cognitive categorization, on the other hand, appear highly related.

Furthermore, the present study shows that there is a close relationship between L1 and L2 proficiency level and the child's age. Moreover, the proficiency level in either language turned out to be positively related to the period of institutional care the child had gone through, the extent of language contact, and to a lesser degree, the socio-economic background of the child.

Another important finding from the present study is that the children's proficiency levels in L1 and L2 were clearly related. As such, positive evidence was found for Cummins' interdependency hypothesis. The strong emphasis on cognitive aspects in the language tasks may have strengthened the corrections between L1 and L2 proficiency levels within each of the ethnic groups.

There are, of course, a number of limitations to the present study. First of all, it should be mentioned that in the present study the construct of language proficiency has been assessed in a restricted way. To arrive at a better understanding of children's communicative competence we also need insight into children's pragmatic behavior. In an earlier study it was shown that in language assessment context-based pragmatic skills can be distinguished from decontextualized grammatical skills (see Verhoeven 1992). Second, the present study deals with cross-sectional research data. In order to explore the linguistic interdependency hypothesis in more detail longitudinal research findings are in order. Finally, the present study gives no account of the consequences of bilingual development. In several earlier studies it was shown that children who acquire a high proficiency in two or more languages at an early stage enjoy an advantage in a number of cognitive domains (for an overview see Bialystok and Ryan 1985; Hakuta 1986; Cummins 1989).

References

Bialystok, E. and E. B. Ryan. 1985. Metacognitive framework for the development of first and second language skills. In D. L. Forrest-Pressley, G. E. MacKinnon and T. G. Waller (eds.), *Metacognition, Cognition and Human Performance.* New York, NY: Academic Press.

Clark, H. H. and E. V. Clark. 1977. *Psychology and Language.* New York, NY: Harcourt, Brace, Jovanovich.

Cummins, J. 1983. *Heritage Language Education: A Literature Review.* Toronto: Ministry of Education.

Cummins, J. 1984. Wanted: A theoretical framework for relating language proficiency to academic achievement among bilingual students. In C. Rivera (ed.), *Language Proficiency and Academic Achievement.* Clevedon, Avon: Multilingual Matters.

Cummins, J. 1989. Language and literacy acquisition in bilingual contexts. *Journal of Multilingual and Multicultural Development,* 10, 1.

Cummins, J. 1991. Conversational and academic language proficiency in bilingual contexts. *AILA Review,* 8.

Edelman, G. M. 1992. *Bright Air, Brilliant Fire.* New York, NY: Basic Books.

Extra, G. and L. Verhoeven. 1993a. *Immigrant Languages in Europe.* Clevedon, Avon: Multilingual Matters.

Extra, G. and L. Verhoeven. 1993b. *Community Languages in the Netherlands.* Lisse: Swets and Zeitlinger.

Hakuta, K. 1986. *Mirror of Language: The Debate on Bilingualism.* New York, NY: Basic Books.

McLaughlin, B. 1985. *Second Language Acquisition in Childhood.* Hillsdale, NJ: Lawrence Erlbaum Associates.

Narain, G. and L. Verhoeven. 1993. Development of Papiamentu in a mono- and bilingual context. *AILA-Bulletin* 10 (2).

Tosi, A. 1984. *Immigration and Bilingual Education.* Oxford: Pergamon Press.

Verhelst, N. and T. Eggen. 1989. *Psychometrische en statistische aspecten van peilingsonderzoek. (Psychometric and Statistic Aspects of Assessment Research).* Arnhem: Cito.

Verhoeven, L. 1991. Predicting minority children's bilingual proficiency: Child, family and institutional factors. *Language Learning* 41 (2).

Verhoeven, L. 1992. Assessment of bilingual proficiency. In L. Verhoeven and J. H. A. L. de Jong (eds.), *The Construct of Bilingual Proficiency.* Amsterdam/ Philadelphia: John Benjamins.

Verhoeven, L. 1994. Transfer in bilingual development: The linguistic interdependency hypothesis revisited. *Language Learning* 44 (3).

Verhoeven, L., G. Extra, O. Konak, G. Narain and R. Zerrouk. 1993. *Peiling van vroege tweetaligheid. (Assessment of Early Bilingual Proficiency).* Tilburg: University Press.

16 Development of new proficiency based skill level descriptors for translation: theory and practice

Eduardo C. Cascallar   **Center for the Advancement of Language Learning**

Marijke I. Cascallar   **Federal Bureau of Investigation**
Pardee Lowe, Jr.   **Federal Language Training Laboratory**

James R. Child   **Department of Defense**

Introduction

The set of guidelines described in this report builds on work carried out in the past decade by the members of the Interagency Language Roundtable (ILR). A number of federal agencies as well as outside organizations have developed translation evaluation systems which meet their specific organizational goals. There has not as yet been any agreement reached on a standard set of proficiency guidelines which would provide US translators in both the public and private sectors with a uniform approach to evaluating translation. The guidelines set out in this paper represent a first step toward unifying the disparate translation evaluation systems currently in use.

These guidelines are different than previous systems in two ways. First, where previous systems took into account only the reading and writing skills of prospective translators, these guidelines consider an additional measure: that of congruity judgment – the ability to comprehend a donor[1] text and to select from a number of possible alternatives a receptor language equivalent which most fully reproduces the meaning of the original. Second, these guidelines set out a taxonomy of what will be termed text modes: broad categories of texts divided according to their originator's intent and level of complexity. These guidelines seek to link these text modes to levels of translation ability in a way that is much different than the approach taken by earlier guidelines, which generally enumerated various genres of documents a translator at each level could be expected to translate effectively. By raising the analysis of test genres to a higher level – that of text modes – the authors feel that they are providing test designers and evaluators with a finer-grained measure for evaluating the difficulty levels of translation passages used to rate translation ability.

Translation rating systems

A number of organizations, public and private, need to assess translation ability for the purpose of hiring, evaluating, or certifying prospective translators to meet their needs and objectives. Prospective users of translation services have used or developed various rating systems for translation ability. Some rating systems are holistic in nature in dealing with errors, focusing on the relationship of the content of entire texts or major text segments to that of smaller units. Other rating systems focus on smaller, formal units (at the sentence level and below) in distinguishing error types to arrive at final judgments. Rating systems range along a continuum from simple to complex, ranging from those which simply mark errors, to those which define broad categories of errors, to those which employ a set of translation skill level descriptors. The rating systems which employ skill level descriptors all roughly parallel the American Council on the Teaching of Foreign Languages (ACTFL)/Educational Testing Service (ETS)/ Interagency Language Roundtable (ILR) proficiency guidelines for reading and writing, generally referred to as the AEI proficiency guidelines. In the discussion below of the rating systems, a close reading of the descriptions indicates that many of the systems focus on lower linguistic levels (syntax, grammar, and morphology) rather than on the text as a whole.

Error classification

Various federal agencies and other organizations involved in translation testing have developed error notation systems for grading tests. These systems often make distinctions between a number of different errors, designating major and minor errors that result either from misunderstandings in the donor language or misrepresentations in the receptor language. These systems also allow for the identification of errors that render translations which are too free or inappropriately colloquial when such translations would not be acceptable in the particular professional environment of the receptor text, i.e. contracts, legal documents, or technical writings. Various academic institutions which have translation programs, the American Translators Association (ATA), and some federal agencies employing large numbers of translators all have independent rating systems which attempt to provide useful information regarding translation ability. Some systems describe the translator, others describe the translation, and some attempt to do both. To date, there has been no common metric to rate translation ability.

Department of Defense

This lack of commonality for rating translation ability has created a vacuum in which extremely diverse systems could develop. As an example, over the course of two decades, one federal agency within the Department of Defense (DoD) has employed several versions of a grading system for evaluating translations into English. The current grading system is based on a hundred-point scale from which points are subtracted for errors. Errors are assigned a point value between one and four. One-point deductions involve violations of English usage which render the translation as stilted or unidiomatic. Two-point errors have to do with the area of lexicon and certain kinds of grammatical affix. Three-point errors apply to minor syntactic errors which distort the meaning from that intended in the donor language. Four-point errors pertain to major syntactic errors which significantly alter the meaning intended in the donor language.

Federal Bureau of Investigation

The Federal Bureau of Investigation has developed at least three sets of AEI-type guidelines for translation over the past ten years. All of these sets of guidelines have descriptors for each level, levels zero through five, including plus levels.

1982 Translation guidelines

The first set of guidelines developed in the early 1980s, which bears a great resemblance to the AEI proficiency guidelines for reading and writing, was submitted to the ILR Testing Committee, but did not receive community-wide acceptance and was only used internally by the submitting agency. The Level 3 Translation Skill Level Description, considered the minimum level for professional performance, reads as follows:

> *Able to translate authentic prose on unfamiliar subjects.*
> *Translating ability is not dependent on subject matter knowledge.*
> *Texts will include news stories similar to wire service reports,*
> *routine correspondence, general reports and technical material*
> *in his/her professional field, all of which include hypothesis,*
> *argumentation and supported opinions. Such texts typically include*
> *grammatical patterns and vocabulary ordinarily encountered in*
> *professional reading. Mistranslations rare. Almost always able to*
> *correctly translate material, relate ideas and make inferences.*
> *Rarely has to pause over or reread general vocabulary. However,*
> *may experience some difficulty with unusually complex structures*
> *and low-frequency idioms.*
>
> *In preparing translations, control of structure, spelling and*
> *general vocabulary is adequate to convey his/her message*

accurately, but style may be obviously foreign. Errors virtually never interfere with comprehension and rarely disturb the native reader. Punctuation generally controlled. Employs a full range of structures. Control of grammar good, with only sporadic errors in basic structures, occasional errors in the most complex structures. Consistent control of compound and complex sentences. Relationship of ideas presented in original material is consistently clear.

Although these guidelines describe the type of material a translator at a given level can handle as well as the requisite writing accuracy in the receptor language for that level, they do not directly address congruity judgment, the specific ability required for translation, covered in the guidelines developed in this paper.

Mid-1980s Translation guidelines

In the mid-1980s, the FBI developed another set of level descriptions which used a zero through five scale for *grammatical accuracy*, resembling a discrete point system rather than proficiency guidelines, and another zero through five scale for *thought conveyance* which was subdivided into *lexical choice* and *tone*. The Level 3 descriptions for grammatical accuracy and thought conveyance read as follows:

Grammatical accuracy

Morphology	Present tense	Virtually always correct
	Future, present, imperfect, conditional and subjunctive tenses, irregular verbs and nonverb endings	Normally correct
	Other tenses	Occasionally correct
Syntax	Articles	Normally correct
	Prepositions	Normally correct
	Complex relative clauses	Normally correct
	Passive constructions	Occasionally correct
	Pronouns	Normally correct
Spelling		Consistently correct
Capitalization		Consistently correct
Punctuation	Comma and all other	Normally correct

Thought conveyance

Lexical Choice	Definitional accuracy	Consistently correct
	Contextual accuracy	Normally correct
Tone	Tailors language of translation to	Normally conveys
meaning	correspond to donor text style/mood	with full accuracy
	Recognizes objective view-points, nuances and subtleties appearing in the donor text	

These level descriptions were also submitted to the ILR Testing Committee, but they again failed to become the government-wide standard for describing translation ability. The latter level descriptions were so difficult to apply to rating translation tests that even the FBI never used them to evaluate translation tests.

1992 Translation guidelines

In the early 1990s, in connection with the development of a Spanish translation test (Stansfield, Scott and Kenyon 1990), the Bureau and the ILR Testing Committee collaborated on another set of AEI-type guidelines. These tripartite guidelines have scales for *interpretive information, expression*, and *accuracy*. The interpretive scale describes the type of material which a translator of a given ability level may be able to handle. The expression scale characterizes writing ability in the receptor language, addressing punctuation, spelling, syntax, grammatical structures, word choice, use of idioms, etc. The accuracy scale sets forth the various levels of translation ability in terms of conveying the donor language text and addresses mistranslations, omissions, additions, and conveyance of nuance.

The interpretive information scale for the T-3 level is:

> *Able to translate acceptably most formal and informal written exchanges on practical, social, and professional topics. Demonstrates an emerging ability to translate diverse subject matter.*

Expression at Level 3:

> *Occasionally makes spelling mistakes, some grammar mistakes in low frequency complex structures, sporadic errors in high frequency complex structures, and shows no pattern of errors in basic structure. Uses punctuation that is almost identical to donor document, i.e. sometimes atypical of the receptor language. Moderately good ability to join or divide original sentences as required by receptor language constructions, while still retaining the meaning of the donor document. Moderately good ability to use complex structures, sentence patterns, and vocabulary appropriate for expressing abstract thoughts. Moderately good knowledge of idiomatic expressions and colloquialisms, and some sayings and proverbs, but with occasional misunderstandings. Uses a number of syntactic constructions that are more characteristic of donor language than receptor language, thereby producing documents that appear to be a translation. This person's style and tone are even, but occasionally differ slightly from original.*

Accuracy at Level 3:

> *Produces translations whose accuracy is good, with occasional minor mistranslations or omissions. Can handle clearly identifiable nuances.*

These guidelines were called the Provisional Interagency Language Roundtable Language Skill Level Descriptions for Translation. However, they are not currently in use.

Current rating procedures

The FBI currently uses a combination of the above as well as a detailed Error Notation Key (FBI 1990).This document helps raters identify and mark mistranslations, incorrect additions and/or omissions, and errors in style, spelling, vocabulary, grammar, capitalization, punctuation. The number and type of errors are matched to the level descriptions and are used to provide an AEI-type score.

American Translators Association

In evaluating its translation exams, the ATA uses two graders applying the ATA standards who identify and count major and minor errors. Major errors include those mistranslations which totally change the meaning of the donor text, omit pertinent information, insert information not contained in the original, or represent serious grammatical errors in the receptor language. Minor errors cover mistranslations that slightly distort the original (Teague 1987). Any translation which contains two major errors receives a failing score regardless of the number of minor errors; translations containing one major and seven minor errors also receive a failing grade, although a translation without a major error will pass no matter how many minor errors are identified. The ATA and its Accreditation Committee are engaged in an ongoing effort to refine the accreditation program to ensure that test results properly identify people with translation ability and eliminate those whose skills are inadequate.

SUNY Binghamton Evaluation Scale for Translation

The Binghamton Evaluation Scale for Translation (BEST) was developed at SUNY-Binghamton in connection with its Translation Research and Instruction Program (TRIP) which has awarded the Graduate Certificate in Translation since 1974. BEST draws upon the AEI guidelines for reading and writing and on James R. Child's typology of texts (Mahn 1989). The resulting scale has skill level descriptions which describe the performance and the nature of texts for a given donor language level and assumes that the receptor language is the native language of the translator. For example, a person who is a Donor Language 3/ Receptor Language Native (SL3/TLN) is described as:

> *The SL3/TLN translator also works independently. S/he can handle formal and informal texts, including abstract texts and makes only minor errors that will not distort the author's intent. As we saw in the ACTFL/ETS description, 'misreading is rare' at the Superior level; therefore it is safe to assume that the errors at this level will not be major errors of mistranslation. The phrase 'works independently' is important because it implies that the translator should be aware of any problems and seek ways to solve them. This is not the case at the two lower levels, where the translator obviously is not aware of errors and needs supervision in work. The level 3 translator should comfortably handle any of the level 2 and below text variety.*
> (cited in Mahn 1989)

As to what constitutes errors, SUNY-Binghamton has adopted the ATA's system of major and minor errors, where the former are those mistranslations resulting in a change or loss of the original donor language meaning, omissions and additions which change the essence of the original, and serious grammatical errors and the presentation of alternate translations. Errors are considered minor if they do not distort the original meaning in a major fashion or result in *infelicities* – insignificant changes in wording or inelegant receptor language forms.

Summary

The previous sections have provided an overview of some of the major types of systems used to evaluate or grade translations in academic, federal, and professional organizations. Doubtless there are many other systems in use at other institutions. The ILR Testing Committee's experience suggests that these systems tend to stress two basic orientations: one in which textual wholes are considered in terms of overall intent, with parts identified as they contribute to the totality; the other, and, as was noted above, more frequent, reverses the process, with the result that grammatical structures take precedence over textual ones. While both have specific contributions to make to the elements of translation discussed in these descriptions, experience has shown that it is a well conceived blend of the two which will yield the reliable, valid guidelines essential to the discipline of translation. In summary, this section provides only a sampling of the approaches to translation evaluation that have been developed by many academic, professional and federal organizations involved in translation testing.

Translation terms

The following sections will introduce a number of significant translation terms, describe how translation may be approached from a content/form or a form/content perspective, and briefly treat the question of different translation types. In the following, it is assumed that an effective translator possesses certain knowledge and skills. Translation – the written rendering of a text which is both true to the content of the original donor text and clear and idiomatic in the receptor language text – requires that an effective translator possess both a broad general knowledge base and expertise in the special knowledge areas required by the translation, or possesses the ability to acquire such knowledge. The following guidelines address the separate linguistic skills contributing to the ability to translate effectively, such as reading the donor language and writing the receptor language. It is assumed that this ability exists and that it is present as defined by the relevant separate ILR skill level descriptions.

What then is unique to translation ability? Translation, in our experience, is an integrative ability. Thus, we conceive of it as one that puts all the other abilities involved in translation together. For instance, an individual could possess higher-level reading skills in the donor language as well as higher-level writing abilities in the receptor language and – although uncommon – still be unable to translate effectively. The glue which integrates these abilities would be missing.[2] Child (1990) calls that glue *congruity judgment(s)*: the ability to successfully match donor language features, characteristics, or forms to their most suitable receptor language equivalents. The demonstration of effective congruity judgment requires that a translator control the concepts of *organization* and *shaping*. It is crucial that a translator grasp the organization of the donor text, its connotations and denotations, and use that understanding to select an appropriate receptor language organization. In addition to being aware of organization, a translator should be able to note and reproduce the originator's shaping of the donor text, and to maintain the original subtle guiding of the reader through the choice of single lexical items and longer quotes or by the placement of material within the text. Shaping is a subtle part of organization, while organization has a much greater impact on the visual form of the text. The ability to make congruity judgments, often from among a number of appropriate choices, and to manifest such judgments in the rendering of the receptor text is what the authors believe to be unique to translation, whatever other skills may be required. Consequently, the scale guidelines detailed below focus on the nature of congruity judgment(s) at each ILR level.

Eduardo C. Cascallar

Translation types

A thorny issue in discussing translation is somehow delineating the many possible *types of translation* along what we call below the translation continuum. Between the most literal translation and the freest possible translation, there obviously stretches a continuum with many gradations.

Figure 1

The translation continuum

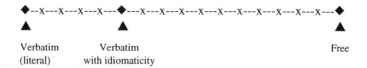

Verbatim	Verbatim	Free
(literal)	with idiomaticity	

The starting point for this discussion (indicated by the leftmost ◆ in Figure 1) is what many have called the *literal* translation. This is the closest word-by-word rendering possible, usually focus on denotation, or the most common rendering into the receptor language, which, consequently, ignores collocation, connotation, and nuance. At its worst, a literal rendering will almost completely mask or obfuscate the meaning of the original, as in the case of word-by-word relexification or glossing. *Word-by-word relexification* is the replacement of a donor language word by a receptor language word in exactly the same position in the sentence. In general, this process is based upon the assumption that there is a one-to-one correspondence between the two languages. Child (1990) terms this process *glossing*. Literal translations in this most extreme sense are generally useless. For the term literal, some have used the term *verbatim* as a synonym, as has been done here.

Moving away slightly from the literal pole, there may be some usable renderings which are somewhat literal. One such intermediate point might be called *verbatim with idiomaticity*; that is, a translation which is as close to the original as possible, yet that is idiomatic in the receptor language. Such translations are sometimes required in legal proceedings, and translators often purposely follow a process which Child (1990) calls *code-matching* – the matching of the same larger segments between the donor and receptor language texts, such that, for example, information embedded in a relative clause in one appears within a relative clause in the other – while avoiding literalness at the vocabulary or phrase level.

Contrasting with the pole *verbatim (literal)* and the intermediate point close to that pole *verbatim with idiomaticity* is the pole *free* translation. This third type of translation is distinct from literalness, from word-by-word relexification/glossing and from code-matching. Thus, a free translation is neither bound to the literalness of the word(s) nor to the literalness of word or phrase placement nor to extreme equivalence of structure.

Testing translation ability

Each organization which requires translation skills must find a way to assess whether a prospective translator possesses this ability. As can be seen from the overview of current rating systems above, the focus of each system currently in use is slightly different. Some approach the ability to translate by describing the prospective translator's language skills, while others attempt to classify the texts to be translated. Others combine both strategies. In the following sections, the authors suggest the format for a battery of tests of translation ability and provide guidelines for raters of the test of congruity judgment.

Test format

Since the very nature of translation involves two languages and a written text, it follows that a translator must demonstrate his or her reading comprehension in the donor language and writing skill in the receptor language. To demonstrate their ability, translators would take a battery of tests. The first phase of this assessment would examine a prospective translator's donor language reading comprehension and receptor language writing. These skills should be tested in advance of the actual translation exercise, and the results should be made available to prospective users of translation services. After this preliminary testing, the prospective translator would next face an exercise of the ability unique to translation: demonstration of *congruity judgment*. Prospective translators must be able to adjust the fit of their rendering to the content of the original text, at both the lexical and discourse level. Meeting that challenge is formidable, especially along the upper ranges of textual complexity: texts may, depending on the views and needs of the user of the translation, include philosophic discourses, scientific and technical studies of topics inaccessible to all but the specialist, or dialogues containing colloquial or slang words and phrases on unfamiliar subjects. The specifications of this congruity judgment exercise must of course require that all of these texts be rendered in the most idiomatic language possible, while rendering the semantic structure and intent. The preliminary tests may show a fair level of linguistic ability, but in a separate translation exercise, the rendering may yet prove to be askew. With this additional information about the language skills, the user can then infer that something has gone wrong in the translation process and not in the other two skills.

Test evaluation

It is essential that raters, however, address the evaluation of congruity judgment in as independent a fashion as possible. It is often assumed that there is a weakness in language skills from an analysis of a translation, since translation draws upon so many language skills at once. Splitting out congruity judgment to be examined separately would prevent this false assumption of lower linguistic skills as the reason for a weak translation. While the rating of translators' reading and writing skills is a necessary initial step, it may not always be sufficient: it must be kept in mind that the result of any donor language reading or receptor language writing test is at best a snapshot, not a comprehensive picture of the examinee's language abilities. In the majority of cases, though, testing procedures of the sort described above, if performed as carefully and thoroughly as possible, should prove adequate.

Translation and a taxonomy of text modes

Translation entails a complex set of skills, and while each of these skills can be identified and described separately in an analysis of the translation process, the contribution that any one skill makes is inevitably blurred in any translation. As was mentioned previously, it is possible to automatically assign tests which fall within a broad text category to a specific ILR reading skill level. Indeed, some of the translation rating systems described earlier include information about what text types translators at each level should be able to handle effectively. Since clear specifications are critical for rating texts and assigning them to skill levels, the authors recommend the use of taxonomy of textual modes, which classifies texts according to the intent of its originators into four larger categories. The sections that follow will define this taxonomy of textual modes, identify issues that pose challenges to translators within each mode, and provide guidelines for assigning texts within certain text types[3] and modes to specific skill levels.

Definition

The taxonomy of text modes by work and level proposed here is generally compatible with the ILR 11-point scale in use for the other language skills. It classifies texts according to the mode (or purpose) of the text: *Orientational* (O), *Instructive* (I), *Evaluative* (E) and *Projective* (P). All texts, regardless of their content type (general interest, technical, culturally-based, etc.) may be assigned one or more of these modes, depending on the particular intent of the originator(s).

Orientational (O) texts are brief and closely linked to the concrete world, and they address issues of space and time. Texts in this mode include the following: schedules; descriptions of places; directions for arriving at a given place; simple references to single or recurring events, which often occur in a highly predictable format; and a variety of other informational messages. These texts are frequently supplemented by pictures, diagrams, or printed forms and are intended to convey information as briefly and efficiently as possible. They reflect the immediate facts and needs of daily life, with the consequence that the message is more important than the originator.

Texts in the *Instructive* (I) mode likewise deal with facts, either actual or perceived, but they usually do so in an extended frame of reference over space and time. A newspaper reports events from the recent past; a planning document outlines projects for the future and proposes a plan of action to reach the desired goals; radio announcers, while covering an event immediate to themselves, are at the same time translating it for a distant audience. This feature of distancing the treatment of facts is critical for the I mode: such texts are required both to compensate for the audience's lack of non-linguistic information and to provide background information. In this mode, the text's originator acts upon the text to impart to it a sense of the spatial and temporal constructs implicit in reporting and narrating. In these situations the originator may play a role in the message greater than that within orientational texts.

Evaluative (E) mode texts, on the other hand, move away from facts viewed as such to their significance for individuals and groups as they respond to either actual or perceived reality. Examples of evaluative texts include editorials commenting on the state of education or the dangers of a given social policy, which may often be accompanied by suggestions for remedy; position papers defending courses of action; or justifications of personal conduct in complicated situations. All of these, while traceable to 'facts' rooted in the world of space and time, transcend the purely factual in favor of conceptualization and judgment on the part of the originator and the audience.

Finally, texts in the *Projective* (P) mode exist in a realm which the originators are concerned with the argumentation or analysis of particular facts or events only to the degree that these exemplify some aspect of the originator's thought. Works of literature or art, philosophic discourse, and sophisticated humor may be considered instances of the Projective mode.

Though this model categorizes texts into four discrete modes, the fact remains that all texts are likely to contain features of language variety, style, tone, register and the like which may be attributed to more than one mode and which must be accounted for in the translation process.

Assigning texts to modes

Congruity judgment has been identified above as the one skill unique to translation, though it may be used in other situations, as, for example, in intra-language paraphrasing. Since congruity judgment must be exercised in rendering any text across languages, it is important for translation rating guidelines to specify problem areas associated with each mode, from both content-form and form-content perspectives, and to establish that each translation is rated against specific requirements associated with each textual mode.

Congruity judgment and the world of facts

Congruity judgment applied to the orientational and instructive modes is generally a straightforward procedure, since the purposes associated with texts in these modes are to make facts, events and situations as accessible as possible to persons functioning in the society for which those texts are intended. The translator must, however, understand the thrust of the message within culture A before attempting to produce an equivalent in culture B.

The case is more difficult with Instructive texts. For one thing, these texts tend to be longer and to demand greater control of the semantics of space, time and circumstance, and the roles language users play in communicating. While the focus of Instructive texts is on factuality rather than opinion or argumentation, the included facts in a donor language text may well reflect a view of daily life and nuts-and-bolts realities quite different from that of a prospective receptor language culture (i.e. a different content-form representation). Obviously, to render these texts correctly the translator must be aware of such dissimilarities and know how to handle differences at the morpholexical (or form-content) level.

Congruity judgment and conceptual structures

As challenging as orientational and instructive texts sometimes are, they are ordinarily much easier to render across languages than are evaluative and projective ones. Evaluative and projective texts serve as standards for Level 3 (evaluative) and Levels 4 and 5 (projective) respectively: a successful candidate at level 3 in reading can read between the lines while candidates at levels 4 and 5 must read beyond the lines because of the very nature of those texts. As difficult as it may be to meet evaluative and projective standards within a single language, doing so across languages is even more so for evaluative and next to impossible for some projective texts.

The discussion of the evaluative mode above suggests the kinds of problems translators face as they translate evaluative texts. The critical feature of such texts is the way in which the originator has shaped information to develop (or contest) a point of view on or rationale for an individual or group position. It follows that the translator must be clear in his or her mind on the social, political or other context of the donor language text(s), together with the relevant position(s) of the author, before attempting to identify a comparable receptor language context.

What is true of the evaluative mode is even more so of projective texts. These are highly individuated expressions of authorial intent: the originator of (or participants in) texts in this mode are neither bound solely to the facts of the world of space and time, nor to the (more or less) institutional rules on addressing such facts. The source of projective texts is highly innovative and often truly creative: the originator transcends narrow time and space considerations to see the world or some part of it in a new light. Philosophic and esthetic discourses are prominent forms in this mode, but surprising collocations of dissimilar or even contradictory ideas vital to humor at its best are likewise important. All of these have in common the fact that content-form uniqueness informs projective texts.

As observed earlier, capturing the spirit of the projective text, with its allusions and metaphors, its oblique suggestions and implications, may in extreme cases prove impossible. However, texts in each of the textual modes pose unique challenges for translators.

Translation testing and language levels

The sections above were written in such a way as to assume ideal performance on the part of translators as they go about their tasks. In actuality, translators are quite varied in educational background, subject matter knowledge, and, most especially, congruity judgment. No clear standard has yet been accepted in the translation profession that can provide guidelines for matching a translator's ability to texts which he or she may be expected to handle effectively. This set of guidelines attempts to provide that guidance.

Classifying texts

While other rating systems assign text types to each level, ILR experience suggests that a specific text mode is often more closely tied to ILR levels than a specific text type is. In general, reading scores of 0+ to 1 allow a translator to handle orientational texts, scores of 1+ to 2 instructive texts, 2+ to 3+ evaluative texts, and 4 to 5 projective texts. For example editorials as a text type are usually assigned to the 3 level, but some editorials are written with the intent to inform, others offer varying amounts of opinion or judgment, and others include language, such as metaphor or analogy, which expresses the author's unique personality as well as his or her opinions. Thus an editorial may fall anywhere along the scale between a 2+ and a 5. By identifying texts by both text types and primary mode, it is possible to more readily approximate a text's level. However, only a close scrutiny of a text and the factors contributing to its difficulty can ultimately determine its level.

In the course of assessing texts for the purpose of assigning them to a given level, however, it frequently becomes obvious that texts are not often purely orientational or purely evaluative; most texts contain elements of more than one mode. The best approach for classifying such mixed-mode texts is to assign them to the level which corresponds to their most complex mode, i.e., if a text is informative and evaluative, that text would be assigned to the 3 or 3+ level because of the additional complexity its evaluative elements add to the translation.

Assessing translators

Mixed-mode texts, though they are slightly more difficult to classify, offer increased efficiency in the assessment of translation ability. By employing mixed-mode texts in tests of congruity judgment, it is possible to identify where the translator's ability breaks down. Mixed-mode texts may be categorized at the following levels: orientational-instructive, equal to about the 1+ level; instructive-evaluative, equal to about the 2+ level; and evaluative-projective, equal to the 3+ level.

An analysis of how well a prospective translator handles these mixed-mode texts would allow raters to place those results on a scale from 0+ to 5 similar to that employed for the other skills. In the case where a prospective translator is rated at a plus level in reading or writing, though, there is concern about how this score will affect a measure of congruity judgment. A translator, for example, who scores a 2+ in reading may be able to process instructive-evaluative texts containing content in his or her area of expertise. In the case of mixed instructive-evaluative texts containing unfamiliar content, though, a 2+ may become ineffective.

Guidelines

Broad descriptions of 11 ranges on the congruity scale (starting with zero) accompany this mode/level overview. These should be of value both for the system of standards set forth here and the rating of prospective or actual translators concerned with the demands of the profession.

These guidelines for assessing translation ability are presented here as a preliminary version. Its main goal is to attempt to characterize the overall ability with particular reference to its two poles – the ability to read and comprehend the donor language and the ability to express oneself in writing in the receptor language – with an overall characterization, a global score, for congruity judgment.

Like the ILR skill level descriptions for the individual skills, speaking, listening, reading, and writing, officially approved by the US Government, these translation guidelines are both theory- and method-neutral. They attempt only to characterize how well the translator accomplished the rendering, not how well he or she did according to a given theory or method. A fuller, more specific evaluation can be carried out according to any such theory or method. The guidelines provide the framework, the theory or method the specifics.

These guidelines are scalar; that is, they refer to different qualities and quantities of ability as levels are compared. Consequently, users should become thoroughly familiar with using the guidelines from both directions: from level 5 down to level 0 as well as vice-versa. Statements in the guidelines, for example, about variety and style are often reflect a comparison of skills to the next higher level, while statements about approaches to translation, glossing, code-matching, are often framed in terms of comparison with what a translator is able to do in either quality or quantity beyond a translator performing at the level down.

The translation scale below will, for those levels below Level 5, concentrate on the Congruity Scale as a true *descriptor of the ability to translate*. For the specific linguistic skills, the reader is referred to the separate ILR Skill Level Descriptions for Reading and Writing 5.

Applying the guidelines

Since these guidelines attempt to be useful to both translators and raters, the following sections provide some guidance to these groups.

To translators

The first step to be taken is to ascertain the level and mode(s) of the donor text since this information may be useful in looking at the text from both a content-form and form-content perspective. It will then be possible to identify the most appropriate receptor text style and to gauge the appropriate level of accuracy or faithfulness to the original required in the receptor text.

To evaluators

The initial step is to ascertain the level and mode(s) of the donor text. This classification will inform the evaluation of the level of accuracy or faithfulness to the original the translator achieved in the rendering. Translation errors or infelicities at level 5 differ in nature from those at levels 1+/2. Level 5 requires a judge capable of evaluating the appropriateness of a variety of styles, while at the lower levels, an evaluator who adheres to a single style will suffice. By selecting raters who possess the requisite language abilities, it is then possible to identify the style the translator elected to use in the receptor text and evaluate its appropriateness for the context of the translation.

Individual level definitions

Ideally, the present paper would describe both the wide-ranging interrelationships between the three scales and the special contributions of the congruity scale to the traditional procedures. Space does not suffice to thoroughly outline the interrelationship between one's reading proficiency in the donor language, one's writing proficiency in the receptor language, and one's ability measured on the congruity scale.

The congruity scale

The congruity scale is divided into three stages: professional, transitional, and pre-professional. At the professional level, the translator's language abilities and congruity judgment are such that he or she can render useful translations on a broad range of general and specialized topics. The transitional stage occurs at the level 2+, which is probably the lowest possible level for a usable translator in the workplace. Below that level, an individual may be conceived of as a learner of subskills involved in translation, but not as someone who may integrate them into any kind of usable performance. Further, it is questionable whether individuals rated in the pre-professional range (levels 2 and below) could be considered professional translators.

Professional stages

Translators whose skills are rated from levels 3 to 5 fall within the professional stages. The following sections outline the level of skill required at each of these levels.

Level 5

Specifically at Level 5, the congruity judgments made are highly appropriate for the type of translation selected. The holistic form in the receptor language is fully adequate to express the holistic form of the donor language. There are no, or only minuscule, infelicities in any rendering; and these may result from cultural, sociolinguistic, or other non-linguistic lack of parallelism between the two languages, societies, or cultures. From a pragmatic point of view, the translation is regarded as fully successful.

The translator is often challenged to devise idiosyncratic approaches to render the original adequately into the receptor language, particularly in highly idiosyncratic texts, such as avant-garde literature. It is the hallmark of such translators that they accomplish this successfully, often producing text just as, if not more memorable than the original. Highly idiomatic words, phrases, and references are rendered accurately.

A Level 5 can render an extremely wide variety of texts accurately and felicitously.[4] This means that a Level 5 can make a wide variety of precise congruity judgments, and these will accurately reflect, and at times even enhance, the original.

Level 4+

Like the Level 5 translator, a Level 4+ translator can render a very wide variety of texts, but is limited either in extent of variety, amount of flair and originality, or by a minor number of infelicities, which reveal an ability close to, but not truly that of a Level 5.

A Level 4+ will often be less successful in devising a suitable receptor language holistic form to render the donor language's idiosyncratic one. Word choice in the receptor language may not meet the demands of highly nuanced or avant-garde language in the donor language. Such donor language nuances may be slightly misunderstood, and their overtones and implications not fully captured. Nevertheless, the high level of the translator's ability would be evident, as would his inability to achieve the skill of a true Level 5.

Level 4

Like the Level 4+ translator, a Level 4 translator can render a wide variety of texts, making suitable congruity judgments. Unlike a Level 4+, a Level 4 will often have to struggle with highly idiosyncratic texts and may not render them with the ability of a 4+ or 5.

Still a Level 4 can make congruity judgments suitable to texts at level. For texts at Level 4, the holistic form in the receptor language will adequately reflect the original holistic form in the donor language. In freer translations, there will be no, or minimal, evidence of the donor language and its structure. In translation intended to reflect the original more closely, say for legal purposes, a suitable ability to reflect the original will be manifest. In either type of translation, focus within the text as a whole and within its individual paragraphs and sentences will suitably reflect the original. Word choice in the rendering will accurately reflect the subtleties and nuances of the original and evince an understanding of synonymy in both languages. Cultural nuances will be accurately conveyed, save for those at a higher level(s). Another way of expressing the totality of these abilities to deal with focus, word choice, and cultural nuances is to say that the translator captures the shaping of the original in highly suitable ways. In summary, the totality of the original will be conveyed, but perhaps lacking the 'originality' and 'flair' a Level 4+ might bring to the same task. The congruity judgments are very appropriate; and the rendering as a whole is regarded as highly dependable.

Level 3+

Like the Level 4, the Level 3+ translator can render a variety of texts, but these may be somewhat more limited in scope. The translator's grasp of the donor language synonymy and its rendering into the receptor language will be evident, but not as fully present as with a Level 4. Similarly there may be limitations on the rendering of holistic form where freer translation may be required.

Renderings, while very acceptable, lack the fullness of features characterizing Level 4. Besides the aspects already noted, these may appear as an inability to render higher-level sociolinguistic or cultural references. There is a lesser ability to render nuanced focus, word choice, and cultural references, so that while the overall organization will be clear and appropriate, the shaping in the

Eduardo C. Cascallar

original may not be fully captured in the rendering.

Level 3

Like the Level 3+, the Level 3 translator is expected to translate in several topic areas, both concrete and abstract. The translator is sufficiently skilled so that the rendering is generally accurate, though lacking some nuances and style. The rendering is acceptable.

Unlike the Level 4, the Level 3's task is often made simpler by the presence of a one-to-one relationship between holistic form in the donor language to holistic form in the receptor language for the same text type. Therefore, unlike the Level 4, the Level 3 does not normally have to search for the connection between the two forms, and, for some 3 Level work, the translation will reflect the donor language holistic form rather than that of the receptor language. Problems with atomistic form are rare. The Level 3 translator accurately renders both the concrete and abstract thought at level, including evaluative aspects of the text, such as hypothesizing, supported opinion, as well as author-intended nuances where present in the original. However, focus within either paragraphs or sentences may occasionally be misrendered, as will be some nuances. The wording chosen is usually congruent with the intent and focus of the original. While the problem of overall organization and form may be simplified, shaping in the donor language may not be fully captured in the rendering. Still, the majority of congruity judgments are suitable for the level. A Level 3 translator renders originals at level in a limited number of topic areas very accurately, and the end product is highly usable.

Transition stage

The transition stage includes only the level 2+.

Level 2+

A level 2+ will normally only be able to translate a very limited number of topic areas, usually containing text in rather predictable sequence. Congruity judgments may still often be based on an atomistic approach, but the number reflecting attention to overall form and particularly to content as required in the receptor language are increasing. A Level 2+ will probably still follow the overall structural outline of the donor language original, while attending to many other, though not all, of the requirements of the receptor language for the same topic. Author-intended inferences may well be missed, as will, occasionally, the overall focus of the article. More likely to be missed are the foci of individual paragraphs; that is, the general meaning of the whole may well be conveyed, while tone, stress on details, and the proper placement of subtler elements in the receptor language may be missed. Along with the overall form reflecting more of the donor than of the receptor language, the translator may render with some difficulty any shaping in the donor language. In sum, we can expect that most of the meanings in the donor language passage are rendered accurately into the receptor language, but a few may be lost or masked, primarily for the reasons cited above.

Pre-professional stage

Translators whose skills are rated in this range are still acquiring skills and may not be able to perform professional translation tasks appropriately.

Level 2

Makes many congruity judgments especially at the upper range, but more based on atomistic form than on overall form or content. Word-by-word relexification is receding, but code-matching persists by an inability to do more than strongly reflect the donor language sentence and paragraph structure. Compared to a Level 1, fewer meanings are lost or masked, and many are accurately rendered.

Level 1+

Makes more congruity judgments than the Level 1, but still is operating primarily by 'word-by-word' relexification, although this is yielding to some sense of receptor language sentence structure at least in its simpler and more straightforward forms, yielding some 'code-matching'. Compared to a Level 1, fewer of the meanings are lost or masked, but many are still inaccurately rendered.

Level 1

Makes a few congruity judgments, but operates by word-by-word relexification or glossing. Meanings may be lost, masked, or inaccurately rendered

Level 0+

Makes congruity judgments haphazardly.

Level 0

Has no functional ability to make congruity judgments.

Absolute 0

No ability to translate.

Notes

1 For consistency, the terms *donor* and *receptor* languages will be used in the following pages. The donor language is that of the original or source document, while the receptor language is that of the target or translated text.

2 For the initial version of these guidelines (November 1993), we assume parallel abilities, such that the necessary ability in the source language skills is, at least, matched by the same level in the target language. Should the target language skills be higher than required, this would introduce fewer problems into the assessment than if the target language skills proved to be lower than required. A topic for further research in this area could be the effects of any offset(s) between source language skills and target language skills along with the way in which they alter the assessment of translation, which this paper does not address.

3 The term 'text type' may be used in two ways. First, it is used as a general designation for texts. This sense of type is rooted in the history of linguistics, where a separate term has typically been defined to refer to any individual text as well as to express broader categories into which individual texts may be placed. Under this definition, any text is therefore a text type by its very nature, though it may be possible to specify its text type more fully by comparing it to other similar texts.

    The second use of the term 'text type' is an indication of a category of texts, usually defined by a qualifier or other designation. These categories of texts are culturally determined, and a category that exists in one language may not exist in another. Further, even if the category exists in both languages, the expected form such texts take in the source language may differ significantly from that of the target language. For example, an 'editorial' is a specific text type; other examples include the following: 'obituary,' 'essay,' 'feuilleton' (in French and German), 'keseri' (in Swedish), or a 'marriage announcement'. The term 'text type' will be used, unless otherwise noted, in its latter, broader sense in the pages that follow.

4 The demands for accuracy, style, and variety placed on a Proficiency Level 5 in Translation are extremely high. As a 5 in translation proficiency is a composite of numerous other skills, all of which must be at Level 5, the statistical likelihood that such translators will be found decreases markedly over the numbers of Proficiency 5s in any single contributing skill, such as compared to Level 5 readers in the donor language. When the number of topic areas in which a translator can perform at his or her highest capacity is also taken into account, the number of possible level 5 ratings of translations decreases even further. Consequently, such high-level ability is more likely to be attained on the performance side than on the proficiency side. It is possible that a Level 5 reader of the donor language who is also a Level 5 writer of the receptor language may not prove to be a Level 5 translator.

References

Child, James R. August 1990. *Language skills and textual norms across languages.* Paper presented at the annual meeting of the American Association of Teachers of Spanish and Portuguese, Miami, FL.

Federal Bureau of Investigation (FBI). 1990. *Error Notation Key.* Unpublished manuscript.

Mahn, G. 1989. Standards and evaluation in translator training. In P. W. Krawutschke (ed.), *American Translators Association Scholarly Monograph Series: Vol. 3. Translator and Interpreter Training and Foreign Language Pedagogy.* Binghamton, NY: State University of New York at Binghamton (SUNY).

Stansfield, C. W., M. L. Scott, and D. M. Kenyon. 1990. *Spanish-English Verbatim Translation Exam.* Final Report. Washington, D.C.: Center for Applied Linguistics.

Teague, B. 1987. ATA accreditation and excellence in practice. In B. Teague (ed.), *American Translators Association Scholarly Monograph Series: Vol. 1. Translation Excellence: Assessment, Achievement, Maintenance.* Binghamton, NY: State University of New York at Binghamton (SUNY).